A FAREWELL TO ARMS, LEGS & JOCKSTRAPS

A FAREWELL TO ARMS, LEGS & JOCKSTRAPS

A SPORTSWRITER'S MEMOIR

DIANE K. SHAH

RED ⚡ LIGHTNING BOOKS

This book is a publication of

RED LIGHTNING BOOKS
1320 East 10th Street
Bloomington, Indiana 47405 USA

redlightningbooks.com

© 2020 by Diane K. Shah
All rights reserved

The paper used in this publication
meets the minimum requirements of
the American National Standard for
Information Sciences—Permanence of
Paper for Printed Library Materials,
ANSI Z39.48–1992.

*Manufactured in the
United States of America*

Cataloging information is available from
the Library of Congress.

ISBN 978-1-68435-115-2 (hdbk.)
ISBN 978-1-68435-116-9 (web PDF)

1 2 3 4 5 25 24 23 22 21 20

Contents

A FAREWELL TO ARMS, LEGS & JOCKSTRAPS

1

Call Me "Tolerated"

I WAS EARLY, OBVIOUSLY.

Through the open ballroom doors, I could see a handful of men seated at round banquet tables covered with starched white cloths. I consulted my watch again. 6:03 p.m.

I had checked into the hotel maybe an hour before and, after dropping off my suitcase in my room, rode the elevator down to the second floor to pick up my credentials. There had been a bit of a fuss when I had phoned a week earlier to request them. The man I spoke to had put me on hold, presumably to consult a higher authority, then finally came back on the line and said, "Hell, why not?"

Even so, I worried they might give me a hard time when I showed up. I was wrong. I was handed my credentials for the All-Star Game and told, with a chuckle, "Well, this is a first." The man then gave me a goody bag. I carried it to the lobby and sat down, hoping to see a familiar face, someone I could have dinner with. The thought of eating a room-service meal by myself was depressing.

I opened the goody bag and began pawing through it. The contents made me smile. A Gillette razor, a pack of razor blades, a tie-pin, men's deodorant, a pen and . . . wait, what was this? A square, sealed envelope.

I tore it open. Inside was an invitation to a dinner that evening for sportswriters and the baseball players selected for the game to be played the next night. Salvation! *No room-service meal after all*, I thought. I reread the invitation. The dinner was called for 6 p.m.

I checked my watch. It was 5:45. I hurried back to my room and grabbed a reporter's notebook. This would be fun! I could chat with other sportswriters, meet some ballplayers, and maybe extract a colorful quote or two. Pausing in front of the mirror, I ran a comb through my long, dark hair; applied pink lipstick; and studied the navy cotton dress I had on. It was wrinkled, but it would have to do.

Now, as I was about to step into the ballroom, a man standing off to the left quickly intercepted me. He gave me an unwelcome look. "This is a private dinner," he announced. "Sorry."

I pasted on my best smile. "This is the Baseball Writers' dinner, right?"

"Yes. Obviously, you have the wrong ballroom."

"No, I have the right ballroom." I made a move to enter.

He moved with me. "I can't allow you in."

I put away my smile and pulled the invitation from my purse. "I'm invited."

He barely glanced at the invitation. "Clearly, there's been a mistake. This dinner is stag. Women are *not* allowed."

"I'm allowed. I'm a writer with the *National Observer*. I'm here for the All-Star Game, and this invitation was given to *me*."

"It shouldn't have been."

My eyes slid from his frown to his jacket lapel. The name on the badge pinned to it identified him as Hal Middlesworth, the public relations director for the Detroit Tigers. Since the game was being played in Detroit, he had apparently been given door-approval duty. I brightened. Paul Hood, the senior managing editor at the *National Observer*, had told me he and Middlesworth had been army buddies.

I smoothly reapplied my smile. "Paul Hood is one of my editors," I said sweetly. "He sends his warmest wishes. He also said I could come to you if I have any problems." I paused. "Apparently, I have a problem."

Middlesworth nodded. "Paul's a good guy. Tell him I said hello. But this is not something I can help you with." He offered me a pretend smile. "I'm sure Paul would understand."

"Mr. Middlesworth," I tried again, "this invitation was included with my credentials. Nowhere on the invitation is the word *stag*."

Middlesworth turned his head to check the invitations of two men who were allowed to waltz right in. Then he returned his attention to me.

"You may be credentialed for the game, but not this dinner."

"Really?" I said. "So you mean to tell me that 500 sportswriters are coming to Detroit, just for the dinner? I doubt it. They are here to cover the game and this, by extension, is part of it."

"Miss, you are only credentialed for the game. The dinner is separate. And as I said, the dinner is strictly a stag affair. Men only."

I grinned and lowered my voice. "You mean . . . they tell dirty jokes? Do naked women pop out of cakes?"

Middlesworth reddened. "Of course not!"

That he had blushed gave me hope that he realized how ridiculous this situation was. But having been in the army, he had learned to follow orders, I assumed, and he wasn't going to break rank. Frantically, I tried to think of something else I could say, but I had run out of arguments. While every other sportswriter in town was attending an event from which I was being excluded, I would be sent to my room like a naughty child, to choke down a lukewarm dinner. I felt humiliated. I started to turn away.

Then I stopped.

Suddenly, from out of nowhere, a voice that sounded strangely like my own announced, "Well, I'm going in. You'll have to bodily remove me!"

Where that came from I will never know. But I strode into the ballroom, my two-inch heels clicking loudly on the floor. And with each step, I was sure my arm would be yanked and I would be hauled out of there. But then I was standing at the first table, where the Cincinnati catcher Johnny Bench was sitting by himself. "Johnny," I said, "remember me? May I join you?"

Bench smiled. "Of course, sit down."

—⁓—

The dinner, it turned out, was almost not worth the effort it took to bust in. The speeches could not have been duller, and not a single naked lady jumped out of a cake. There were three other men at my table who said little. Thankfully, Bench had invited country and western singer Bobby Goldsboro, and the two of them were fun to listen to.

Afterward, Bench said, "Why don't you all come up to my room? I've got beer."

So the four of us, plus Goldsboro and Bench, trooped up to his room. And it was there, *Mr. Hal Middlesworth*, that I found the lead to my story. I wrote:

"Johnny Bench was, as usual, stealing the show. There he was, the night before the All-Star Game, in his hotel room, host to a party; and the fact that singer Bobby Goldsboro was the guest of honor hardly daunted Johnny. Goldsboro wound up in a dark corner, strumming his guitar as accompaniment for, who else? Bench. *'When you're hot, you're hot. When you're not, you're not,'* bellowed the catcher, who wouldn't know what it's like to be 'not.'

"Sure enough, next night he was hot," I continued, and I went on to describe his second-inning two-run homer and his tug-of-war with Baltimore Orioles third baseman Brooks Robinson. In the fourth inning, Brooks made a sensational play on a grounder by Bench, throwing him out at first. In the seventh, Bench retaliated. First, he faked a bunt down the third-base line. Robinson moved up and closer to the line in case Bench was serious about bunting. But on the next pitch, Bench smashed a grounder past Robinson's outstretched left hand for a clean single.

Several days after my article appeared, I received a letter from Middlesworth. "Dear Diane: Congratulations on your excellent story on the All-Star Game. It was a fine piece of writing and it certainly captured the essence of the event.

"I hope I did not offend you—and I assume I did not—about your presence at the usually stag dinner. You set a precedent, apparently with no serious results. Congratulations!"

He sent a slightly different version to Paul Hood:

"Your young lady wrote a fine story on the All-Star Game. She also knocked down the writers' barrier at the social events. No damage was done, and I assume women will now be welcome—or at least tolerated—in the future."

—∿∿—

That dinner was the first of many "let-me-in!" farces I had a starring role in. Still, each time a door was slammed in my face, I was genuinely surprised. I had never focused on being a "female" sportswriter or how the world would react. I didn't care. I was a sportswriter, period, and all I ever wanted was to get the story. Whatever it took.

I had no idea—*none*—what those stories would be. It never occurred to me that I would break into the White House—literally—or pick up my phone to hear the startling voice of *Cary Grant*. Or cause California Angels manager Gene Mauch to break into tears. Nor could I have imagined Paul Newman slamming the phone down on me. Or that one October night I would go out on patrol with three newly minted Moscow cops, rusty Kalashnikovs splayed across their laps.

Nor did I have an inkling that one morning, while driving to work along the Santa Monica Freeway, I would spot, right in front of me, a Los Angeles city bus with my face plastered across the back window. And I certainly never imagined that, according to the Boston Red Sox, I would—apparently, all by myself—destroy the American family. *Me?*

In the end, it wasn't a matter of hurdling a few barriers. It was so much bigger than that. To me, it was all showbiz, pure and simple. One riveting tale after another played out in real time. And I had muscled my way to a seat in the audience. Right up front.

2

Can't Hire a Girl for That!

I HAVE OFTEN WONDERED WHO THAT WOMAN WAS, THE ONE who strode so boldly into the forbidden dinner, the one who declared, "You'll have to bodily remove me!" Had I heard that line in a movie? Certainly, that wasn't me. I was shy. As a child I had a hard time making eye contact. My father was strict. You didn't talk back. You *obeyed*. But in time, I realized the professional me bore little resemblance to the kid growing up.

I was born in Chicago, but my family moved to Highland Park, an upmarket suburb north of the city, when I was eight. Although I had a younger sister, my parents used to joke that I was an only child, because I would plant myself in my bedroom, door closed, reading Nancy Drew and other books—or talking on my Princess phone—until I had to emerge for dinner. In fact, soon after we moved into our two-story house, I woke up my four-year-old sister one Sunday morning and said, "How would you like your own bedroom!" Without waiting for a reply, I began moving her bed and dresser out of our bedroom, down the hall, and into the guest room.

My Brooklyn-born father had been deployed to Navy Pier during World War II, met my mother, and they married. When I was four, my mother pointed to an airplane flying overhead and told me we were going to travel in one of those to New York. How, I asked, looking upward, could I fit into that little-bitty plane? In New York I met two cousins and became a pen pal with one of them, Danny, who was my age. At some point we began writing to each other. Whenever one of Danny's letters arrived, I would race upstairs to my bedroom and quickly pencil a reply. I found I loved writing back.

When I was 12, a friend of my mother asked what I wanted to do when I grew up. I said I wanted to be a writer but added I didn't think I was creative enough to write a book, so I wasn't sure. The friend suggested journalism. I said, "What's that?" She explained it was writing stories for a newspaper. This sounded incredibly dull, but it gave me something to consider. Even at that age, I didn't think I could write books like Nancy Drew. But newspapers? *Hmm.*

I think it was seventh grade when I discovered that maybe, just maybe, I could be a little creative. For English class I wrote a short story called "The Car of Life and Death." I don't remember the plot, but since I read mystery novels, it probably was suspenseful. The teacher called on me to stand in front of the class and read my story aloud. Before I could finish, the bell rang. I paused, expecting everyone to jump up and bury me in the stampede for the door. But not one student moved. I finished reading the last page and a half. Only then did everyone dash out.

Wow! I thought. *Wow!*

—◦◦◦—

Although I soon became obsessed with being a journalist, pretty much the only journalism I read as a kid was in the sports pages. I had few qualities that portended journalism would be a wise career choice. I read books about famous reporters, and they all stressed that you needed to be curious, aggressive, and familiar with the dictionary. I had little curiosity outside of baseball, I was painfully shy, and looking up words in the dictionary seemed too much trouble. I only wanted to write.

My misguided outlook was hammered into me my senior year in high school, when my guidance counselor summoned me to his office. By then, I had earned my first real byline, in my hometown paper, the *Highland Park News*. I was 14 years old and chosen to write a story about students taking over the town's government for a day. After school I worked on the Highland Park High School newspaper and somehow landed a bimonthly column for the *Waukegan News Sun*. It was called HPHS *something*, and I haven't a clue what I wrote.

This guidance counselor asked about my plans after college. I said, "I want to write for *Time* or *Newsweek*."

He shook his head. "*Time* and *Newsweek* each have about fifteen writers, all middle-aged, all men. What else would you like to do?"

In truth, I hadn't thought any of this through, so I blurted out the only thing I could think of. "Then I want to be a sportswriter!"

He rolled his eyes. "Dear, no editor will hire you. Sports reporters have to go into locker rooms, and girls can't do that." He sighed. "I suggest you go home and start thinking *sensibly* about your future."

For some reason, this blast of cold reality did not faze me.

I was going to be a journalist no matter what.

—◦◦◦—

Although women's lib hadn't surfaced yet, I began to realize there were jobs women were not allowed to do. Had I been a man, I would have applied for a copy boy's job at the *Chicago Daily News* or *Sun-Times* or *Tribune*. That was how many male journalists got their start. But something told me I would not be hired for that. Nope, I would have to get a journalism degree.

In a hurry, I graduated from Indiana University in three and a half years. I wrote for the *Indiana Daily Student* and, the summer between my final two semesters, I carried a bunch of clips to the oddly named *Bloomington Herald-Telephone*, where I was hired as a reporter for the summer. Then, that fall, a new paper appeared, the *Bloomington Tribune*. I hadn't even heard of it when I got a phone call offering me a part-time job until I graduated in January; then I could work full-time. I agreed and was handed the education beat. In June, I announced I was leaving. My boyfriend was graduating, and I wanted to go to Europe for the summer. The editor said I mustn't leave and offered to make me the highest-paid writer on the staff. But despite this inexplicable offer, Bloomington was not my kind of town. I wanted the big time—Chicago or New York. When I again said no, thank you, he said, "You're making a big mistake. Someday, you could be the most famous woman journalist in Indiana!"

I gulped, smiled, and fled.

—◦◦◦—

I got married, moved to Washington, DC, and began to hunt for a writing job. Nobody wanted me. I could not help noticing that most of my male classmates had secured newspaper jobs, while I kept trying to find one. I had no trouble reaching managing editors to ask for a job. Back then you simply dialed the newspaper's number, asked for the M.E., and were put right through. Also, back then, managing editors did not mince words.

"Just got married, eh? Well, soon you'll be having babies. Sorry."

Or "Only thing available is the four-to-midnight shift. Can't hire a girl for that."

I didn't know what to do with myself. We didn't have much furniture in the one-bedroom apartment we rented, so there wasn't much I could do at home. Lacking anything meaningful to occupy me, I was horrified to discover I was having trouble stringing coherent sentences together. When my husband came home from his job as a TV director at a local station, he could tell me about his day, but all I had to offer was that the price of tomatoes had gone up.

Desperate to do *something*, I took a job selling sportswear at Lord & Taylor in Bethesda. And every lunch hour I carried a handful of coins into a payphone booth. Over the next two months, I called every newspaper, magazine, wire service, and radio and TV station in the DC metropolitan area. Sometimes a managing editor would tell me to call back. "Something might be opening up soon." And call back I did—to no avail. Meanwhile, I had put together quite a résumé. After Lord & Taylor, I wrote newspaper ads for a department store under the tutelage of two men who screamed at each other all day, and at Christmas, I sold cosmetics at Saks.

I might add that I struck out completely at *Newsweek*. Ignoring my guidance counselor's advice, I wrangled an interview with the Washington bureau chief, who asked what I wanted to do. "Be a writer," I declared.

Two weeks later, I received a letter saying that I didn't have the experience to be a *Newsweek* writer, but might I be interested in a reporting or research job? I hastily wrote back that I was. Two weeks later, another letter arrived. I really wasn't qualified to be a reporter or researcher, it said, but I might consider applying for an opening as the bureau's part-time librarian. Yes, of course, I eagerly wrote back. The third and final letter said, "Sorry. We just hired a college guy for that position."

At 23, I was clearly washed up. And miserable. All I had ever wanted in life was to be a writer. (Okay, after I figured out that being a cowgirl wasn't going to happen.) I had grown up in a wealthy suburb, and I prayed—actually prayed—that I wouldn't end up getting married and living in a house with two powder-blue Mercedes in the driveway, as one of my classmates had. I didn't want *that*—I wanted adventure.

This was the end of the 1960s, a topsy-turvy decade filled with rebellious youngsters, long tangled hair and ratty clothes, blaring music, communes, shocking assassinations, and a war everybody seemed to hate. My husband and I lived in a three-building complex called Eldorado Towers in Silver Spring, Maryland, not far from where he grew up. Some nights his brother and several of their friends—including a young Catholic priest—would come over, smoke marijuana, and talk about overthrowing the government. The priest would tell us how he agonized over the church's ban on birth control and how many in his poor parish desperately desired it. What to do? What to do about America? Leave it? Go to Canada? All this was debated amid plumes of pot smoke.

Twenty years later, I met a lawyer in Los Angeles who, after getting his law degree, worked several years for the FBI. I mentioned Eldorado Towers, and this lawyer, Jay Grodin, said he had lived there too, at about the same time. "That's where they housed us during our first year at Quantico," he said. I burst out laughing. If only we had known we were breaking the law just down the hall from dozens of FBI agents!

Eventually, I did land a journalism job with *Roll Call*. A sort of *Politico* before *Politico*, it was an inside look at doings on Capitol Hill that I wasn't sure anyone read. After routinely getting lost on DC's alphabetical one-way streets, I would walk into a federal building and stare down a hall that stretched for blocks and then turn right, only to start down another hall that stretched for more blocks. *Maybe*, I thought dismally, *I ought to find another career.* But I couldn't come up with anything. Some nights I could hardly sleep.

Then everything changed.

My first job interview after arriving in Washington had been at the *National Observer*, a Dow Jones–owned weekly like *Time* or *Newsweek*, only in newspaper form. I had spoken with the managing editor, Roscoe Born, and he—like most of the others I would soon meet—took a few notes on a three-by-five index card, slid it into a metal card file box, and said he would be in touch if something opened up.

Eight months later, shortly after I had begun working at *Roll Call*, he phoned to say he had a job that might interest me. Dow Jones also published a weekly current events newspaper called *Spotlight* for junior high school students. The staff consisted of one editor, one art person, and one writer. The writing job was available. "And maybe," Mr. Born said, "in a couple of years, we could give you a story for the *Observer*."

Good God, I thought, how boring this sounded. Writing for junior high school kids? But my husband thought it was a gamble worth taking, the pay was enticing, and there was a chance I could write for the *Observer*—someday. The paper was extremely well written and highly regarded, so I took the job. I gave the boredom factor three months to kick in.

After two and a half months, I was already twitching when Mr. Born summoned me to a large conference room with a desk at the far end. He was seated behind this desk, and it seemed to take me forever to reach it. He had bad news. *Spotlight* was folding, leaving him with two choices. He could put me on the *Observer* staff or he could let me go. "I know you gave up a job to come here, so I am going to put you on staff."

Later I learned that Born had tossed me up for grabs and that no editor would take me on—except for one, Lionel Linder, who, it turned out, was the best mentor any reporter could wish for. The first story he assigned me was to fly to New York to interview Jean Nidetch, the founder of Weight Watchers. I turned the story in late one afternoon. The next morning, he called me over.

"Kid, you did a great job," he enthused and carried on for several minutes praising my work. Then he said, "Pull up a chair. I think we can do a couple of things to make it even better." He tapped my story with a blue pencil. "Here, look at the fifth graf. That's your lead. See? Now the second graf should be . . ."

Basically, we rearranged—rewrote—the entire story, though he left me feeling I had created a masterpiece all by myself. Normally, the *Observer* ran five stories on page one. My Weight Watchers piece was good enough for front-page consideration, I was told, but according to one editor in the room, "It came in number six."

My second story, about a weird yoga camp in Canada where you couldn't talk, did land on page one, and after that, so did most of my stories.

I was stunned by my good fortune; not only was I the youngest staff writer (also the lowest paid) but one of the first female journalists Dow Jones had ever hired. Indeed, two years before, when an editor from the *Wall Street Journal* came to Indiana University to interview prospective hires, a department secretary called me two hours before my meeting to inform me the *Journal* did not hire women. "You should go anyway," she said. I decided not to bother.

Six months into this job, a new editor-in-chief arrived at the *Observer*. He was Henry Gemmill, a highly regarded writer and editor from the *Wall Street Journal*. During one of our first meetings, he said, "I really don't know what to do with you. I not only have never worked with a woman, but I never considered that I was writing for one."

Despite these ominous words, I got along well with Henry although—as it turned out—maybe too well. From time to time, he asked me to lunch. We'd talk about stories I might do, or he would comment on stories I had done. One day he took me to lunch at a pricey French restaurant in Georgetown. Afterward, as we got into his car (the first Mercedes I had ever ridden in), I realized we had not talked about story ideas or the paper at all. Why, I wondered, did we have lunch? But as soon he started driving up Connecticut Avenue, he "proposed"—he was quite the gentleman—that we have an affair.

Oh god, I thought. *It will take 25 minutes to drive back to the office . . . what am I to do?*

"Henry," I said, "I am so flattered that you are interested in me. A man like *you*. But I am married. And I work for you. Sometimes I get a little crazy. Like, if I got a pay raise, I would wonder if I really deserved it. Or if I didn't get a raise, I would think, Oh dear, he's punishing me. I'm so sorry, Henry, but I don't think such an . . . er, arrangement could work."

I don't remember what else was said during that interminable ride, but when I walked into the newsroom, Nina Totenberg, our amazing Supreme Court reporter (who would go on to become one of the best in country) grabbed me. "Is Henry hitting on you?" she asked. I nodded. She said, "Me, too." That night, Nina came to my apartment—my husband was working—and we camped out in the kitchen. I opened a bottle of wine, and while Nina sat on a countertop, I made us something to eat.

"What if we went to New York?" I said.

"You think they would believe us?" Nina said. Since we were the first—or among the first—women reporters Dow Jones had hired, and since Henry was a Dow Jones star, we couldn't imagine Dow Jones executives in New York, specifically *Wall Street Journal* executive editor Warren Phillips, doing anything to help. Unable to concoct a strategy, we finished our wine and put our problem on hold.

Yet my success at the *Observer* had made me think, *screw it. If Henry tries to interfere with me, I'll quit and go to the* Washington Post. (Assuming, of course, they would hire me.) To my relief, Henry never raised the subject again, and I kept getting good assignments and pay raises. But this experience taught me two things. One, I could think on my feet (or in a car). And two, I could take care of myself. Both lessons would serve me well when I plunged into the macho world of sports.

3

I Didn't Fall Far from the Tree

ONE OF THE COOLEST ASPECTS OF BEING A REPORTER IS THAT your press credential can be a backstage pass to anywhere you want to go. You love music? Become a music critic. Art? An art critic. Science, business, medicine, politics, showbiz? It's all there for you to delve into. For me, it was baseball.

Apparently, I inherited baseball genes—from both sides of my family. My mother, grandmother, uncle, and aunt lived and died with the Cubs (mostly died), and my mother once complained that when I was a baby it took me *four innings* to finish a bottle. She brought me to my first Cubs game when I was four. Beginning to fidget, I said, "When are they going to start?"

"Honey, it's the fourth inning."

"But," I said, "where's the voice?" I was referring to broadcaster Jack Brickhouse, whose play-by-play descriptions filled our apartment, and I didn't understand how there could be a game without his voice.

(Years later I was on the field at Dodger Stadium before a game against the Cubs when I saw Brickhouse walking toward the batting cage. I hurried over to him and blurted, "Mr. Brickhouse, you were the third voice I ever heard after my mother's and father's." He laughed and shook my hand.)

What really attracted me to baseball, I always believed, was the connection I desperately sought with my father. A brilliant man who looked down on most average people, he brought his high standards home with him. He wrote best-selling books on electronics—his first, *Television Simplified*—long before most people knew what electronics were or even owned a TV. With his two daughters he was strict and demanding. Not in words, but in his grimaces and his expectations. When I would tiptoe down the stairs to his basement writing room, homework in hand, he would be impatient with my questions about science and math. I would feel a knot in my stomach if my report card ever included a C. He wouldn't punish me; worse, he would dismiss me.

But a different father would greet me when I walked into the den while he was watching baseball. A transplanted New Yorker, he still worshipped the Yankees and their recently retired hero, Joe DiMaggio. If the Yankees lost an important game, we tried to stay out of his glowering way.

I can't explain what impelled me, but when I was 12, I found myself wandering into the den while he was watching a game. And in this room, something changed. No matter how many questions I asked each inning, he would turn from the TV and patiently answer, never showing his usual disdain for my lack of brilliance. In this room, he taught me the infield fly rule and how to fill out a scorecard. And then, because I too became a rabid Yankees fan, he would take me to Comiskey Park whenever the Yankees came to play the White Sox.

Joe DiMaggio was gone, but in his stead stood Mickey Mantle. So, like my father, I became a fan of the New York Yankees' star center fielder.

With my newly printed press pass to anywhere, I headed to Yankee Stadium. It was September 1970.

4

This Was My . . . *Hero*?

HIS LEGS SHOT, MICKEY MANTLE HAD RETIRED IN 1968. IT WAS a sad ending to a storied career, but he couldn't run anymore, nor was he smashing those tape-measure home runs, nor was he making spectacular catches in the outfield. Now, two years into his retirement, he was returning to serve as the Yankees' first-base coach. Mantle a coach? Would Joe DiMaggio do this? Babe Ruth?

No matter. This was an opportunity to meet my hero. The Yankees had even given me a press credential.

So there I stood, on the field near the Yankees' dugout, half-paralyzed with fear and excitement as baseballs whizzed past my head and players dodged around me as if I were the main challenge on an obstacle course.

"Who are you looking for?" yelled Elston Howard, the former Yankee catcher and now coach, from the dugout.

"Mantle."

Howard disappeared into the tunnel that led to the locker room, only to reappear moments later, motioning for me to step down into the dugout and into the tunnel. I followed cautiously. There, in the shadows of the dimly lit tunnel, materialized a tall, broad-shouldered man—very blond and very handsome. Howard vanished, and I found myself face-to-face with Mickey Mantle, the godlike hero of baseball, worshipped by kids and grown-ups alike.

"I forgot you was waitin' for me," he apologized. Then he let loose the most incredible wad of spittle—it just kept flowing, no *unraveling*, through the air like a lopsided missile until it exploded against the wall. No tape-measure home run had ever left me as speechless.

Somewhat hesitantly I plunged into my pitch for an interview, just as a paunchy locker room attendant waddled over and started to shoo me away. "You can't be here," he said indignantly. "You're a woman!" Mantle, who was far more cooperative than I would have imagined, said I could call him at his hotel at six thirty that evening, and we could talk then.

—⁓—

I arrived at the St. Moritz Hotel on Central Park South and called Mantle's room from the lobby precisely at six thirty. The hotel operator asked for my name. There was an ashtray in the phone booth, and I quickly lit a Carlton to ease my nerves. The seconds ticked by, and just as I was ready to give up, Mantle's Oklahoma drawl twanged in my ear and I was invited to join him in the bar.

Even though I had already met him, I was still really, *really* nervous. I had been such a rabid Yankees fan growing up that I had the *Chicago Sun-Times* delivered to my cabin at summer camp in Menomonee, Wisconsin, so I could check the box scores. Mantle, of course, was my hero. In Highland Park, I would walk into town and buy a copy of *Sport* magazine. I would ask that it be put into a brown paper bag so that if I ran into friends they wouldn't think I was weird. (Ok, maybe I was.) While my girlfriends papered their bedroom walls with pictures of Elvis and movie stars, my bedroom featured Mantle. And now I was going to interview him! I knew he was married, he had four sons, and he was known to drink, supposedly showing up for some games highly inebriated. (He often hit home runs anyway.) I also understood that he could be crude. But he was . . . *Mickey Mantle.*

I ran my fingers through my hair, took a deep breath, smoothed my skirt, and headed for the bar, where he had apparently been parked for some time.

Once my eyes became accustomed to the dark, I saw only one person in the whole place: Mantle, sitting alone at a table, gazing out the window. He was nibbling peanuts and was halfway through a rum and Coke. I set my bulky tape recorder on the table, sat down, and—unsure how to start—asked him the very question I had heard every sports reporter ask: "So Mickey, how are your legs?"

Mantle grinned. "Not so nice as yours."

Oh dear. Okay, it was a dumb question, and maybe I should have expected that, but I was so nervous. I quickly looked down at my notepad and asked how he felt about his new role with the Yankees.

"Today, I was happy," he said. "I felt really good to be with the club again. When Roy White hit that home run, I had goose bumps."

"Really?"

"Yeah. I was excited, but I was also nervous. Last night I dreamed I couldn't get into the stadium. Nobody recognized me to let me in. I tried to squeeze in under the fence, but I was too fat. All the while they were announcing my name on the loudspeaker. Finally, they put [Elston] Howard in to coach. I woke up clutching my pillow and sweating."

"Was it difficult to participate from the sidelines?"

"Sure. It's sad to me that I can't play anymore. I dream that I'm still playing. I guess I always will."

Mantle, I thought, had not changed noticeably from his playing days. He said his uniform felt a little tight, but at 38, he still looked trim in his black-and-white checked suit. He called for another drink, and the barman hustled to please him.

"When I quit baseball, I was glad I didn't have to play anymore because my legs hurt so bad after a game, you know? And then I lay out of baseball for a year, and it looked like everything was going good. I had the Mickey Mantle men's shops and restaurants, and that looked like it would keep me pretty busy. And then all this money got tight, and first thing I know, I haven't opened a restaurant or a men's shop in two months. All I've been doing is sitting around my house and playing golf. And really, it just seemed to me like my life was wasting away."

He leaned forward and glued his blue eyes to my face. Not so long ago, he wouldn't make eye contact but would mumble into his stomach.

Also not so long ago, it would have been farcical to imagine Mantle as a first-base coach. "When I was a player, I paid no attention at all to the first-base coach," he said with a chuckle. "In fact, I ignored the third-base coach too. Both my managers, Casey [Stengel] and Ralph Houk, let me run when I wanted to. My average for stealing second was something like nine out of ten tries."

Another round of drinks arrived, along with a platter of hors d'oeuvres specially prepared for Mantle. He selected a couple of fish tidbits and waved the rest away.

I don't recall how long we sat there, and while I managed to ask appropriate questions, I could not forget that I was sitting across the table from my childhood hero. I noticed Mantle was eyeing my tape recorder. "You better start making notes," he admonished. "What if this thing isn't working? You're getting a pretty good interview, you know." In celebration, he called for another drink.

He had reminded me of my biggest fear—a tape recorder that didn't work. The little green light was on, and the spools were moving, but I felt too self-conscious to pause and play some of it back. *Please, god,* I thought.

I asked about his family, curious about his four sons and if any might play baseball. He said something about his wife, Merlyn. I asked, "How long have you been married?"

"Too long," he said. Then he reached inside his jacket and pulled out a greeting card. He handed it to me. The front showed a picture of flowers, and I assumed this was a card he intended to give his wife. I opened it. Inside it said, "Wanna fuck?"

He grinned.

I stared at the card. Had he bought this specially for me, or was this something he did all the time? I suddenly felt bad, but I wasn't sure if it was for me or for him. I closed the card and—without a word—handed it back.

Thankfully, at that moment, two of Mantle's buddies walked in, and I was invited to join the three of them for dinner at a restaurant up the street owned by one of the buddies.

The table reserved for celebrities was already taken by actor Sean Connery. Mantle feigned indignation. "How's come I never get to sit at that table?" he asked the owner. "I'm a star. Besides, he doesn't even have any socks on."

Everyone in the restaurant was looking at Mantle. Connery may have been James Bond, but Mantle was New York. As we walked past tables, I could hear the whispers like a constant drone. "Say, isn't that Mickey Mantle?" But Mantle had learned to put on a good deaf-mute act and ignored the sensation he was causing. One of the patrons happened to be a distant acquaintance of his, so Mantle obligingly postponed his dinner to sit at the bar with the fellow for what turned out to be a good hour.

After he returned to the table, it was some time before a waiter came to take our order. Buddy number two was about to grouse to the owner-buddy, when Mantle stopped him. "Don't do that. If you're hungry, we'll say we have to leave and go around the corner to eat. But don't say anything to him."

As the evening wore on and Mantle kept drinking, he became tipsy and, at one point, nearly fell off his chair. Later, as we walked along Central Park South, he tripped on the curb at Sixth Avenue and—for one fleeting moment—*oh, God*—there was my hero, lying in the gutter. Mantle scrambled to his feet. "New shoes," he mumbled. He crossed the street—a little wobbly.

—◦◦◦—

I left several things out of the story that ran in the *National Observer*, though I can't remember why. I know my editors did not take them out; I simply chose to omit them. The *Sporting News* contacted me and asked if they could reprint the piece. What I left out of the *Observer* I included in the *Sporting News*. Two of Mantle's comments that I did not use in the *Observer* I have already mentioned. The first, when I asked about his legs, and the second one was the so-called greeting card. I also wasn't able to bring myself to write for the *Observer* that he had fallen in the street, but I did include it in the *Sporting News* story.

Finally, I added that I had asked what he did during the off season, and he had replied that he liked to hunt and fish.

I asked what he hunted, thinking maybe deer, grouse?

"Pussy," he said.

The next time I caught up with Mantle, nine years later, he said his favorite part of the story was the pussy comment.

5

Pots, Pans, and Me

AUGUST. MIAMI BEACH. HOT, HUMID, MISERABLE. BUT weather was the least of my concerns. I had landed at the airport an hour ago, and now I was standing in the hotel lobby waiting for Jim Dickenson, one of my *Observer* colleagues. We, plus three other *National Observer* staff writers, had been assigned to cover the 1972 Republican National Convention.

Not that I knew the slightest thing about politics. Aside from the two months I spent at *Roll Call*, I hadn't even been to Capitol Hill, let alone met any politicians. But with President Nixon's assured renomination, my editors figured politics would not be the main event anyway. Dan Greene—or Daniel St. Albin Greene, as his byline read—was one of the paper's most talented writers, and he had been assigned to cover the demonstrators who had come to protest "the coronation of King Richard the Last." Jim Perry and Jim Dickenson, our top political writers and analysts, who knew all the key characters lurking on the Hill, led our team; Mark Arnold would write about Miami Beach's eroding beaches.

Then there was me. My assignment was to cover the *real* action at the convention: the social events. And the rich people who attended them.

Although I was thrilled to be chosen to go to Miami Beach, I believed covering parties was reminiscent of the old, though still being printed, "woman's page" stories, the last type of reporting I wanted to do.

Editor Henry Gemmill had announced our team eight months earlier. That day, the men thought we should celebrate over lunch. We piled into two cars and drove the short distance to a hamburger joint where *Observer* people often ate.

No sooner had our orders been taken than Jim Dickenson looked at me and said, "Glad you're coming with us. You should talk to my wife about how I like my collars starched." Everyone chuckled.

"I want my eggs over easy," Jim Perry piped in. "By the way, we get our eggs from a farm, so you'll have to bring those too." More laughter.

"You can unpack my suitcase," Dan Greene said. "And the clothes need to be hung a certain way."

"Oh, and I'll need you to bring the special detergent my wife uses to wash my shirts," Dickenson added. And on they went, with more and more demands. Followed by peals of laughter.

Go ahead, call it outrageous sexism. But this was 1972, at the beginning of the women's movement, and both sexes were trying to understand the implications. Maybe I was naive, but I believed my colleagues were merely teasing me. After all, they had included me in their lunches many times before without poking me. And I had learned that even an innocent lunch with a female coworker was a new experience for many of them, because there were few women in the Washington press corps. Once, as lunchtime drew near and not many people were in the office, I asked Jim Dickenson if he would like to go eat. He squirmed. He said he had never had lunch with a female colleague and wasn't sure it was proper to do so. He mumbled something, looked embarrassed, but finally agreed. I also didn't mind the teasing because I believed I was well regarded at the paper. And in a way, I thought their making fun of me was a sign of acceptance. So I decided to play along. Sure, I said, I would be happy to bring an iron, an egg-frying pan, and all the other things needed for my long list of domestic chores—I think one even wanted his special reading lamp.

They kept at this throughout the months that followed, laughing hysterically with each new demand.

Now we were finally in Miami Beach. When we checked into the hotel, Dickenson told me to meet him in the lobby in an hour. To do what? Iron his wrinkled shirts? Make him lunch? But when he came down, he said he wanted to take me to the convention center and show me around.

There, he formally introduced me to Ron Ziegler, Nixon's press secretary, and a handful of famous journalists who covered the White House and Capitol Hill. He led me onto the convention floor and said I would be free to walk among the delegations. He took me into the press room. He also introduced me to several socialites.

After that, I was on my own. And so, for the next four days, I ran from one social function to the next, sneaking in when necessary. To set the tone, here are the second and third paragraphs of what I wrote:

"Like a royal procession, the Republicans filed into Miami Beach to lend their glamor to the festivities. As nobility will, they cut a dashing court. From the titled classes came the likes of Cornelius Vanderbilt Whitney, Chicago multimillionaire W. Clement Stone, Diners Club executive and department store heir Alfred Bloomingdale, and real-estate heiress Mrs. Carling Dinkler, who showed up with no fewer than three yachts, appropriately rechristened 'The Nixon Navy.'

"The entourage of court jesters was equally impressive: Charlton Heston, Frank Sinatra, Pat Boone, Ethel Merman, Jimmy Stewart, Art Linkletter, and Peyton Place doctor Ed Nelson. John Wayne obliged fans with small cards bearing printed autographs."

But before I began elbowing my way into parties, I made some local inquiries. The Democrats, who had held their convention in Miami Beach in July, apparently had not been as good for business. Rent-a-Bird escort services ($50 for six hours) had not sent any of its nubile merchandise to them, I was told. "I guess the Democrats were just too busy working," said Bird co-owner Betty Skarl. "The Republicans have had a lot more time to party."

Oh, and did they. One cabinet member, joining an evening cruise for newspaper and magazine publishers, slipped topside and necked with a comely hostess. John Wayne and Jimmy Stewart stopped by the Playboy party to catch comedian David Frye's impersonations of them. Clement Stone, the insurance tycoon, threw a lavish luau around one hotel pool for some 1,000 guests, which was hardly worth mentioning, considering his bash for 90 diplomats aboard the 123-foot yacht, the *Blackhawk*, which he borrowed from Chicago Black Hawks owner Arthur Wirtz. He also contributed a half-million dollars to each of Nixon's presidential campaigns. "If a family has wealth of $400,000,000," he said to me, "what's a gift of a million?"

Despite the opulent settings and the princely guests, most of the parties, like the convention itself, were unmercifully dull. Ears perked as

Frank Sinatra encountered Henry Kissinger. "Hello, Henry. Nice to see you."

"Nice to see you, Frank," went the entire exchange.

Here is a sampling of how my week went.

Reception and dinner for members of the Republican National Committee and spouses. Eden Roc Hotel.

A combo plays but nobody dances. Men wear dark suits and white shirts—except for the bartender, who is resplendent in a blue matador jacket, black pants, red leather boots, and shoulder-length kinky hair. He is chewing gum. A rebel in a gray suit stands like a praying mantis over the hors d'oeuvres, deciding which goodies to bag.

I am approached by a sweet-faced old lady in a green print dress and green crocheted stole. "Hello, we're the Broyhills of North Carolina. I have a son who's a congressman and a grandson who's in the Singing Sergeants in Washington. Isn't that nice? You know, it's wonderful to see all my old friends, though frankly I'm surprised they can all stand up. We've been coming to conventions for over 30 years." Her white-haired husband says nothing.

The dinner is off limits to the press. I slip in anyway but don't quite fit in—I am under 50. The meal comes: cold roast beef. The woman next to me frets. "I've been going to parties all week, and this is the worst food yet, though the music is better than last night." Then she clutches her chest as if stricken and intones, "Did you hear that those nondelegates [euphemism for demonstrators] are actually going to swim *nude!*"

One party I wanted to attend was held by media mogul Gardner Cowles and his wife on Indian Creek Island for 100 of their closest friends. Guards stood at the foot of a bridge leading onto the island. "What is your name?" asked one, rattling a typed list of invited luncheon guests. From the back seat of my cab, I tell him. He runs his finger down the list—which, of course, wouldn't have had my name on it—grins, and waves me on.

A half-acre of lawn fronts the mansion. A uniformed footman hands me out, comments that only Art Buchwald has arrived, and invites me to join the Cowleses at poolside. I tell the footman I think I will wait on a black wrought-iron loveseat next to a Pucci umbrella. It didn't seem an opportune moment to crash a party.

A Porsche moves slowly up the driveway. With military precision, the footman hauls out a horsey-looking woman with saddle-molded legs and a thoroughbred reputation; a young man slides behind the wheel and disappears with the car; a second young man follows in a golf cart to retrieve the driver; and a uniformed maid appears at the front door to escort the guest down the half-block-long veranda, around the corner of the mansion, and out to the pool.

The footman eyes me dubiously. "Perhaps you would care for a drink, madam? It's rather warm out here, don't you think?"

More guests arrive. The William F. Buckley Jrs., the Stewart Alsops, Nancy Dickerson of NBC News, Barbara Walters, ambassador to Britain Walter Annenberg, and New York governor Nelson Rockefeller with his wife, Happy. "What will I do with this briefcase?" worries Rocky. An aide sets it down next to me and the Pucci umbrella.

The homemade bouillabaisse is almost ready when a water pipe breaks at the pool, dousing some of the guests. Rockefeller offers to rush to the basement and fix the leak. "There is no basement," says Gardner Cowles. A utility man is called. Other trouble is brewing. Around the corner of the veranda strolls Jan Cowles.

"And who are you?" she asks me. "Never mind, I know. And you may just join that group over there." She points over her shoulder to four persons emerging from the pool area. Delighted to be admitted, I walk over to them. One man is wearing a press badge. "Are you all press?" I ask incredulously. The fourth estate had been warned it would not be welcome on this estate.

"Yeah. And we just got kicked out."

The night Nixon's renomination was announced, I stood on the convention floor as people danced and cheered, balloons fell from the ceiling, and the band struck up *Happy Days Are Here Again*. Somehow, I was pancaked against NBC reporter Garrick Utley, a very tall man who stood straight as a ramrod. I wondered if I would be able to escape. Although Bob Woodward and Carl Bernstein had been breaking Watergate stories in the *Washington Post*, nobody here seemed concerned.

I was. But not about that. The next day, I had to write my story. And as I fell into bed, I wasn't sure I had one.

—✺—

I awoke before the sun and ordered up a pot of coffee. I showered, threw on a blouse and skirt. (Calvin Klein hadn't invented jeans yet, nor had athletic wear become the go-to wardrobe.) I took the lid off my typewriter—word processors were still nine years away—slid a piece of paper into the roller, and began to hit the keys. Wadded-up papers fell to the floor as my ashtray filled with cigarette butts. Another pot of coffee was ordered. A mound of crumpled up papers rose higher by my chair. The ashtray overflowed. Hours passed.

Sometime around six thirty or seven, I carried my typed pages to Jim Perry's room. He was charged with the initial editing. Stories would then be sent by Telex to our office in Silver Spring, Maryland. Jim asked me to sit down as he went through the story quickly, making an occasional pencil mark. He then looked up at me and smiled—a rare Jim Perry sight. "This is terrific," he said. "Go get something to eat."

To my surprise, my story ran on the top of page one, with Dan Greene's demonstrators story next to it. All the preconvention teasing was merely, as I had assumed, a form of acceptance or, as I would soon learn, typical locker room taunts. I didn't believe the *Observer* guys were testing me, but athletes certainly did.

Oh yes, they did.

6

Taming the Green Monster

DESPITE WHAT I TOLD MY HIGH SCHOOL GUIDANCE COUN-
selor, I had no desire to write sports full time. When Doug Looney, our
sportswriter at the *Observer*, was hired away by *Sports Illustrated*, I was
offered his job. I declined. I was free to do stories about anything that
intrigued me. I wrote about famous people—Vietnam War protester Jane
Fonda, soon-to-be first lady Rosalynn Carter, *Washington Post* publisher
Katharine Graham, Warren Beatty, politics, national fads that I made fun
of. I trekked down the Grand Canyon on a mule in search of the nomadic
Havasupai Indian tribe, struggled through an Outward Bound trip in
the Mexican desert with ten men, and attended New York City fashion
weeks, after which I ripped many designers' creations to shreds. I also
talked to Joan Little, a tiny 21-year-old woman in North Carolina who
was about to go on trial for murder after plunging an ice pick 11 times into
a jailer who was trying to rape her. Being cooped up in a press box hardly
seemed as much fun as the other stuff I was doing.

Besides, at the *Observer* I could write a sports story whenever I wanted
to. In the fall of 1972, I wanted to write about the Boston Red Sox, one of
four teams in a close race to win the American League pennant.

What I ended up writing was a comedy in three acts.

—♦♦♦—

ACT 1

A Tuesday morning.

I called the Red Sox public relations office to request credentials for
six home games starting that Friday. I asked for a pregame field pass and

access to the press box. (Locker rooms hadn't been invaded yet.) Bill Crowley, whom I referred to in my story as SuperFlack, harrumphed. "I'm not sure what our legal status is," he coughed, "but around here, we don't let women into the press box. Or onto the field. Or into the dugout."

"You're kidding," I said. I don't know why I was surprised, for I had been through this routine with several teams before. Eventually, the other flacks gave in, skeptically, but with a fair amount of grace.

"Tell you what I'll do," Crowley said. "I'll get you a special box seat, and I'll arrange interviews with any players you want to talk to."

Right. I could just imagine Carl Yastrzemski or their hotshot out-fielder Reggie Smith lumbering through the stands—at some appointed hour—to reach my seat for an interview. "That won't work," I said. "I need to be on the field and in the dugout to get color."

"Well, I'm sorry," Crowley said, "but we never let a woman onto the field. We did let one into the press box earlier this season. It was a disas-ter. Never, *never* again." (The maligned female, it turned out, was from the *Waukegan News Sun* in Illinois. It wasn't her fault that a foul ball struck her on the shoulder in the press box.)

"Why can't I go onto the field or into the dugout?" I asked.

"The language," Crowley replied. "Not the proper atmosphere for a young lady. Besides, you'll make the ballplayers uncomfortable."

"That's ridiculous," I said. I had become increasingly annoyed with Major League Baseball's attitude toward women. Back then they were lured to the ballpark with pantyhose giveaways (really) and half-price tickets. In Philadelphia they could roam the stands in cute little mini-skirts as ushers. In Baltimore they could rush onto the field between innings to sweep off the bases and even Brooks Robinson's feet. Those were baseball's concessions to women.

"Look," I said, "I don't want to cause any trouble, Mr. Crowley. But I do not think your position is legally defensible. I'm afraid we're going to have to look into this."

"Well," he hedged, "tell you what. You have your editor—you are a legitimate reporter, aren't you?—write me a letter giving your credentials and telling me what you want. I'll take it up with some people. But I don't think anybody is going to change their minds."

As it turned out, I had two obstacles blocking my way. SuperFlack and the Press Box Lord. SuperFlack determined who got field passes, while the head of the local baseball writers chapter decided who could, or could not, sit in the press box. While awaiting a reply to the letter that Henry Gemmill sent to SuperFlack verifying my legitimacy, I phoned the Lord of the Press Box. I couldn't tell if it was a personal affliction, but he sounded like a nervous wreck. As if the decision was suddenly dumped in his lap whether to drop the atomic bomb.

"Uh, um, er, just a moment please," he stuttered. He was gone a long time. Long enough, I later learned, to call SuperFlack's underling, Mini-Flack, asking, "Who is this dame?" Eventually, he tut-tutted back on the line.

"No problem, miss. I'll have your passes at the gate. Uh, do you have some kind of identification? Just so there won't be any embarrassment. And, uh, you won't be allowed into the press lounge for dinner." As if I had a communicable disease.

By Friday morning, we still hadn't heard back from SuperFlack. We had called him Thursday, but he was tied up in meetings all day, his secretary said. Friday, it so happened, he was likewise engaged. But he had left a message. I probably wouldn't be allowed onto the field—not because I was a woman, of course, but because I was from a weekly publication. In fact, two male *Observer* reporters had previously been on the Fenway field.

At this point, with the clock winding down, I picked up the phone and called in the cavalry: a Dow Jones attorney named Bob Potter. He phoned the Red Sox lawyer, and they haggled on through the day. Finally, at 5:30 p.m., two hours before game time, a decision was handed down. Let her in. But tell her she'd better behave herself. Honest, that is what I was told. Which meant, I supposed, I had better leave my squirt gun at home.

———

ACT 2

That night.

Rookie Dwight Evans stood at the batting cage, thrashing his spikes with a bat to loosen some imaginary dirt. He was billed as the greatest thing to turn up on the diamond since Mickey Mantle, and in his first Major League minute of play the day before, he had made a spectacular diving catch in right center. I was talking to him about that play. Or trying to.

He fidgeted, scratched his stomach, bent over to rub dirt on his hands, clouted his spikes again, and punctuated the act with a mesmerized stare to center field.

"Look," he finally mumbled, "I'm not used to talking to girl reporters. I just don't know what to say to you."

Apparently, they had all come down with the same ailment. "We have to watch what we say around you," admitted catcher Carlton Fisk, one of the few Red Sox brave enough to speak with me.

"Why?" I asked.

"Because we feel we should act like gentlemen when ladies are around."

Upon learning I would be setting foot on their hallowed grounds, MiniFlack had rushed into the locker room to give advice on proper girl-reporter etiquette. And so, for six straight days while covering the Boston Red Sox, I heard the purest language since kindergarten. It made me anxious. For had *I* let an expletive escape, the whole team surely would have fainted.

With my reporter's notebook containing scarcely a scribble, Mini-Flack walked over to the batting cage and offered to give me a tour of Fenway—read: get me off the field. He was a nice, nervous-looking man named Dick Bresciani, who had clearly been given a job from hell. We rode the elevator to the roof, where the press lounge was located. Outside the door was a round wrought-iron table with one place setting and a sign that read—I swear—"Ladies Pavilion." I said I wasn't hungry. Bresciani then opened the door to the press lounge but did not enter. "You can't go in here," he warned, then pointed to his left. A sign on a door read *Ladies.* "Except to use that bathroom."

If the Red Sox plan was to sweep me under the rug, it failed. For by the time I had reached the ballpark, everyone knew I was coming. The ticket takers, the peanut sellers, the bat boys, the press. Would I pose for a picture with the boys in the dugout? Would I appear on the pregame radio show? Would I give interviews to sportswriters? You'd have thought Ted Williams had come home.

It was inevitable that I would meet SuperFlack, although the Red Sox brass was trying to delay the confrontation as long as possible. Thus, I was given the tour, which lasted until the first pitch was thrown. When at last I entered the press box, I was told to sit next to MiniFlack, who was seated next to SuperFlack.

No introductions were made.

Finally, after four innings, I introduced myself to Crowley. "Do you realize what you've done?" he barked. "Tomorrow there will be fifty girls on the field!"

"I don't think there are that many female sportswriters in the country," I answered mildly.

"Maybe not," he grunted, "but they'll say they are, just so they can get at my players!"

Later he hissed at me, "Because of you, the American family will be destroyed!"

Meantime, the Red Sox were off to a horrendous start. I said to Bresciani, "Do you suppose I'll be blamed if the Sox lose?" I laughed. He didn't.

"You know," he said, "I was down at the batting cage earlier, and instead of going onto the field after they hit, the guys just hung around home plate."

"The novelty will wear off," I said.

"And the language!" He groaned. "I guess the boys were testing you, but it got so bad I had to leave." Funny, I thought, for I hadn't heard anything out of the ordinary.

That night I was the lead story on the local ten o'clock news, and the next morning, the *Boston Globe* wrote about me too.

ACT 3

A plot twist.

The next day, the rules were relaxed, and I was told I could now eat dinner with the other writers in the press lounge. MiniFlack explained that Tom Yawkey, the Red Sox owner, had called him first thing that morning. "He said he'd been up all night worrying about this situation.

Said what the hell, she has credentials like anyone else. Let her go where she wants to."

I went into press lounge and sat down. Nobody came near me. But then Mr. Yawkey sent word to me to join him at his table.

By week's end, they had all pretty much come around. When I didn't show up for one game (I was sitting in the stands with my husband), SuperFlack actually remarked, "Where is that girl? She's been good luck. Get her up here!"

Perhaps the American family will survive after all.

7

Back at the Ranch

IT IS OFTEN SAID THAT WOMEN DO NOT KNOW HOW TO ASK their bosses for raises or promotions. Again, for reasons I cannot explain—from a little girl who did not dare ask Daddy for a bigger allowance—at the *Observer*, I did not see this as a problem. If there was a story I wanted to pursue, I asked. Sometimes I was told no. So what? The next day, I would propose another. When it came to money, I also asked. Respectfully.

At first, I didn't have to ask; I kept receiving nice annual raises. One day Henry called me into his office to congratulate me for a 10 percent raise. At the time, this was standard, but my salary still lagged the others. I thanked him and said, "You know, Henry, it's still not enough." He mumbled a bit then said he'd see what he could do. Later, he called me in again. With a big smile and a chuckle, he said he had wrangled more money out of Dow Jones. I said thank you, "But it's *still* not enough."

Henry just stared at me. "Few people ever get two raises in one year, and you just did," he said sharply.

"Yes, and I appreciate that, Henry. But I really think I deserve to be paid more." I pointed out that most of my stories were on page one, and this should be taken into consideration.

He dismissed me then. Later, he summoned me back. Shaking his head, he said, "Well, you got it. Three raises. Nobody has ever done that."

Unlike journalists today, if we weren't out reporting a story, we were at the office. We didn't work at home, and the camaraderie was special. Often, one of the men would stop by my desk to chat. One might complain he did not like his beat. Another thought he should be making more money or didn't work well with his editor. But unlike me, they didn't make a fuss. In time, I came to realize the one important advantage I had over most of the men: they had families to support. They were terrified they might get fired and didn't want to risk asking for more money or a different beat or something that might antagonize the boss. I didn't have their responsibilities. I was married; we had two incomes and no children. In short, no one was dependent on me financially. So I could take chances. I could ask for things without worrying I might lose my job.

In that newsroom I learned another lesson. Women, the antifeminists would exclaim, suffered *that* time of the month, had stomachaches, were emotional, couldn't do tough work, etc. I had heard these slurs so often that I resolved never to show signs of weakness. One day my editor was missing; oh, he had a stomachache, went home. Once I saw a male colleague cry in the newsroom. I, one time, went to the ladies' room and sniffled for a few minutes before returning, dry-eyed, to my desk. My favorite moment, though, was when I went to a doctor with an infected thumb. He ripped off my thumbnail. He put a large ball of cotton and tape over it, and back to work I went. The men asked what's with your thumb? Oh, I had the nail ripped off. Each turned green. Each told me I should go home. *Now.*

Instead, I went to work that night—covering a party at the White House.

8

My Seven-Dollar Formal Gown

IT ALL SOUNDED SO VERY GLAMOROUS. IMAGINE. I WAS GOING to the White House to write about a party for visiting royalty: Prince Charles and Princess Anne. Surely this would be one of the highlights of my career.

The 21-year-old prince and his 19-year-old sister were winding up a two-and-a-half-week visit to the New World, most of it in Canada. But before returning to England, they would spend this one night at the White House. It had been forever since such a swinging bash had been held at 1600 Pennsylvania Avenue, and the daughters, Tricia and Julie Nixon, had meticulously planned each detail. The party would be on the South Lawn: 57 round, yellow-clothed tables, a dance floor, and two bandstands, one for the red-coated Marine Corps Band, the other for a bell-bottomed Canadian rock group, the Guess Who.

What fun! There was only one problem: reporters and photographers had been directed (more like ordered) to wear formal attire, just like the real guests. I did not own formal attire, and I didn't have the money to buy a fancy gown. Luckily, I found a rental store, and after picking through the slim selections, settled on a full-length turquoise nylon . . . gown? In truth, it looked like a nightgown, but I rented it for $7 and then bought a pair of silk heels that I had dyed to match.

For our trouble, nobody ever saw us. Before the 550 invited guests arrived, we were shepherded around the grounds then herded back to the press room. I felt sorry for the photographers, loaded down with equipment hanging over their stiff tuxedos on a hot night. We sat and waited. And waited. Eventually, the press entourage was chaperoned up to the second floor for its last observation of this socially noteworthy event. With stopwatch in hand, Mrs. Connie Stuart, staff director to the first lady, allowed relay teams of five reporters out onto the balcony to watch—from behind—as the guests shook hands with the Nixon girls, David Eisenhower, and the prince and princess. For two whole minutes. Then we were shooed away so the next relay team could observe the scene below.

Later, as I was walking to my car, I stepped on soft grass and one of my heels broke. I returned my "formal gown" the next day.

9

Where Is That Damn Shark?

THE SCENE WAS UNFOLDING TEN FEET AWAY. NOTEPAD IN hand, I stood mesmerized. It was early morning, and already trouble loomed. Down the road from the East Chop lighthouse, in the dining room of a small oceanside bungalow, the young director was staring a crisis in the face. Literally. The entire day's shooting schedule involved a one-minute dinner scene. And one of the diners, actor Richard Dreyfuss, had—dear God!—a *pimple*.

The director swept the hair out of his eyes and calmly pondered the situation. "We could make it into a shaving accident and write in a new line," he suggested.

Dreyfuss groaned.

"Okay, so maybe we could send everyone home and let the insurance company pick up the day's tab," the director said, referring to the film's $30,000-a-day budget. "But maybe," he decided, "we'd just better shoot Dreyfuss from the left side."

I scribbled furiously, only to look up and discover Dreyfuss had another problem. He was supposed to be telling a story about a shark that once attacked his small boat. "He ate everything, the seat cushions, the oar-holes, the . . ."

"Cut!"

Once Dreyfuss got his oarlocks and oar-holes squared away, filming resumed. I was on Martha's Vineyard observing the making of *Jaws*, directed by Hollywood's latest fixation, 26-year-old Steven Spielberg. Fresh from his first major motion picture, *The Sugarland Express*, Spielberg was now in his fourth week of filming a movie all Hollywood was yakking about. Could Spielberg make Peter Benchley's best-selling novel into a blockbuster movie? Would sharp-toothed sharks lure people to buy tickets? The budget was high, $3.5 million, and the shark—or sharks—would swallow an enormous chunk of it.

The problems began even before shooting did. The permanent residents of Martha's Vineyard made it known immediately they did not want these interlopers sashaying around their precious island. Indeed, the 7,000 year-round inhabitants still referred to actor James Cagney, a resident of 25 years, as "that off-lander," and to the Kennedys as "those *nouveau riche.*"

Meanwhile, the weather proved as unfriendly as the locals. Said one crew member, "This is going to be a swell film. Every other line is going to be, 'Hmmm, looks like rain.'"

But the filmmakers' biggest headaches began when production manager Jim Fargo ferried into town and hung a two-foot sign outside the production office that said, "Jaws—a Zanuck/Brown production—Universal Pictures." Folks were scandalized. Soon Fargo was brought before the Edgartown selectmen, the Chilmark selectmen, the Gay Head selectmen, and so on until, like a traveling road show, he had presented himself before the governing boards of each of the Vineyard's six towns. When the legalities were finally cleared away and the list of financial penalties for overstaying the June 15 deadline was approved, *Jaws* became the biggest social "do" in memory. The cold-fish islanders showed up in droves to vie for the 70 cameos and 800 extras.

One woman, cast as the aggrieved mother of a boy who got eaten by the shark, was instructed to slap Police Chief Brody (actor Roy Scheider) in the face. "The cameraman asked me not to drop my head too far back," Scheider said. "But after she whopped me, practically knocking me over, the cameraman said, 'Forget it, I understand.'"

Oddly, each of the principals has a different take on the story. Scheider considers himself the star of the film; Spielberg sees it as a story of tension between the leading actors. Producer Richard Zanuck views it as a picture about a shark that is not a villain but a mindless Frankenstein's monster that doesn't mean any harm and is, Zanuck insists, the real star.

I was talking to Zanuck as we sat on a deserted beach. I had never been on a movie set, so I didn't know that my freedom to move around as I pleased and talk to whomever I wanted to was unusual. Still, no matter how convivial everyone was, no one would reveal the whereabouts of the killer shark. If, as Zanuck maintained, the shark was the real star of the movie, I obviously had to find it.

But then, so had the producers. For casting the shark, I learned, had been quite difficult. Obviously, Universal could not hire a real killer white shark, and the chilly Vineyard waters were about as shark-infested as a bathtub. Hoping to at least find a stand-in, stuntman Ted Grossman was dispatched to Sarasota, Florida, where he managed to obtain a 12½-foot, 715-pound tiger shark. He carefully packed the dead animal in a crate with rock salt and Airwick and hired a private jet to fly it to the Vineyard. By the time it arrived, "Oscar" had deteriorated, as Grossman put it, "into a wrinkled prune."

Next, Universal hired Bob Mattey, formerly of Walt Disney Productions, to make a stand-in for some scenes. At a cost of $200,000, Mattey devised three mechanical monsters, each 25 feet long, which reportedly were so lifelike that shark expert and *Jaws* author, Peter Benchley, gushed, "They're perfect. They even feel like sharks."

These then were my prey, if only I could find them. But because Spielberg believes films should be fantasy, the sharks were hidden in a secret location with a round-the-clock guard. Could I have a peek? No! Then, noticing my long face, one crew member pulled me aside and gave me an address. I hopped into my rental and took off. The address led me to a boat shed in Edgartown. An old-timer was sitting in a lawn chair on the front porch.

"Hi," I said, approaching him with a big smile. "I heard three sharks are inside. Is that true?"

Maybe the old guy was bored, but he immediately got to his feet and motioned me to follow. He led me inside and up a flight of stairs, past walls lined with signs saying "Do Not Enter." The stairs opened onto a large loft. And there, on the floor, lay three great whites, open-mouthed, revealing their horrible, jagged teeth. But they didn't look scary. They looked like three fake sharks. I figured Spielberg's movie magic would somehow turn them into terrifying beasts. I asked if I could snap a picture, the old guy nodded, and I did.

Apparently, the mechanical shark revelations in my *Observer* story did not deter moviegoers. *Jaws*, which opened in the summer of 1975, grossed $260,000,000 as of 1982, second only to *Star Wars*. It lost the Oscar for best picture to *One Flew Over the Cuckoo's Nest*. None of the sharks was nominated for a best acting award.

10

Ladies' Home Journal, Miss?

WHEN I SET OUT TO WRITE THIS MEMOIR, I HAD NO INTENTION of making it a compilation of the sexist snubs thrown my way. Sure, I would recall tales of locker room "situations" and tell the story of my colleagues "preparing" me for the Republican National Convention. But as I poked through old stories and notes, I was surprised how often sexism popped up. The following story—about an *airline*—amused me, and I had fun writing about it for the *Observer*.

It went like this.

Once again, I am sitting on an airplane, peering squinty-eyed at the magazine-bearing stewardess. She is only two rows away now, and I tug at my seat belt in preparation for yet another in-flight floor show.

"Magazine, sir?" she asks the man next to me.

"What do you have?" he inquires.

"*Sports Illustrated, Business Week, Fortune, Time, Newsweek . . .*"

"*Time,*" he says.

To me she offers, "*Ladies' Home Journal, Better Homes and Gardens, Vogue, McCall's . . .*"

"*Sports Illustrated,* please."

She pretends not to hear.

"And, oh yes, *Bazaar!*"

"*Sports Illustrated,*" I repeat.

She regards me suspiciously, no doubt wondering how this one got past security. "I think," she coldly informs me, "that you'll find more to read in something like *McCall's.*"

Okay, so I have come to accept the fact that all my husband need do is grimace and three stewardesses miraculously appear with aspirin and headcloths, while I, I could be bleeding all over the plane before anyone thinks to ask if I might want something. And well, okay, so maybe most women never request *Pro Quarterback* (wrestling that magazine from one scandalized stew is my biggest coup to date)—but the fact that stewardesses rarely even offer *Time*, *Newsweek*, or *US News & World Report* to their female passengers is preposterous. It is even more preposterous because these very flight attendants have formed their own groups to protest what they consider to be sex discrimination practiced by their employers. Then they go squealing and oinking down the aisles, passing out recipes and hairstyles to their very own sisters. Terrific.

I finally dispossess the outraged stewardess of *Sports Illustrated*, but before I can even flip it open, the man next to me is tugging at my elbow.

"I've never seen a girl read *Sports Illustrated*," he marvels. "Do you, uh, like sports or what?"

"Not really," I tell him. "I just like to look at the underwear ads."

He doesn't hear me. "You know," he plunges on, "I know four girls who play handball every week. And you know what?"

"What?"

"Boy, do they ever smell when they're through."

Yeah, I tell him, it's a pretty smelly business. Then I open *SI*, which, of course, I'd already read.

Shortly after this piece appeared, I received a letter from the president of American Airlines, apologizing for the "misunderstanding," and promising to retrain his staff. I never had that problem again.

11

A Hat and a Purple Note Card

SPECIFICALLY, IT WAS A NOTE-SIZED PURPLE SHEET OF stationery tucked inside a matching purple envelope. It came to me at the *Observer*. The writer introduced herself as literary agent Roslyn Targ, and she wondered if I might stop by the next time I was in New York to discuss book ideas.

Book ideas? Me? What, like a cookbook or how to arrange a proper table setting? What could she possibly have in mind? And who wrote a business letter on purple stationery? Still, I figured it wouldn't hurt, so I did go to see her.

Some weeks later, I found my way to her office in a brownstone in the West Village. A tall, striking blonde, she wore a fitted wool dress and—I swear—a hat. If Google had been around then, I would have learned that Mrs. Targ was quite well-known or, as she was called, the "Grand Dame of the Book Industry." She had sold Mario Puzo's *The Godfather* and represented Harold Robbins and Norman Mailer. Moreover, she was the go-to agent for selling foreign rights, and she was married to well-known book editor William Targ. And, it turned out, she *always* wore hats.

To my surprise, she did not suggest the kind of book I might write. Instead, she asked me what kind of book I would like to write.

I said I didn't know. Maybe someday . . . a mystery novel?

"Someday?"

"Yes, I'm not old enough." (I was in my midtwenties.) "I don't know enough about life."

"When do you think you will be old enough?"

"Um, when I'm forty?"

Roslyn Targ smiled. "If you think you will suddenly wake up one day and say today is the day I will start my book, I promise you, you never will. If you want to write a book, start writing it today."

But...

She then explained all she needed to sell a book was two chapters and a plot outline.

As I raced back to my hotel, I remembered hearing that a writer should stick to a subject he or she knew well. I doubted I knew anything well. Okay, maybe baseball. *Murder at Home Plate? The Mystery of the Broken Bat?* When I got to my room, I immediately called my husband. If you want to write a mystery set in the sports world, Bruce said, it should be about football. And betting. "Yes!" I exclaimed. "Brilliant!" A mystery involving a football player. Perfect.

I thought for a moment. Then I said, "Um, can you teach me football?"

—◦◦◦—

I wasn't kidding. I knew little about football, had never been interested. But now I was on a mission. Every Sunday and Monday night, I plugged myself into the TV, all the while badgering poor Bruce with question after question. What's a nickel defense? A prevent defense? A play-action pass? Bruce would laugh and say, "The same thing it was when you asked last week." Learning the strategies and the lingo took me that whole season. Plus, I sneaked in a couple of football stories for the *Observer* about Baltimore Colts quarterback Bert Jones and Patriots five-foot-six running back Mack Herron. And then—still pummeling Bruce with questions—I began writing chapter 1 of my novel about a kidnapped quarterback.

12

"I Am My Arm"

NOT THAT BASEBALL NO LONGER INTERESTED ME. IT WAS September, and the pennant races were heating up. So were the Baltimore Orioles. I phoned their public relations director and said I wanted to interview Jim Palmer, one of the best pitchers in the American League.

I had dealt with the Orioles before. Unlike the Red Sox, they were the nicest, most accommodating team I may have ever dealt with. The previous September, I had traveled with them to Milwaukee. They beat the Brewers to win the American League East. Since I couldn't go into the locker room, after the game I went outside and sat on the team bus, which the PR guy had allowed me to ride. Boog Powell, who played first base and the outfield, trotted out in his underwear and through a window handed me a glass of champagne. "You should help us celebrate too," he said.

The following year I rang Jim Palmer's doorbell.

———※———

At 5:20 p.m.—I wrote in my notebook—Jim Palmer is in the laundry room of his 12-room house, searching frantically for a clean pair of socks. White socks. For some reason—maybe a superstitious one—the socks absolutely must be white. He flips through a pile of folded towels, shakes his head.

It's late September, and Palmer is having a typical Palmer season. Already he has won 20 games. He has won 20 or more games in five of the last six seasons. His lifetime ERA is 2.68. His current ERA of 2.18 is the lowest in the American League. He's won a Cy Young Award. *(And now he is pawing through his dryer.)*

In fewer than two hours, he will take the mound for the Baltimore Orioles against the division-leading Red Sox. The year before, Baltimore had made up 5½ games to overtake Boston for the American League East title, and it seems the same might happen again. *(If only he could find his socks!)* He is supposed to be at the ballpark by now. But, he says, "I see no point getting there at 5:30 and worrying for two hours."

Anyway, Palmer has already completed most of his pregame prep. He downed his traditional breakfast of pancakes (after scouring Baltimore at 1 a.m. for the required quart of milk), donned this year's good-luck charm—a hand to ward off evil on a chain—and went so far as to remind his wife to watch the game not from her seat behind home plate but on the TV in the Orioles' front office. This season, for some inexplicable reason, Susie Palmer has rained runs upon her husband's head when she sits in the stands.

So, at 29, Palmer seems to have it all. Not only is there his superb pitching, but Palmer also has the good looks of a movie star—6'3", slender, reddish-brown hair, big blue eyes, and a dimpled grin—not to mention a beautiful wife and, ah yes, those Jockey underwear magazine ads. Yet . . .

"Found them!" With socks in hand, Palmer slides into his Datsun 280Z and sets off at a speed slightly under that of his breakneck fastball (while I try to follow in my rental) to do battle with those other Sox. The ones from Boston.

Yet . . . despite his many attributes, Palmer seems to hold grudges—lots of them. I noticed this shortly after he greeted me at the front door. He was holding a scythe. As he led me through the living room, out a sliding glass door, and onto the patio, he explained Susie had complained that one of the trees on their 1½-acre lot was dripping pine tar onto her new patio furniture, and he and a neighbor were trying to chop off the offending branches. Palmer insisted he was eager to do the work himself, but this being "the season," he had to babysit his right arm, which, I learn, he treats like an exotic pet. Finally, after flailing at one branch with his left arm, and being overcome with embarrassment, he bravely lifted the scythe once more and hacked off a tree limb.

At this point, the neighbor looked down from his perch in the tree and said, "You know if you guys win tonight and tomorrow night, you'll be back in it."

"How's that?" said Palmer. "By scoring two runs?"

"Well," said the neighbor, "you'll have to shut 'em out."

"Yeah, Weaver already thought of that. And no walks either. Sure." Palmer was referring to his manager, Earl Weaver.

Palmer insisted he was being realistic. The Orioles were not hitting. "If they give me three runs," he said, "I'll win it."

If Palmer sometimes has reservations about his teammates, he seems never to have them about himself. Even the year before, his worst, when he suffered a 7 and 12 season after injuring the ulnar nerve in his right elbow and missing six weeks, he never doubted his ability. "Although I lost seven of eight games before going on the disabled list, I *still* only gave up 12 runs in nine games," he is quick to point out.

Then he says, "It did not seem to matter how good or bad I pitched. It was that kind of year, and it really opened my eyes. I began to realize for the first time you had to deal with fate. I always believed that if you pitched well you automatically won. Now I know it's not hard to lose 2 to 1."

Palmer's acceptance of fate extends only so far. He has meticulously arranged his life—and apparently his wife—around one thing: his arm. He does everything but lock it up in a safe at night. For as he nonchalantly noted at one point, "I am my arm." Thus, he trained himself to sleep on his left side by piling pillows against his back because, "What if my right arm should go to sleep?"

During the season, he tells me, he performs household chores with his left hand because "Even using a hammer involves different muscles." He taught himself to play tennis left-handed; he abstains from golf during the summer because "It's not what I'm paid to do, and it's got to take something out of you."

"He's not a pitcher who works once every four days," manager Earl Weaver testifies. "He's in the ball game nine innings every night, sitting on the bench studying pitchers' motions and watching how the other teams hit."

Weaver does not handle Palmer like a Fabergé egg—or anyone else. A master umpire baiter, he once had this exchange with Ron Luciano after Luciano called an Oriole out at first on a close play. When Weaver stormed out of the dugout and questioned the ump's eyesight, Luciano pointed to his right eye. "See this eye? It's insured for ten thousand dollars." Pointing to his left eye, "See this eye? It's insured for ten thousand dollars." To which Weaver shot back, "So what did you do with the money?"

As with umps, Weaver tends to get the last word in with Palmer too. He recalls starting Palmer during a spring-training game. "The wind was blowing in at about forty miles an hour, and there was no way nobody was gonna hit a home run. But Palmer's out there in the first inning, pitching outside, and he walks four batters. I went out to the mound and told him to just throw over the plate. He wouldn't do it. When he came back to the dugout, I said, 'That was terrible. Anybody can do that.' And he says, 'Well, if anyone can, then *you* pitch.' I brought in someone else. I think he was surprised."

This night, at Memorial Stadium against Boston, Palmer had ten strikeouts; he also did something he had never done in the big leagues: he walked four straight batters in the second inning, giving up the first run. In the tenth, he served up a home-run ball to Cecil Cooper, and Boston won 3–2.

Afterward, Palmer walked jauntily out of the locker room and shrugged. "They," he said, referring to his teammates, "blew two, and the umpire made a bad call, and that was the game. Just like I said. Three runs and we would have won it."

Palmer was wrong. He would not have won no matter how many runs Baltimore had scored.

Susie Palmer had been sitting in the stands.

—◦◦◦—

That I'd spent all day with the best pitcher in baseball before he would start a must-win game was not unusual. Unlike the sound-bite age of today, in the '70s and '80s, a writer could spend significant time with an athlete or a celebrity. Lots of it. Can you imagine Tom Brady or LeBron James chilling with a reporter, hours before the big game? Here's another way things have changed. I flew to Cleveland one blustery day to interview Browns quarterback Brian Sipe. We were supposed to meet in the coffee shop at my hotel, but there was a blizzard and I wondered if the roads were even passable. One half hour late, his knit cap caked with snow, Sipe hurried in—and *apologized*.

But those days evaporated as salaries skyrocketed and TV and smartphones made athletes more cautious with reporters and less generous with their time. Why spend hours with a print reporter when one could reach millions of viewers in a two-minute clip on ESPN? In the late '90s, Tim Brown, then the highly respected Lakers writer for the *Los Angeles Times*, told me, "If I want to interview Kobe or Shaq or anybody really, I get to practice or the game early and sit in my car in the parking lot. When one of the players pulls in, I jump out and talk to him as we walk toward the locker room door. That's it."

While I could spend hours in locker rooms chatting with players before and after games, now reporters anxiously shuffle their feet—with nary a player in sight.

13

Moving On

FOUR YEARS AFTER I JOINED THE *OBSERVER*, MY HUSBAND WAS offered a job at the PBS station in Boston. The *Observer* had no bureaus then but I pleaded my case to Roscoe Born. "Why not Boston? I rarely report stories in Washington. I'm usually on a plane anyway." In the end, the top editors agreed and arranged for me to work out of the *Wall Street Journal*'s Boston office. Soon after I had another request. Waking early, I would punch out a few pages of my novel before going to work, and often I wrote at night and on weekends. I was obsessed! A year after moving to Boston, I had completed a (very) rough draft. I asked Roscoe Born, could I have a short leave of absence to polish it?

Like the move out of the main office, this request would be a stretch. Dow Jones policy, I was told, only allowed leaves for pregnancy or education. Before I could say anything, Roscoe asked, "Why don't you find a writing seminar? Boston College, Boston University? It shouldn't be difficult."

Several inquiries led me to Boston College English professor Richard Hughes, who agreed to create our own "seminar." Each Tuesday afternoon, I would go to his office and bring one chapter. He would then return my previous week's chapter and discuss it. I always looked forward to our sessions. It was autumn, and outside his windows the beautifully colored leaves danced and swirled in the breezes. Professor Hughes would pour me a glass of red wine and make invaluable suggestions. "How can your first-person narrator be looking at a bookshelf and comment on something a man is doing behind her back?"

He told me he had been trying to write a novel but was getting nowhere with it. The last time we met, he said—with a note of bitterness—"Yours is a very commercial book. I'm sure it will do quite well."

The Mackin Cover, as I titled it, was a terrible book, one I refuse to ever read again. It probably should have died in my bottom desk drawer.

—⁓—

After my leave was over, the *Observer* assigned me two big stories. One was on presidential candidate Jimmy Carter's wife, Rosalynn, the other about *Washington Post* publisher Katharine Graham. Mrs. Carter was a new kind of first-lady-in-waiting. No wife had ever campaigned so relentlessly for her husband. In Jackson, Mississippi, she told a small crowd that the week before, her family had been in 25 states and 97 cities. The week before that, they'd been in 35 states and 127 cities. "Mr. Ford," she said sweetly, speaking of the president, "has been in Washington since 1948. There's *no way* you can be in Washington since 1948 and know what it's like to be out in the country working."

I found her curiously controlled as she spoke. Always she smiled prettily, but it was a smile bereft of emotion. And her eyes—those wide, gray-blue eyes—revealed nothing. Not to me during the five days I spent traveling with her. And, said people who had known her for years, not ever. Even her mother admitted, "I don't know how to describe Rosalynn."

—⁓—

By contrast, when I first contacted Katharine Graham, she said, "The only line I draw is that you can't live with me in my house."

This was 1976, not even two years since the *Post*'s Bob Woodward and Carl Bernstein had broken open the Watergate scandal and made her a heroine for running the stories her reporters banged out . Until 1963, she had been an upper-class housewife married to Phil Graham, publisher of the *Post*. Her specialty was entertaining. But when he committed suicide, this shy, awkward woman edged into the driver's seat and slowly but surely learned how to keep her foot on the gas.

Here is how I started the piece:

"I came from this incredibly high-powered family. My mother was sort of a Viking. Very bright, and utterly contemptuous of everyone else. When I told her I had read *The Three Musketeers*, she said, 'Undoubtedly a waste of time, my dear, unless you read it in the original French.'

"I swear the first compliment she ever paid me was when I was giving a party for my 18-year-old daughter. As we were doing the preparations, my mother said, 'Darling, you're so good at lists!'

"Actually, she was a good mother in that she told us: 'You can't just sit around the house and be rich. You must do something.' But of course she never made me feel I could do anything at all."

I then wrote:

It might be reasonably argued that at 58, Katharine Meyer Graham has indeed "done something" other than sit around her various houses being rich. Perhaps the most celebrated something is puckishly alluded to in the office of *Washington Post* executive editor Benjamin Bradlee—in the form of a cartoon. Gerald Ford is standing at a lectern explaining, "I got my job through the *Washington Post.*"

Deposing one American president, causing at least two others to phone her in fury, not to mention recently turning out the *Post's* entire pressmen's union on its heels, are among some of the "things" Katharine Graham has done. She also holds the dubious distinction of being dressed down, so to speak, in Lyndon Johnson's bedroom.

One person who read my story was an editor at Dodd, Mead & Company publishers. "Great piece," he told me over the phone. "How about doing a book about her?"

I said I doubted she would agree, but I would ask. And indeed, she did say no. She wasn't ready for a memoir, and when the time came, she thought she might write it herself. (She did. *Katharine Graham: Personal History*, which was universally lauded.)

The editor sounded disappointed but said he would welcome any ideas I might have for a book.

"As a matter of fact," I said, laughing, "I just finished a mystery novel."

He asked me to send it. I relayed the message to Roslyn Targ and—to my astonishment and delight—received an advance of $2,000 plus a publishing agreement for a hardcover book! Playboy Press printed the paperback edition.

———✦———

Although I was doing really well, the *Observer* was not. At the time, only the *Wall Street Journal* was a national newspaper. *USA Today* was still a few years away, and advertisers were clueless about what kind of ads to place in a weekly national newspaper. In June 1977 the *Observer* folded.

I was contacted by the *Wall Street Journal, Newsweek*, the *New York Times*, and five or six other papers. Over the summer I narrowed my choices to the *Journal* and *Newsweek*. The *Journal* job looked amazing. I would be writing the Page One A-HED column, which was always offbeat and usually funny. But in subsequent conversations, I was told I might be assigned to "culture," whatever that meant. Or maybe do some sports. Back then, business was not nearly as interesting as it would become. *The Predators' Ball* hadn't been written, Enron hadn't happened, and neither had the many headline-grabbing scandals that loomed ahead. But, I thought, the *Journal* was prestigious.

The *Newsweek* job wasn't well defined, but it seemed like a more fun place to work. The money would be about the same. The big difference, however, was that if I left Dow Jones, which owned the *Observer,* I could collect my pension, which, at about $20,000, seemed like a lot of money. If I stayed with the company, I wouldn't collect it.

In August I heard from Ed Cony, the *Journal*'s executive editor. Had I decided what I wanted to do? I told him I was considering both the *Journal* and *Newsweek*, but I was confused about what beat the *Journal* would assign me. He told me not to worry and put in a few words about why the *Journal* would be a better choice.

Then I said, "The money is about the same Mr. Cony, but if I go to *Newsweek* I can collect my pension. Could Dow Jones pay me all—or some—of it?"

Cony launched into a screaming attack. "You think you're such a prima donna! Well, here you'd be just one of three hundred reporters." I tried to explain that I would have to move to New York (along with my husband, who would have to find a job, both of which he was willing to do. But it would be an expensive move.) Mr. Cony kept yelling at me, and finally the conversation ended with me saying I would get back to him.

As I hung up, I couldn't help thinking that if I were a man talking about the need to take care of his family, Cony wouldn't have yelled at me. I wrote him a letter thanking him for the offer, but I was declining.

Then I dialed *Newsweek* and signed on. Not as a part-time librarian or a researcher, but as a *writer*. I proudly framed and hung in my office those three letters of rejection from the Washington bureau. And then, a little more than one year later, I was anointed *Newsweek*'s number-two sportswriter. Of all things.

FINAL SCORE:

High School Guidance Counselor—0

Me—2

14

Into the Woods with Butch Cassidy

STANDING AT THE DOOR, I CHECKED MY WATCH AND, TAKING a deep breath, rang the bell. Immediately, the door swung open. And there he was—*Paul Newman!*—possibly the handsomest man on the planet. The actor's luminous blue eyes sparkled as he smiled and asked me in. Behind him, piled high in the entryway, were cases of Budweiser. He was wearing jeans and a flannel shirt. He was—this was 1978—one month shy of his 54th birthday, but neither his face nor his body showed signs of wear.

"It's such a nice day," Newman said. "How about if we go for a walk?"

It was early December but unseasonably warm, and the sky was clear and bright. I was on the campus of Kenyon College, Newman's alma mater, in Gambier, Ohio. A publicist who handled education stories phoned me at *Newsweek* to pitch the story. Since I hadn't transitioned into sports yet, I was a "floater," writing pieces for any section of the magazine. My ears perked up. Newman, the publicist said, had agreed to direct the first student play to open in Kenyon's brand-new theater. He said Newman had agreed to do two interviews. Would I like to be one of them?

I broke a personal speed record racing down the hall to my editor's office. Approval given, off I went. I had seen many of Newman's films: *Butch Cassidy and the Sundance Kid, The Sting, Hud, Cool Hand Luke, Slap Shot* among them. Even at an age when most movie stars get kicked to the curb, he was still considered one of the handsomest and most in-demand actors in Hollywood.

As always, I had a list of questions written out in my reporter's notebook, but I tucked that into my shoulder bag as Newman led me down a deserted blacktop road. I had been given strict instructions: He didn't want to talk about his movies, his acting, or, really, himself. More importantly, under no circumstances was I to ask about his son, Scott Newman, 28, who had died from a drug overdose only three weeks before. Newman's wife, Joanne Woodward, had been on campus at the time and had immediately left. But Paul had stayed and continued working with the students.

The article, I was told, should focus on the play, *C. C. Pyle and the Bunion Derby*, by Pulitzer Prize–winning dramatist Michael Cristofer; a generous Ford Foundation grant; and Newman's interactions with the students. I had my tape recorder on as we walked.

Newman explained that Kenyon had asked if he would contribute to the construction of its new $2 million theater. "I said no," he related, adding how often he was hit up for money, "but I did promise to direct the first student production for free." To this, one Kenyon official had complained, "It's less than we wanted."

"But more than I can afford," Newman said he replied.

Across the road were woods, and Newman suggested we head into them. The ground was a bit hilly and covered with crisp autumn leaves. I, assuming we would have a routine sit-down—would you like a cup of coffee, a beer?—type of session, was wearing a skirt, stockings, and two-inch heels. Newman quickly moved out in front of me as I slip-slided along. Realizing I wasn't right behind him, he stopped, looked back, and waited for me to catch up. Then he casually looped his right arm through my left one and walked on.

Rarely did celebrities unnerve me but . . . *Paul Newman*? Strolling through the woods, *arm-in-arm* with this movie idol? And I was supposed to continue my interview? Newman talked about why he had decided on a sabbatical from films. "I took so much out of this place," he said. "I wanted to give something back." And he was intrigued by Cristofer's play about a shady sports promoter of the '20s. Once on campus, Newman was amazed by his charges. "They act with a built-in naturalism. The only explanation I can think of is that they've been exposed to so much on the idiot box."

As we left the woods, he caught sight of a student passing nearby. "Hey, remember I bring the hamburgers tonight, you supply the rest," he called out. The student nodded solemnly.

"You, too," Newman said, inviting me to the cookout, something he often did for his students.

I remember asking about his well-known ban-the-bomb activities, but there is little else I now recall. After an hour or so, he told me he would see me later, adding, apropos of what I didn't know, "I'm in a very whimsical state these days. Joanne is home doing a needlepoint for me. It says, 'I will not *should* on myself today.'"

I raced back to my motel room to check the tape and . . . *oh no! No, no, no!* A reporter's nightmare. It wasn't that my recorder had malfunctioned, it had worked perfectly. But I had been holding it in my right hand, swinging it back and forth as I walked. And all that it had recorded was the crunching of those damn leaves.

I sat down on the bed, grabbed my notebook, and scribbled furiously, trying to recall everything he said. I got a lot of it, but not all. *Okay, okay,* I thought. *I will have more time with him to fill in the blanks.* But I was furious with myself and embarrassed.

—⁓—

Newman had arrived in October, without his wife and with no props except for a portable sauna. No one knew what to expect, least of all spinster Kate Allen, who turned over her antique-filled house to him. "He's a bit disorderly," she told me, as she surveyed the cases of beer stacked in her front hall, "but nice, forever apologizing for not having made his bed." Locals who had hatched grandiose schemes found Newman disappointingly uncooperative. He declined to appear at the Beekeepers' Association luncheon in exchange for a hive of bees, and balked at a real-estate woman's request that he pose in front of a house she had for sale.

Instead, he reserved his charm for the students. That evening, as he stood over a grill, flipping hamburgers, I learned he was a patient, gentle coach, sitting in the theater night after night, calling out, "Hold it, guys," and bounding onto the stage.

A loose intimacy soon grew between the star and his protégés. After Newman wore a Band-Aid on his chin to cover a fever blister, the entire cast appeared on stage with Band-Aids on their chins. "You mean you all have the clap too?" Newman exclaimed.

When I asked how Newman had reacted to the news of his son's death, one student told me he assembled the cast and said, "It would help me if you'd all be as rowdy as possible." Later that night, several students put on silly costumes and rang his doorbell. When Newman greeted them in his nightshirt, they handed him a case of beer and a bottle of Jack Daniel's. Newman grinned, took one swig of the whiskey, said, "It's the first time I've touched hard stuff in eight years," and quietly said good night.

My last day there, a Friday, I spoke briefly with Newman before heading out. "Here's my phone number," he said, handing me a piece of paper. "Don't hesitate to call if you need anything."

Monday morning, back in my office, I wasn't sure if I should write about what the students did the night Scott died. It didn't seem right to use this anecdote without talking to Newman. I dialed the number he gave me, and he answered with a sleepy voice. It was 10 a.m., but clearly I had awakened him. I apologized. He said no problem; what did I need? I threw out a few fact-checking questions. Then I said, "Several students talked about the night Scott died and how they went to your house with beer and I was wondering . . ."

"*Goddammit!*" Newman exploded. "The kid is dead! Why do I have to keep talking about it?" With that, he slammed the phone down.

I was mortified. It is never fun when someone hangs up on you, but *Paul Newman*? I felt terrible that I had upset him and was, frankly, shaken. After a moment and a few deep breaths, I decided to try again, if only to apologize. He had been so nice to me, so helpful. Slowly I dialed the number and held my breath.

The phone rang and rang. Newman did not pick up.

My story may have been the nicest one I ever wrote. But it pleased no one. As I was writing it, my editor stopped by to say that due to a big news week, my story would be cut to barely half a page. Thinking that readers would be more interested in Newman's role, I only mentioned the name of the play, the playwright, and left out the Ford Foundation grant altogether. This displeased the publicist. I did not mention Newman's hanging up on me, but I did write about the students going to his house the night Scott died.

A few days after the story ran, one of *Newsweek*'s top editors burst into my office waving a telegram. "What should we do with this?" he demanded.

The telegram said: "I'm canceling my subscription to *Newsweek* and subscribing instead to *Screw* magazine. Paul Newman."

I handed the telegram back. "I think you should run it in letters to the editor. He's upset, and he should be heard."

Newman's anger did not go away. Four years later, when his movie *The Verdict* was about to open, both *Time* and *Newsweek* wanted to put him on their covers. Newman refused to deal with *Newsweek*, and *Time* got the story.

15

If I Ever See That Girl Again, I'll Spit in Her Face

I DID NOT KNOW ANYTHING ABOUT LARRY BIRD.

Okay, I knew a little. It was late summer 1979, and Bird was about to begin his NBA rookie season with the Boston Celtics. I knew his college team, Indiana State, had lost the national championship game to Magic Johnson's Michigan State months before in what was considered a big deal. In my defense, I might note that the NCAA title game hadn't flourished into what it is today; in fact, few TV viewers had ever seen Magic or Bird play.

Although I had recently moved into sports for *Newsweek*, we now had a sister publication. It was called *Inside Sports*, and the editor, John Walsh, had asked me to write a cover story about Bird. I was thrilled; it was a big assignment. I did my homework and phoned two or three Boston sportswriters who had been supportive of me years before when I had infested Fenway Park.

Then off I went off to Massachusetts to meet Mr. Bird.

―⁓―

Not far from a sign that reads "Dave Cowens Basketball Camp," the Celtics' center is standing amid a throng of teenage boys shooting from the outside, one ball after another—*whoosh, whoosh, whoosh*.

Slowly, a gray Cadillac rolls up alongside the court. The door swings open and out steps a tall blond man wearing white tennis shoes. Cowens is still shooting... *whoosh, whoosh, whoosh*. Suddenly the youngsters are no longer watching him. He turns, squints into the sun, and breaks into a big grin.

All the chatter stops. The boys stand motionless as Cowens lets the ball dribble away and lopes across the court, his arm outstretched. He claps his new teammate on the back. "Good to see ya, buddy, hey! Wanna go get taped?"

The stranger mumbles something, and Cowens guides him down a leafy path to a trailer. The campers—with eyes as big as basketballs—watch the two large men saunter off. Then, as if they had been rehearsed by Cecil B. DeMille, they begin to follow, dozens of them, not saying a word, trooping down the dirt path into the trees, walking faster now . . . running.

Finally, the two men reach the trainer's trailer. By now, 50, 60 boys have clustered, some gaping, others—the shy ones—pretending not to look at all. The cockier ones strut as if nothing extraordinary is happening. But nobody budges. The taping finished, the tall blond man with one bandaged finger climbs into Cowens's van, and the pair drives off. The boys follow, at first on foot and then with their eyes, until the van disappears from view.

"Wow, did you see him?"

—∿∿—

This opening to my story, I hoped, would demonstrate that Bird was already a big deal, which I already knew. What I soon learned was why. The Celtics had drafted him the year before, but Larry said nah, he wanted to stay for his senior year at Indiana State. His team, the Sycamores, made it to the finals, as noted above. Theoretically, he was still a Celtic draft pick, but he had the freedom to go to any other team. His negotiations, known locally as "The Hundred Days War," were chronicled blow by bloody blow. At one point, Bird's attorney, Bob Woolf, threatened to take his star elsewhere—only to be given the finger every time he walked down the street. Bird finally agreed to a five-year contract for $3.25 million, making him the highest-salaried rookie ever in any sport and, before the first game of his pro career, one of the richest players in the NBA. The Signing Event drew 31 TV and radio stations, plus a small division from the *Boston Globe*. The signing of Bird was the most closely watched Boston news story since Paul Revere dropped by Lexington.

Before Bird even checked into rookie camp, he had taped a spot for 7UP and made a commercial for Ford. While Celtics vice presidents were debating what number to put on his uniform (33), Converse signed him to a $125,000-plus contract to wear their sneakers for three years, and

Spalding agreed to pay him $200,000 so they could make a basketball with his name on it. *The Gong Show* wanted him. The *Today Show* was desperate to book him. It took Pete Rose 16 years and 3,000 hits before anyone wrote a song about *him*. Already such catchy tunes as "Larry the Great Bird" and "Indiana Has a New State Bird" had hit the airwaves. Could *The White Shadow* be far behind?

Once I began my reporting, I learned that all this money and all this attention heaped onto "a hick from French Lick," as Bird liked to refer to himself, left him flummoxed. He had left a burg of 2,000 to play basketball in a sports-crazed city of 640,000. He brought his southern Indiana twang to an area rife with three-piece suits from *Hahvad*. But worst of all was the city's octopuslike press corps. At Indiana State in Terre Haute, the local press consisted of two dailies and a student newspaper. Bird treated those reporters like lepers. Teammates who tried to speak for him—or worse, about him—were given a severe Bird-lashing until, at last, the locker room doors were locked after every game.

Meanwhile, the *Boston Globe* fielded a sports staff of 50; there was the *Herald American* and a zillion other New England papers that were sniffing around for the Definitive Interview. Always, I learned, Bird had been protected from the outside world. In Terre Haute, away from home for the first time, he was "adopted" by five or six families, "who had dinner waiting for me anytime I wanted it." He also had a volunteer committee of five of the town's biggest businessmen spend months screening more than 45 agents to find just the right man. Woolf underwent seven straight hours of grilling before he was called back to meet Bird.

From then on, Woolf became the central figure in Bird's life. When Bird flew into Boston to sign with the Celtics, he had advised Woolf he wanted no press at the airport. One enterprising reporter showed up anyway. "I'll introduce you if you promise not to tell him you're a reporter," Woolf pleaded. When Bird got off the plane, he walked up to Woolf and said, "Are there any fucking reporters here?" Woolf assured him there were not. At the baggage claim area, Mrs. Woolf turned to the reporter and said in a loud voice, "So, how's the hardware business?"

In July, Bird returned to Boston to look for a house. Right away he found a three-bedroom, six-figure, split-level in Brookline—right next door to Woolf's. Then came the interior decorator with a fast tongue and expensive taste. Less than 24 hours after Bird signed the papers for his house, there she was on his doorstep. Bird, whose idea of fancy is a clean T-shirt and a fresh pair of jeans, was suddenly being sold wall-to-wall carpeting, wallpaper, and custom-made furniture, right down to the table for his TV. He excused himself from the hard sell, went out back, and began mowing his new lawn.

The heart of my story would be, of course, an interview with Bird. Despite being a "fucking reporter," my endeavor seemed off to a promising start. I was invited to have lunch with Bird, Woolf, and his assistant, Jill Leone, at a private club on the 43rd floor of Boston's Prudential Center. A sort of meet-and-greet type of thing. Here, listen in.

Woolf is talking. "Last night around ten o'clock, my doorbell rings. I turn on a light, and I go see who it is. Only when I open the door, nobody's there. A minute later, the doorbell rings again. Now I take a few steps outside, and I still don't see anybody. I'm just about to go back in when—all of a sudden—*he grabs me!*"

"I was behind the bushes," Bird says. He puts down his tuna fish sandwich and giggles.

"Boy, did he ever scare me," adds Woolf, who is 51 years old.

Leaving the restaurant, Bird rushes over to the bank of ten elevators and pushes all the down buttons. Then he races over to one elevator. "This one, Mr. Woolf," he shouts. "I bet this one will come first."

"No," says Woolf, hurrying to another elevator. "This one."

Bird is again on the move, gazing at all the elevators as if he is searching for an open man down court before racing over to a third sure bet. The game continues until at last an unpicked elevator arrives. The men disappear inside it, laughing, as the doors close.

Jill Leone watches them go. "He's got so much charisma," she says with a sigh. "He's just like Joe Namath in that respect. I think it's because there's a mystique about Larry Bird. That's what Mr. Woolf says. He has a definite mystique."

—◁∿▷—

Neither his charisma nor his mystique did Bird waste on me. My interview was scheduled for 8:30 at the Celtics' training camp. After an hour or so, I was told Bird would not be coming. Could we reschedule for the next morning?

The next morning produced the same results—or lack of them. Could I come back Friday? In the meantime, I found other things to do. I got on the phone and made calls to Indiana.

—∿—

I learned that Bird spent his early childhood traipsing after his two older brothers, Mike and Mark. As soon as he could walk, he was playing ball. "We always needed another player, so we got Larry," said Mike. "They babysat for me," Bird would later say. "Everywhere they went I had to go. Sometimes I would have to pitch for both teams, and sometimes I just had to chase balls. They were always pushing me and knocking me, always beating up on me."

"I think," said Mike Bird, "he just reached the point where he didn't like to be beat anymore. So he began looking for ways to beat you."

At Springs Valley High School in French Lick, Bird was a competent basketball player but too small and too slow to stand out. A fractured ankle sidelined him his sophomore year, but he joined the varsity as a junior. In what would become his ticket to the NBA, he worked hard at his ball-handling, teaching himself to shoot and pass left-handed, making himself a more complete player.

That year his parents divorced. His father was a piano finisher for Kimball Piano & Organ Co. "He was real good," recalled Mike. "Once he was chosen to finish the piano that would be played by someone, I don't remember who, on national television, and we all watched the show just to see the piano." When the marriage broke up, Bird's father went to live with his own parents. A year later Larry moved in with his grandmother while his mother worked to support her five other children.

The summer before his senior year, Bird grew four inches and then had the size and the strength to go with his exceptional passing and shooting. That spring he was recruited by a Florida college, but when Bird set out to visit the school, he took one look at the airplane on the runway and bolted for home. He wound up on the 31,000-student campus of Indiana University in Bloomington. One month later, he bolted again.

He made yet another attempt in January, at a junior college in West Baden Springs, Indiana, but that didn't work out either. So he went back to his grandmother's house in French Lick and took a job collecting garbage.

Not long after Bird returned to French Lick, his father shot himself in the head, with his folks in the next room. In the years since, people who know Bird well say he has never spoken of the suicide.

Nor did he confide much about his brief marriage to Janet Condra, a former cheerleader and high-school classmate he married in November 1975. This was less than a year after his father died and two months after he enrolled (successfully) at Indiana State.

That winter Bird was often out with the boys, leaving his wife alone, she told me, in a big new city. As problems developed, he refused to discuss them. "We were both too young," she said. "We tried to make it work, but it got pretty bitter in the end."

Deciding that life "shouldn't be like this at 19," Janet filed for divorce. It came through in September 1976. She got a job working as a secretary to police detectives, supporting their 2-year-old daughter, Corrie Bird, on little more than $100 take-home pay a week. She was also studying computer programming three nights a week. She filed a paternity suit against Bird for child support, but the case was postponed three times. "Larry is a very nice person, but sometimes he just forgets about other people," she said. "He sort of forgot about us."

—⁓—

It is now 8:15 Friday morning, and I am losing it. I have a deadline looming, and I must be back in New York this afternoon. Despite the reporting I have done, I still didn't have an interview with Bird. Unless the subject of a story gets run over by a bus, no editor is going to sympathize with an interviewless reporter. I could feel my blood pressure rising.

8:30. Still no Bird. I am in a conference room with no one to confer with. I pick up a phone and dial Pete Axthelm, my *Newsweek* sportswriting colleague. Pete, who had been turning out masterpieces week after week for years, would surely know what to do.

From the sound of his voice, I had awakened him. "He was supposed to be here Wednesday, no show. Same thing Thursday. I absolutely have to get back to New York today."

Pete tried to calm me down but without much success.

"I mean," I said, "he's a goddamn rookie, and the Celtics can't make him show up?"

"Did you try calling Woolf?" Pete asked.

"Not yet, but I will. I'm not sure when practice starts, but I have to see him before. What a jerk! I mean, who the fuck does Bird think he is?"

As Pete was saying something, I turned. And there, standing in the doorway, staring at me, was Larry Bird.

"Oops," I said to Axthelm, "gotta go."

I put down the phone and smiled brightly. "Hi. Why don't we sit down," I said, pointing to a sofa. I placed my cumbersome tape recorder on the floor and began asking questions. Despite my tirade, Bird seemed relaxed and happy to talk.

I asked about his already superstar status, and he unleashed a diatribe.

"They keep wanting to pry into your personal life, and that's one thing I do not tolerate. I wouldn't want no reporter coming to my house, or I wouldn't even want 'em going around my family, which has happened. And people who go around my family, their names I remember, and I will not interview with them. They're probing into my personal life, which has nothing to do with basketball."

Two things immediately struck me. He said all this and more without taking a breath, and when I transcribed it later, it took up half a page, single-spaced, with no punctuation. The second thing: because I had poked into his personal life, he was never going to forget my name.

The story ran, and the Boston sportswriters were ecstatic. They had been trying to get Larry to talk about his father's suicide and his brief marriage, but he had refused. Since my story mentioned both, they approached him, saying since it was out, why not deal with it? And he did. He sat down with the reporters and answered their questions. Celtics beat writer Bob Ryan told me, "He said if I ever see that girl again, I'll spit in her face."

Although the remark amused me, I found myself sliding lower in my chair—sportswriters sat at long tables under the basket—whenever Bird dribbled down court in my direction. After the games ended, I would go into the Boston locker room and stand in a scrum of reporters. If I yelled out a question, Bird always answered. I wasn't sure if he recognized me.

We never spoke one on one. In 1987, the Celtics and the Lakers played each other for the championship for the third time that decade. The Lakers won in six games at home.

Afterward, I waited patiently outside the Celtics' locker room.

It had been eight years since I wrote the *Inside Sports* piece. Back then, I had no qualms about making fun of the Hick from French Lick. But as time passed, he had developed into one of the best players in the NBA, and he had matured as well. Although I would not have changed one word of my story, I realized now that I was picking on a kid who had a rough start in life and had lifted himself up to be a role model. But now, because I would soon be changing jobs and might not see Bird again, I wanted to say something to him.

When I walked into the locker room, it was empty, except for Bird. "Larry," I said, "after all these years, I wanted to say you have been amazing on the court and off it. I have always enjoyed watching you play, and I want to wish you all the best."

I honestly couldn't tell if he knew who I was, but I extended my hand and he shook it. "It's been a real pleasure," I said.

I never saw Bird again.

16

I Wanna Make It Whichoo

THE YEAR AFTER I PROFILED LARRY BIRD, *INSIDE SPORTS* again assigned me a cover story, this time on Boston Red Sox slugger Jim Rice. Then in his sixth season, he was averaging 34 home runs a year, along with a .310 lifetime batting average. In 1978, he won the American League Most Valuable Player award, as he led both leagues with 213 hits, 46 home runs, 139 RBIs, and 15 triples. Thirty of those home runs either tied the score or put the Red Sox ahead. Oh, and he'd also collected 406 bases, the first American League player to break 400 since Joe DiMaggio in 1937.

Here was my lead:

"First time I ever saw him, he was 15 years old. He and a couple of other black boys come over to the ballfield and asked if they could play. We didn't have any black kids in American Legion at that time, but my feeling was, a kid wants to play, it doesn't matter what's his color. So Ed, we called him Ed then, he comes up to the plate, and I throw him five pitches to see what he can do. Well, the ball just jumped off his bat. Four went over a tree, 400 feet away. Next day, he doesn't come back. I ran all over town looking for him. Only time I ever went after a kid. Finally found him up the street from his house in this little store having a Coke and some cookies.

"I said, 'Why aren't you down at the ballfield?' And he said, 'I'm not going to play. I'm going to get a job. I want some clothes.' And I said, 'Look, son, some things I know nothing about, but one thing I do know is baseball. And you listen to me. One day you'll be wearing silk underwear.'"

The quote was from Olin Saylors, Jim Rice's American Legion coach in Anderson, South Carolina. It was a terrific quote, but I probably would not have led with it—or even thought to search out Saylors—had my dealings with Rice gone smoothly.

I started my reporting in Arlington, Texas, where the Red Sox were playing the Texas Rangers.

It was a hot, muggy night, and the game had been held up 45 minutes due to one of those sudden downpours that makes a sponge of the field and fills the tunnel to the locker room ankle-deep with water. Then the thing blew over, leaving the air to dry itself out. So it felt pretty good after that to walk into the air-conditioned bar on the 21st floor of the Doubletree Inn around midnight to interview Jim Rice.

Only Rice wasn't feeling especially good, and he didn't much like bars. "Kahlua and cream," he told the waitress, jerking his head around to see who was there.

"Beer," said Ken "Hawk" Harrelson, the Red Sox broadcaster, who was drinking with him.

Rice carefully placed two red apples he had been carrying on the table. Then he leaned back into the cushions of the banquette and watched the apples hold still.

"Nice throw, Jimmy," said Harrelson, referring to Rice's long toss from left to nail a runner at the plate in the eighth inning.

His eyes downcast, Rice shook his head. When you're three for thirtysomething, nothing seems to go right. "It went up and down," he said miserably, replaying the ball's wobbly journey with his hand.

Rice sank back into the cushions and stared glumly around the bar. After a while, Hawk got up. "Night, Jimmy." Seconds later, from the blackness of the room, a shapeless blonde in thick glasses slipped onto the banquette beside Rice. In soft tones, she asked about his night's plans.

"Got to do an interview," he grumbled. "What do you want?"

She ordered a drink, and Rice pulled out a handful of bills. He held on to them until the drink was on the table. Then he blurted, "I've got to make a phone call." He jumped up, grabbed his apples, and was gone, leaving behind the blonde, the reporter (me), and the Kahlua and cream.

The next day, during batting practice, I was standing behind the cage when Rice sauntered up and said, "I want to make it whichoo." Then he walked away.

Well, well, well, I thought. *This will be fun to tell my friends.*

—∿∿—

"That son of a bitch is so strong it's ungodly," Ken Harrelson said. "I've never heard a bat louder than his. You hear it going through the strike zone, and the sound is unmistakable. It goes *vump.* That's when he *misses.*"

The man was sort of a Mount St. Helens at the plate, a motionless mountain of pent-up forces—ready to explode. Off the field, he is a curious blend of half-finished personas. He has few, if any, friends on the Red Sox, but maybe that figures on a team whose motto is, "Twenty-five men, twenty-five cabs." Says teammate Fred Lynn, who arrived the same year as Rice, "I came from four years at USC. Jimmy came from a small town. He didn't have the background to handle the pressure cooker. I think he felt trapped. And he just clammed up."

But it is impossible to draw meaningful conclusions about him. During spring training, after the players voted to strike, Rice went up to rookie Glenn Hoffman in the locker room. "He told me we wouldn't be paid or get any meal money and that if I needed a place to stay or some money to tell him."

Recently, during batting practice, a middle-aged woman in the stands yelled at Red Sox star Carl Yastrzemski to hold still while she took his picture. Yaz froze, and the woman sighted through the lens. Rice, watching this, suddenly called out, "Wait, you're too far away. She'd need a telescope to find you." Yaz continued leaning on his bat, smiling. Rice grabbed the camera and snapped Yaz. Then he jogged the camera back to the startled woman and said, "I hope it turns out."

—∿∿—

Jim Rice walked into my hotel room the way a man enters a dentist's office for a root canal. He turned on the TV, sat down at a table, and began watching a western, in a last-ditch effort to delay the drilling. His discomfort was contagious. I began reading the paper. Eventually, Rice took the paper away and, section by section, folded it into neat packages.

Soon there were five perfectly constructed rectangles on the table. He looked miserable. "What do you want to know?" he said.

For two hours, I asked questions, and this is what came out of Jim Rice: "I'm really very sensitive. I get hurt easily. So I've learned to keep everything to myself. I guess I got that partly from my mother. Whenever I had a problem, she'd say, 'You can tell me about it, if you want to. But in the end, you've got to do for yourself.' My father was busy just bringing home money. There were nine of us, five girls, four boys. But one thing he always said, 'You've got to respect your elders. Black, white, or blue.' I always spent a lot of time alone. After playing ball, I'd just go home. I wasn't in a group or a gang. I didn't smoke or drink. Most of the kids were four to six years older than I was. Being black . . . it just means I got to be better than the average person."

When Rice stood to leave, he suddenly turned and grabbed my shoulders. He pulled me to him and tried to kiss me. Despite his size and strength, I wasn't afraid, only surprised. I had learned that in such situations, flattery often works best. I wiggled out of his grip and said, "You're very handsome and you've got a killer body. Under different circumstances I would be tempted. But with us there's a line that cannot be crossed." Then I walked to the door, opened it, and Rice, glaring at me, left.

I had no intention of "reporting" him to the Red Sox—for what? Again, my goals were only two: let me in and give me a chance to write my story. How athletes behaved was inconsequential—unless it interfered with my goals or they physically harmed me. Once again, I had dealt with a situation—or so I thought.

But from then on, Rice would not speak to me. I still had many more questions, but each time I approached him, he walked away. I followed. I sat next to him on the team bus to the ballpark, I sat next to him on the plane back to Boston. Not a word did he speak to me. I didn't feel like I had my story yet, and I didn't know what to do. Would the story be killed? Would it be seen as an example of a girl not able to do the job?

Back in New York, I met with *Inside Sports* editor John Walsh. I didn't tell him why Rice wasn't talking to me. I didn't want him to stop assigning me stories.

"Rice won't cooperate? Who cares?" said Walsh. "Go to South Carolina. Talk to his parents, his friends, his high school coach. They'll give you better stuff than Rice would anyway."

Walsh, who went on to revolutionize sports broadcasting by creating *SportsCenter* on ESPN, was absolutely right. Rice's parents, Roger and Julia Mae, happily pulled out scrapbooks and talked about how they didn't favor Jim any more than their other eight children. And I spoke to Olin Saylors and Jim Roberts, president of Sir Pontiac in Anderson, South Carolina, one of Rice's closest friends. I spoke to John Moore, Rice's high school baseball coach. All the men I spoke with, of either race, recalled the prejudice Rice faced growing up and that still existed in Anderson to that day.

John Moore, the high school coach, mentioned that some golf courses in town were still restricted. "The day after the Yankees beat the Red Sox in the playoff game of 1978, I was playing golf. There was a white foursome nearby, and one of the men called over, 'I guess your boy blew it. He didn't get a hit when it counted.' And I said, 'Nope. And neither did Yaz.'"

—◊—

After the story came out, the Red Sox were in town to play the Yankees, and I went out to the stadium to say hello to Rice. He saw me and started to walk away. I caught up and said, "I enjoyed talking to your folks. They're really nice." Silence. "Did you see the article?"

He nodded. And then he spoke: "What's in your mouth?"

"Gum."

"Yeah. You always have to have something in your mouth."

Which is when I pulled a Jim Rice. I turned and walked away.

17

Mickey Mantle (Yep, Again)

"You know that song by Roy Clark, 'Yesterday When I Was Young'? Well, that's what they're going to play at my funeral. Every time I hear it I could just cry."

—MICKEY MANTLE

I DON'T REMEMBER WHY I WANTED TO REVISIT MANTLE NINE years after I had first written about him, 12 years after his magnificent career had collapsed on him. One of baseball's all-time heroes, the one-time King of New York City, was reportedly struggling. I typed up a proposal and sent it off to Bill Broyles, the editor of *Texas Monthly*, one of the nation's finest magazines. Broyles said go.

———

The Longview Mall in Longview, Texas, has barely shaken awake at nine o'clock on a muggy Saturday morning. Everywhere there are signs: APPEARANCE—MICKEY MANTLE. Inside, in a small business office, half a dozen local reporters are sitting around a conference table studying the "Official Mickey Mantle Agenda."

Mantle was delayed on his 140-mile drive from his home in Dallas by a sudden downpour. When he finally appears in the doorway, 50 minutes late, he apologizes, smiles weakly, and slouches into a chair. He is wearing tan slacks, a pastel plaid shirt, and the look of a man who has been railroaded into coming to a party he didn't want to attend. Otherwise, he looks much the same as when I first interviewed him. The broad shoulders, the thick neck, the sun-faded blue eyes. But the stomach is soft with middle age, and the face has aged too quickly—either from all those summers in the sun or all those nights on the town. He hikes his left ankle onto his right knee and looks gloomily around the room. "Aren't you supposed to ask me questions?" he says.

The questions are the same ones he's heard a zillion times. What was his biggest thrill? Wouldn't he like to manage? Doesn't he wish he could be playing at today's high salaries?

He answers every question politely, and when he finishes, if no one jumps in with another one, he continues to belabor it.

"We were going to give you some pictures to look at ahead of time to help you but . . ."

"Pictures?" says Mantle. "Of what?"

Mickey, it seems, had no idea what his appearance at the mall entailed, only that it would take four hours and pay him $2,500. As he is escorted from the press conference, Mary Lator tries to explain the look-alike contest. There would be two: one for children, one for middle-aged men.

Mantle stops short in the hallway. "You mean," he says incredulously, "I'm supposed to pick out some guy who looks like me?"

"The thing is," Mary says apologetically, "only one man entered."

Before several dozen curious shoppers, Mantle lumbers onto a makeshift stage and comes face to face with his look-alike. The man, a 43-year-old dime-store manager from nearby Marshall, Texas, is wearing pastel-green slacks and a face wreathed in a smile. He is overweight, his ears stick out, and if he resembles anyone, it is a middle-aged Howdy Doody.

"Congratulations," mumbles Mantle.

"I used to play ball in high school with your twin brothers," the man gushes.

Mantle hands him a letter telling him where to collect his $100 reward, then looks around helplessly. Below him are the upturned faces of a dozen youngsters participating in the "then" look-alike contest. "Pick out the one who most looks like you did at that age," someone prompts him.

Mantle turns and studies the children. He hesitates before a blond, freckle-faced boy of 11. "Best I can remember," he drawls, "Stanley here looks like me."

Stanley Woods, shy and as embarrassed as Mantle, collects the ball player's autograph then scampers off to join his aunt, a fat woman with a ponytail and a white T-shirt. "I used to be married to a pitcher for the White Sox," she sings happily, "but he died." Then, patting Stanley's head, she says, "I just knew he would win. He looks exactly like Mickey did."

Schlepping around shopping malls is not what Mantle intended to do with his life, even though it pays him well. He is a vice-president of Reserve Life Insurance Company in Dallas. He has to show up at company "victory" dinners, where agents who have sold a lot of policies get to rub his elbow over cocktails. In addition, he does a week-or-two-long "informal golfing excursion" each year with Allied Chemical, and in the spring, Yankees owner George Steinbrenner pays him to throw out baseballs at Yankee-farm-club openers. He also makes appearances. These, his TV commercials, and his Reserve contract pay him more than the Yankees ever did.

Mantle knows he should not complain. He is flattered that people even remember him. Recently, a New Jersey housewife paid him an appearance fee to show up at her husband's 40th birthday party. When Mantle arrived, the man, once an avid fan, burst into tears. Mantle was so moved by this that when he got home, he shipped the man the uniform the Yankees had given him when they retired his number.

Still, he dreads public appearances. When Gerald Ford invited him to the White House for a state dinner honoring the president of France, Mantle's response was to throw out the invitation. "Why do they want me there?" he kept complaining as the White House barraged him with phone calls. "I don't know anything about politics." Mantle finally relented and was seated at the president's table, his wife beside Vice-President Nelson Rockefeller. Ford talked golf with Mantle; Rocky inquired endlessly about Mantle's four sons. "They were so elated that they had such a good time," says his attorney, Roy True, "that they hopped a plane to Las Vegas as a sort of dessert."

This afternoon's activity consists of two autographing sessions—one for an hour at Dillard's department store, the other at J. C. Penney. The local radio men cover Mantle's arrival like a papal visit. "He's entering the housewares department . . . he's climbing onto the platform."

The lines stretch from housewares into bedspreads and sheets, past shower curtains and gift wrappings, along the cafeteria, beyond the credit desk—all the way to the restrooms at the back of the store. Dan Whyte, a retired marine, has been anxiously awaiting Mantle's visit all week. A native of the Bronx, he brought with him a yellowed scrapbook filled with pictures of the Yankees of yore. "Mantle," gushes Whyte, "is like the John Wayne of baseball. Still looks good, doesn't he? Too bad about his knees. He would have made a good marine."

At last, Whyte's moment comes. He steps up to the platform and thrusts his scrapbook under Mantle's nose. Mantle starts to sign "Mickey Mantle"—for his hand is too tired now to pen "Best Wishes"—but Whyte is flipping through the pages, trying to show him the pictures. Mantle stares blankly, smiles, and reaches for the next piece of paper.

"I guess he was kind of busy," sighs Whyte, as he steps off the stage.

At three o'clock, with the lines still stretching, Mantle is escorted from the platform, visibly tired, his official engagement over. He walks out into the heat of the parking lot and climbs into his gold 1979 Cadillac Eldorado for the long ride back to Dallas.

—◦◦◦—

"Mickey and I were in New York on a business deal in the spring of 1969," says Roy True. "We were sharing a suite at the St. Moritz. One morning I woke up and found him wrapped in a towel, standing in front of French doors that opened onto a balcony. I said, 'What are you doing?'

"'Just looking out at the city,' he said. 'It's some city.'

"'Yes, it is,' I told him.

"'And that son of a bitch used to be mine,' Mantle said, 'all mine.'"

—◦◦◦—

Mantle's transition into the appearance business came largely from True. Mickey first approached the Dallas attorney ten years earlier on a Florida land deal, but True quickly realized Mantle was hardly going to galvanize Wall Street. "Mickey is not a businessman," True says. "He hates meetings. He isn't interested in the ongoing process. He just wants to know the results."

Before True came along, the results had been abysmal. His first big "deal" came the very day he arrived at Yankee Stadium, when a fast-talking stranger "grabbed me and said he could make a million dollars for me in five years. All I had to do was give him half of everything I made for ten years," Mantle recalls. "A million dollars is a lot when you're making $7,500. I signed right away."

Mantle was not legally old enough to sign a contract, so he got out of it. But he never learned to distrust strangers. Even at the end of his career, he was boasting about an investment that would make him rich for life. He bought 12,500 shares of a stock at $10 each. Years later he sold them at $4.

True figured Mantle should start promoting himself. Mantle balked. "The problem was he felt he didn't have anything to contribute," True says. "So I talked strong and long to him. Once he found out that people were interested in what he had to say, he gained the confidence that he was something other than a ballplayer."

—◦◦◦—

I arrive at True's offices right on time to interview Mantle, and to my surprise, he is there waiting, fidgeting like a well-behaved child who has been told to say a few polite words to grown-ups. He is nicely dressed as usual, wearing tan slacks and a yellow knit shirt. He seems uncomfortable in his chair, clutching a batch of letters. But as he talks, I begin to understand: he was, and remains, a modest man who worked hard at the game he loved, wanting to excel but never quite comprehending the acclaim that came with it.

Mantle is still fidgeting—though he has finally put the letters down—alternately scratching his still-enormous biceps, stretching, and yawning. "Golf," he says, "is the only thing I can still do. I can't play racquetball or tennis or even ride a bike. And I have this need to compete. What bothers me is that my knee is getting worse, and when I'm 55, I may not be able to play at all. Then I don't know what I'll do." His eyes look sad.

"Don't you still hunt and fish?"

"Yeah."

"What do you hunt?" It was the same question I had asked during my first interview.

For the first time, Mantle grins. "Pussy," he says again, yet the old devilishness is not there, and after a moment the smile fades. "The one thing I would have done different in my life was to take better care of myself while I was playing. I really burned the candle at both ends. And it caught up with me."

Suddenly he stands. "Let's drive by the house. You can meet Merlyn." The interview is over. The jailer has released him.

—⁓—

The Mantles' four-bedroom beige house sprawls on an acre of emerald-green lawn in an exclusive section of North Dallas. Its two wings wrap around a sparkling turquoise swimming pool that looks as if it hasn't been used for some time.

Merlyn Mantle, a tiny platinum blonde with large blue eyes, is in the den talking to Joe Warren, a regional sales manager for Reserve Life, who dropped by with two boxes of baseballs for Mantle to autograph. Mutely, Mickey carries the boxes to an easy chair. Balancing the boxes on his knees, he begins scrawling his name.

As Warren is speaking, Merlyn turns and says softly to her husband, "Do you want your glasses?"

"No," mumbles Mantle, embarrassed.

Later, I am led through a spotless white kitchen to the back of the house, where, stuck on like an afterthought, is the trophy room. It's a treasure trove of memorabilia, every wall crammed with mementos of Mantle's achievements. Encased behind glass are an enormous sterling tape measure honoring his longest home run—a 734-foot blast that missed flying out of Yankee Stadium by inches—a solid-silver bat denoting his American League batting titles, the big jeweled Hickok Belt for athlete of the year. Trophies that didn't fit into the credenza spill out into the far corners of the room. One wall is plastered with magazine covers of Mantle. Another holds a framed swatch of the number 7 pinstripe uniform.

Throughout Merlyn's tour, Mantle stands impassively in the doorway. He rarely goes into the room he says, and seems uninterested in it.

"When Mickey first retired," Merlyn notes, "I thought it was really great—he'd be home all the time. But he isn't."

"The last three months I haven't been home hardly at all," Mantle concedes. "That promotion I did for Cameron Wholesalers? I went to twenty cities all over Texas. They had this deal called Mickey Mantle

Grand Slam Specials. You buy fifty doors and get one free"—he laughs—
"or something like that."

It is only quarter to twelve, but itchy as ever, Mantle suggests we go
out for lunch.

At the restaurant, the Mantles pick at their food and apologize that it
is not very good. Mickey reports that he weighs 205 pounds—not much
over his playing weight. "But it's shifting," he says with a small, sad smile.

Then abruptly he puts down his fork. "I just hate getting old," he blurts.
Merlyn Mantle nods and looks away.

———

It is, sadly, the wrong note to end on, I wrote. But perhaps that is how
it had to be. "Mickey comes to me from time to time and says this guy
or that guy wants to write a book about him," says Roy True. "And I tell
Mickey it's not time. And Mickey says, 'Well, what are we waiting for?'

"And I tell him," says True, "I'm waiting until we can have a happy
ending."

———

It was a hard story to report and to write. I was still too young to understand the process of aging, how the years creep up and steal your finest
youthful moments. As I wrote, I had flashbacks of Mantle in his prime,
his home runs electrifying me, the grinning face, the hero of the Yankees
and all of New York.

So when Bill Broyles sent me a letter saying he was rejecting the story,
I was crushed. It was, he said, too bathetic. Obviously, it was a sad tale . . .
but wasn't it an important story? David Rosenthal, an executive editor at
New York magazine, believed it was. He grabbed it and ran it.

Yes, I thought, *New York City is where the Mantle story should be told.*
Even if it had the wrong ending.

18

The *Her-Ex*

I'D BEEN AT *NEWSWEEK* 3½ YEARS AND WAS STILL HAPPY TO be there—more or less. The hours could be brutal. The magazine came out on Monday, which was usually a light day; either no story had been assigned yet or, if you had one, you made a few phone calls, sent out queries to any bureaus that might do some reporting, cleared the detritus off your desk, and called it a day. Tuesday, the editors met, and often Katharine Graham would fly up from Washington to attend that gathering. Assignments were handed out, though—who knew?—by Thursday an editor might tell you to dump that story and take on another. Friday, you would turn in your article, and then you would wait. And wait. And wait—for the three or four layers of editors to pick at your story.

Often, some of the waiting took place at a restaurant over dinner, always at an expensive restaurant (we had expense accounts!) and included too much alcohol. Then, back to the office, only to wait some more. Or if you got your story back, there might be a note saying you had to cut X many lines because the accompanying photo had been enlarged or simply that space was tight. Which is how I came to love widows. Widows are one or two words that form the final line of a paragraph, and if you could cut one or two words from anywhere in the paragraph, there was one line gone. Sometimes you had to come in Saturday morning to finish up, but after so many late nights and so much pressure, I often spent the weekend recovering in bed.

To be honest, a large amount of energy was spent socializing, if that is the right word. Each day after work, a group of us would start our evening at The Cowboy, a restaurant/bar across the street, where the drinking began. Then to dinner—more liquor—and finally to one of two media meccas for nightcaps—Runyon's or maybe Elaine's—hoping she wouldn't throw us out because we'd chosen to eat dinner elsewhere. I sometimes left Elaine's at 3 a.m. Cursed with a pitiful metabolism that did not tolerate much alcohol, I became adept at nursing one or two glasses of white wine and pretending that the silliness around me was hysterically funny. (I must add that everyone seemed to show up at work the next morning clear-eyed and ready to go.)

As I mentioned, it was not unusual for a story I was assigned to blow up. I had two cover stories tossed before I could even write them. One was about the Dodger rookie sensation Fernando Valenzuela, the 19-year-old source of national Fernando-mania. He had won his first eight games when I flew to Los Angeles to interview him. He lost his next game, and *Newsweek* dumped the story.

In 1980, I was assigned another cover, this one on Kansas City third baseman George Brett, who was flirting with a .400 batting average. Did I mention that being a female reporter did have its advantages? I walked into the visitor's clubhouse in Arlington, Texas, where the Royals were playing the Rangers, and joined the reporters surrounding Brett. He was sitting on a stool, looking down as he talked. Suddenly, his eyes moved slowly upward, clearly along my bare legs, and he sat up and grinned. Later, he happily agreed to meet me in the hotel bar for a drink.

Brett and his brother Ken, a Royals pitcher, were great fun, and I flew home with notebooks full of reporting. Only then Brett's average dipped into the .380s, and *Newsweek* lost interest.

The next time I saw George was in Kansas City three months later when the Royals were playing the Yankees for the American League championship. As soon as I entered the Royals locker room, Brett came charging toward me.

"What happened to the cover story?" he demanded, clearly angry and rightly so. He had given me a lot of his time.

"I'm sorry," I said. "But when your average dropped—"

"To .388? Are you fucking kidding me?"

"I know, George. It wasn't my decision."

"What was on the cover instead?"

I cringed. "Um. Teenage sex."

Brett stared at me for a long moment then turned and strode away.

Aside from moments like these, I still liked my job. Because I was writing sports, I could travel to the biggest sporting events—the Olympics, the US Open of tennis and golf, the World Series, the Super Bowl, the Final Four, or to wherever my story would take me. Also, *Newsweek* let me write occasional freelance pieces if they didn't rob the magazine of a story it wanted.

That's why I wasn't planning to leave *Newsweek* anytime soon. Only then I did.

The week between Christmas and New Year's 1980, I was in Los Angeles to report two stories: the Los Angeles Kings and the new owner of the Lakers, Jerry Buss. There I ran into my friend David Israel of the *Chicago Tribune*, in my opinion the best newspaper sports columnist in the country. He confided that he was going to leave the *Trib* to take a city columnist job with the *Los Angeles Herald Examiner*. Years before, he had worked for the paper's editor, Jim Bellows, at the *Washington Star*. Bellows was a legend who either discovered or helped develop terrific writers. I mentioned that I had always hoped to meet Bellows. That week there was a Chargers playoff game in San Diego that David was covering, and I decided to tag along.

On the plane back to Los Angeles, David said Bellows was having a party that night and would I like to go with him? He gave me directions to Bellows's house on Rockingham Drive in Brentwood, and at LAX we each headed for our cars.

The parking lot was jammed with drivers trying to pull out. As I inched toward the street, I suddenly felt exhausted. I decided to skip the party and go straight to my hotel. But—and this is where the story turns weird—when I finally reached the street, I could only turn left. I needed to turn right to go back to my hotel, but I didn't know Los Angeles well enough to figure out how to do this, so I turned left—which sent me in the direction of Bellows's house. Okay, I thought, but I wouldn't stay long.

I found a parking spot on the street and headed up the walk to a one-story stucco house and rang the bell. A dark-haired man of medium height opened the door and smiled. "Diane, nice to meet you. I'm Jim Bellows. Please come in."

He led me through a swarm of people to a sofa and asked me what I'd like to drink. He brought me a glass of wine and sat down beside me. "So," he said, "what do you plan to do with the rest of your life?"

What an odd question, I thought, to ask someone you had met only minutes before. (I later learned this was a typical Bellows opening.) I replied, "I want to write books and magazine articles," and sipped my wine.

Bellows shook his head. "Nope."

"Yes," I said. "At some point I will leave *Newsweek* to do magazine pieces and write mystery novels."

"Yeah, I don't think so."

Now I was beginning to feel defensive. Did he not think I could do this stuff? "I've already written for *Inside Sports, Washingtonian,* and *New York* magazine, and I published a mystery novel, so . . ."

Bellows rattled the ice in his drink. "No, that's not what you're going to do."

Now I was growing angry. Who was this guy talking to me like this? "Okay," I said, "what do *you* think I should do?"

He leaned back on the sofa and grinned. "You're going to be my sports columnist for the *Los Angeles Herald Examiner.*"

Huh? What?

But Bellows seemed quite serious. I told him I had never worked for a daily newspaper, had no idea how to write a column, and knew nothing about Los Angeles.

"I can teach you," he said and got up to refill his drink.

—⁓—

Almost every sportswriter would like to become a columnist. You are no longer a byline but a Name. Sports fans know who you are. The money is better. And I was being offered this dream job in the second-largest market in the country.

Still, I couldn't decide. *Newsweek* was a widely read magazine, and the *Herald Examiner* was not even close to being in the same league. I went home and consulted four of my best friends, all men, and they said *go!* But I had to be realistic. I did not even read columns, let alone know how to write one. I began to study the New York sports columnists and realized—aha—you had to have an opinion! Then, when I went to games, I tried to have an opinion—but about what? In desperation, I invited Dave Anderson, a *New York Times* sports columnist who, in two months' time would win a Pulitzer Prize, to lunch. He said the column would be great for me and encouraged me to accept the offer.

My editors at *Newsweek* insisted it would be a big mistake. Huge. For one thing, the *Her-Ex* was a money-losing Hearst paper in a city dominated by the *Los Angeles Times*. My editor said, "You'll fall off the edge of the earth. No one will ever hear of you again." Gulp.

Finally, after putting off Bellows for almost four months, I called and hesitantly accepted the job. This was a challenge I decided to take on—not to mention the allure of the weather. And Bellows had said he would help me. This would be like a master class in column writing. I imagined myself sitting in his office as he brilliantly guided me through my flawed attempts.

But almost immediately, I began having freeway nightmares. I would wake up in a panic after imagining myself stuck in traffic and late to the game. Or I would be crashed into. Or I would become hopelessly lost. I wouldn't be able to find parking. I would miss games and blow deadlines. I realized I had made a terrible mistake and would have to call Bellows to say I wasn't coming after all. Once again, I sought advice from my four friends, and they were split: two said go, two said no. Pete Axthelm wouldn't hear of my backing out. "Di," he said, "you want to *reneg*? *Reneg*? You can't reneg! Look, go for three months, and if you don't like it, you can quit."

Lester Bernstein, the editor of *Newsweek*, said there would be a job for me if I chose to come back. I kept my rental apartment just in case. I had my safety nets in place.

And so, in June 1981, I became a sports columnist.

19

What Does a Columnist Do Again?

ON JUNE 23, 1981, I BECAME THE FIRST FEMALE SPORTS COL-
umnist in the country for a daily newspaper. Or so I was told. And Jim
Bellows did all he could to make my ascension known. I understood from
the moment he made his offer that I would be used to draw attention to
the paper. TV stations were scrambling to hire comely female sports
reporters, many of whom knew little about sports. But I did believe that
Bellows chose me rather than a sexier version because he thought I could
do the job. With his considerable help, of course.

I had no idea what the 25 or so people in the *Her-Ex* sports department were told. But I suspected I was described as a big deal from back
east who was making a lot more money than they were. Worse, I was to
become the number-two columnist after Mel Durslag, which dropped
Doug Krikorian to number three. Despite all this, everyone was polite,
and when I asked questions they were always helpful.

While Bellows made sure all columnists now had their pictures next
to their columns (for some reason, the top of my head was cut off) and
plastered newspaper boxes with my picture *and* displayed my face in the
back window of city buses that spewed black smoke into the L.A. smog,
I now had to produce my first column. I could not have picked a worse
time. What are the staples of sports coverage in the summer? Baseball
stories, of course. In Los Angeles, I had two teams—the Dodgers and
the Angels—to poke. Except I couldn't. Marvin Miller and Donald Fehr,
heads of the Major League Baseball Players Association, greeted my
arrival with what would become a 57-day strike.

Figuring he would have the time, I chose Dodgers manager Tommy Lasorda for my first attempt at column writing. Lasorda, I would learn, was always available and cooperative with columnists, and when I arrived at a deserted Dodger Stadium, I was greeted by management with big smiles and led into the executive dining room.

There I found Lasorda, chin on his hands, looking glum. "This is so hard for me to believe or accept. I'm really sad," he began. "There isn't anything else I seem to be able to get interested in. I just keep praying this will end soon."

I had given myself plenty of time to do the column—a week. I wrote it on a typewriter at home. Computers were just beginning to plunk down in newsrooms, but I had never worked on one and didn't want to be sidetracked by—I don't know—whatever computers could do. I began:

He was a man of 53 years who managed a baseball team in Los Angeles, and he had gone eight days now without making out a lineup card. It had been years since he had gone eight days without penciling in his batting order; four decades since he had gone that long without putting on a uniform.

When the day came to turn my column in, I went straight to Bellows's office and gave him three typed pages. He was leaning back in his swivel chair, shoes off, stocking feet on his desk. "Go back to the sports department," he said. "I'll come find you."

Walking into the sports department, I looked at the clock. One fifteen. Deadline was five. I hoped I would have enough time to make the changes he would suggest. I was both nervous and excited; I always liked it when an editor improved my work. I simply hoped I would not have to do a total rewrite. *On a computer.*

Anxiously, I watched the minutes tick by. Finally, an hour later, Bellows slunk into the sports department. Surreptitiously, he handed back my three pages, now folded into quarters. Then, without a word, he slunk out. Oh dear. Slowly, apprehensively, I unfolded the pages, my eyes racing across them. Then I did it again. I could find only one pencil mark—to correct two transposed letters. That was it. No suggested changes? Not a single word crossed out or replaced? This was Bellows teaching me? I sighed and turned my column over to Allan Malamud, our executive sports editor.

My second and final shot to "learn" from Bellows occurred a few weeks later. I sat across from his desk—his shoes off, feet on it—and told him I was at a loss on how to write my column. It concerned the lawsuit the Raiders had brought against the NFL to allow them to move from Oakland to Los Angeles. I had spent time with both NFL Commissioner Pete Rozelle and Raiders owner Al Davis, but I had no idea how to write it. Bellows listened patiently. Then he said, "You'll figure it out."

Six months later, he left the *Her-Ex* to run *TV Guide*.

20

Hey, Kareem! I'm Talking to You!

BECAUSE OF THE BASEBALL STRIKE, SOME OF MY ATTENTION landed on the Lakers. It was being reported that Kareem Abdul-Jabbar, their seven-foot-two center, was unhappy about *something* and had confronted owner Jerry Buss in his office.

Before the source of Kareem's unhappiness could be determined, the two men stepped out of Dr. Buss's office. (He insisted on being called *Doctor* because he had a PhD in chemistry, although his chemistry with his star center apparently wasn't too good.) Both men were wreathed in smiles. "Fortunately, after talking with Dr. Buss," Kareem said, "I realize the situation hasn't gotten that extreme."

To which Dr. Buss added, "I am glad that Kareem had the presence of mind to make matters clear."

Matters? What *matters*? To dig deeper into this drama, I asked to see Kareem. A meeting was arranged, and Tom Collins—his agent, not the drink—offered some helpful advice. "Don't count on a whole hour," he said. "More likely you'll get half an hour. You might want to start by talking about history or oriental rugs or the Egyptian mare he just bought. But remember, when he starts to fidget, that's it. Leave as quickly as possible.

"Also," Collins warned, "don't expect much eye contact."

At the appointed hour, Kareem entered Collins's conference room and sat down at the table. Quicker than a fast break, he swiveled his chair round until he was facing the window—and I was facing the back of his neck. From that point on, in my column, I referred to him as The Voice.

Right away he cleared up the mystery. Earvin "Magic" Johnson, who had just completed his second season with the Lakers, was the source of

Kareem's angst. Specifically, the source was Magic's contract. "Nobody knew what the contract meant," Kareem said. "Earvin could be the general manager if he wanted or the coach."

Suddenly, Kareem whipped around, startling me. "We didn't know," he said and spread his hands in a gesture of helplessness . . . or possibly a warning fidget?

"We know how close Earvin and Dr. Buss are," he continued. "So I wondered, how does this affect me? Is my status on this team reliant on what I do on the court or how friendly I am with the boss?"

At which point, Kareem swiveled back around.

"Nobody could really understand what Earvin's job was," he said to the wall. "The way it seemed was as if Dr. Buss adopted Magic, and he could do what he wanted. This team was just something for Magic to play with."

Whoa. I began to scribble faster.

Kareem started rubbing his hands on the arms of his chair. It looked like a definite fidget. Fearing my time was elapsing, I asked what he had said to Dr. Buss.

Kareem replied that he told Dr. Buss it was important the way he did things. It could be a danger if he made too many bad decisions.

A player *chastising* his owner? Seriously? "And how did Dr. Buss react to that?"

"I don't know," Kareem said. "I am, after all, no more than an employee. I was walking on thin ice."

If the business with Magic's contract was not cleared up, would Kareem ask to be traded?

"That's professional pride," he answered. "I said if the climate isn't right where good basketball could be developed, I would go somewhere where it was right."

By now, Kareem was fidgeting so badly that I worried he might fall out of his chair. Suddenly, he stood and turned to me. "People should be allowed space to be human, and to excel." Then he was gone.

Thirty minutes, to the second.

—⁓—

It was rare for a player to be so open, even then.

Apparently, Magic's contract matters were worked out to Kareem's satisfaction because he and Magic went on to win four more championships (plus their previous one) under Coach Pat Riley. But because I had made fun of him in writing this column, I assumed he wouldn't speak to me again.

That season, spurred by Magic's play, Kareem once again sprang to life and was playing brilliantly as the Lakers headed into the playoffs. It was time to write another column about Kareem, but I was reluctant to ask him directly for an interview. Instead, I went to the Lakers' publicist who, to my surprise, said Kareem would be happy to talk to me. But, he added, because Kareem had a dental appointment after practice the next morning, could I interview him over the phone?

Seriously? Talking to him in the same room had been like pulling teeth (*sorry*), but on the phone? Still, having no choice, I agreed.

Kareem called me as scheduled. And talked and talked and *talked*. He mentioned that he had a home on Kauai, and we talked about that, his fondness for jazz and his interest in history. An hour or so later, when I was finally able to hang up, I had learned a valuable lesson; *always* interview Kareem Abdul-Jabbar on the phone.

He *was* different for sure, perhaps eccentric. It must have been awkward to be so tall in a game that wasn't yet peopled by seven-footers. One day, while walking with him through an airport, a middle-aged man came up to him and actually said, "Hey, how's the weather up there?" which is what I used to get—in junior high. I can't say his physical appearance accounted for his social awkwardness, but at the time, it was hard to know what to expect from him.

One time, during another round of playoffs, the Lakers were on the road, and I phoned Kareem in his hotel room from my hotel room. We spoke of many things—even basketball—and once again I had to tell him, "I have to go now." When does a reporter do *that*?

Five minutes later, I left my room and was waiting for an elevator when Kareem came up beside me. He did not say hello or acknowledge me in any way. We rode down to the lobby in silence.

One final note. The Lakers were holding their training camp in Honolulu and I followed them there to report a *GQ* cover story on their coach

Pat Riley. Kareem agreed to meet me in his room after morning practice. We spoke for a few minutes, then he called room service. Once his lunch arrived, he ate while we talked. After he was finished eating, he curled up on a sofa, his hands under his head, and continued the interview.

I left before he fell asleep.

21

Lunch with the Ladies

FROM TIME TO TIME, I POKED MY HEAD INTO THE NFL-RAIDERS trial in downtown Los Angeles. There, I would run into Carrie Rozelle, the commissioner's wife. A Los Angeles native now living in a wealthy suburb north of New York City, she quickly attached herself to me as my personal guide who could tell me where to shop, which Beverly Hills store sold the "most fantastic" pants, and the best people I should get to know: that is, her friends. Despite this charm offensive, I understood where she was going with it. If we became besties, surely I would write glowingly of her husband.

I responded politely to her entreaties but brushed most of them off. The last day of the trial, when it was declared a mistrial, she urged me to have lunch with her and six of her closest friends. I figured, why not? I doubted it would produce column material, but who knew where their gossip would lead? Off I went to join them at the Biltmore Hotel.

I assumed I wouldn't fit in. These women were married to wealthy men who, I learned, didn't *let* their wives work. Still, being more naive than I ever imagined, I couldn't believe what I heard.

One by one, the Beverly Hills ladies recounted their clever ploys to squirrel away extra cash. Apparently, whatever "allowance" their husbands provided was not nearly enough. One woman told of buying expensive jewelry, which her husband wouldn't mind, and charging it on his credit card. Then she would secretly return the jewelry for cash. "He'd never notice if I wore the necklace or not," she declared. Another woman passed along a story about the wife of a well-known celebrity who ordered large amounts of filets mignons from a catalog—putting them on her husband's credit card—then selling them to a grocery store or to her friends. But it was Carrie Rozelle who took the cheatin' wife prize.

One September she went into Manhattan to buy clothes for her fall wardrobe. She did not go to stores but to the showrooms of famous designers. She couldn't help herself and ended up spending $13,000, which, given that it was 1981, would have cost ten times more today. Carrie knew her husband would be furious.

"So what I did was sell my car to pay for the clothes."

The women stared at her in astonishment. What? But . . . wouldn't Pete know?

Carrie smiled impishly. Her car, she said, was always parked in their garage, his in the driveway. "One day, months later, his car wouldn't start, and he came into the house and asked to use mine."

Oh no, the women chorused.

"I told him I didn't have my car, I had sold it"—here she paused dramatically—"and used the money to invest in the stock market!"

I attempted to unfreeze my face and laugh with the others, but at this point—thank goodness—the check arrived. It was $400. Had I still been at *Newsweek*, I would have picked it up, no questions asked, but I knew the *Her-Ex* would not cover this expense. Each woman opened her wallet. No one removed a credit card. But like my grandmother paying a check, they each slowly, painfully withdrew one bill at a time until they had the exact amount.

As I drove back to the office, I realized I didn't have what it takes to be a lady who lunched.

—⁂—

In fact, I began to wonder if I had what it took to adjust to life in Los Angeles at all. It never occurred to me that its culture could be so different from what I had known in the Midwest and on the East Coast. There, your calling card was how smart you were. I often joked that everyone at *Newsweek* had double degrees from Yale and, since I had only a bachelor's degree from *a Big Ten school*, I stayed in the closet about my education. But in L.A., I would learn, your calling card was charm.

Few of the people I met seemed interested in what was going on in Washington or overseas. If news was discussed at all, it was L.A. news.

The guys in the sports department were unlike those I had befriended in New York. Those men—from NBC, CBS, the *New York Times*, *Sports Illustrated*—wore sport coats and ties, and no matter how long the evenings stretched, sports were rarely mentioned. Have you seen the new play on Broadway? Have you heard Willie Nelson's new album? I'm reading an amazing book, etc. Maybe Dan Jenkins, *Sports Illustrated*'s brilliant football writer, might go on about a drinking bout he'd had with a certain quarterback. Pete Axthelm would talk about jockey phenom Steve Cauthen, with whom he was writing a book. Pete Bonventre, formerly of *Newsweek* but now with *Inside Sports*, would regale us with stories about hanging out with Muhammad Ali after the Rumble in the Jungle in Zaire.

By contrast, my colleagues in the sports department at the *Her-Ex* often wore flip-flops, T-shirts with a product logo, and spoke most often about teams and stats. Some had attended colleges I had never heard of. None of this is to say they were not excellent at their jobs; they were. It merely said I often felt like an East Coast alien.

Also, sadly, I couldn't find women like me, women with interesting careers. In fact, I had trouble finding any friends at all.

One Saturday night, shortly after arriving in L.A., I was feeling sorry for myself, having no one to spend the evening with. *Aha*, I thought. *I'll go get an ice-cream cone, a big one, to cheer myself up. The hell with the calories.*

I jumped into my white Saab ("It looks like a bathtub," someone once said) and drove to a 31 Flavors on Santa Monica Boulevard. The place was empty except for a man and a woman at the far end of the store. I ordered a giant waffle cone with two scoops of chocolate ice cream. As I was paying, the couple walked by. The man stopped, stared at my cone, and said—without a trace of humor—"You eat like that, you'll get fat." And walked out.

The man was Jerry Brown, the *governor* of California.

Such was my warm welcome to L.A.

I ate my ice cream cone anyway.

22

Georgia Out of Her Mind

MY FIRST SPORTS PROBLEM IN LOS ANGELES WAS THE RAMS. More to the point, my problem was with the owner of the Rams, former showgirl Georgia Frontiere. She was the only female who owned a team in the NFL, but she could not understand my request. "I see no reason why women should go into the locker room," she declared. "They can do their job just as effectively without going in the locker room. And if they must go in, there's plenty of time for them to go in while the players still have their clothes on."

Yeah, right.

I tried to explain that going into a locker room is no trip to paradise; everything is kind of smelly and sticky and damp. And it's not quite true that a sportswriter can report as effectively without entering the inner sanctum. When you're on deadline, you don't have time to swap stories with the burly guard blocking the door, while several dozen of your male competitors interrogate the quarterback inside, then hope that eventually the exhausted athlete will be hauled out for one more tedious interview.

In a column written as a letter to Mrs. Frontiere, I said that keeping me in the hall outside the Rams' locker room would be like an NFL policy that a woman could own a team but could not attend league meetings in which crucial business was done. Rather, they would place a chair for her outside the meeting room door. When the session ended, she could request that certain owners come out and answer her questions about what went on inside.

This got me nowhere. But then, Mrs. Frontiere had far more to deal with than one persnickety female sportswriter.

She inherited the Rams when her husband, Carroll Rosenbloom, drowned. She then married a musician named Dominic Frontiere. Rather than admit she knew nothing about the business of running a football team, let alone anything about football—she once told me she needed a quarterback, "you know, a running back who can throw"—she took control of the Rams, or so we were led to believe. Her husband, who had sworn he wanted nothing to do with the team, reportedly made many phone calls not connected to music and often showed up in her stead for meetings when "Georgia wasn't feeling well."

I didn't get serious about kicking down the doors to the Rams' locker room until the week of November 16, 1981. The Rams were 5–6 and would be playing the San Francisco 49ers next. On Monday, I called general manager Don Klosterman, who seemed sympathetic to my cause, and told him I really *really* needed locker room access on Sunday. He said he would talk to Mrs. Frontiere but didn't sound hopeful. Actually, he sounded nervous. I often suspected Don worried about holding on to his job.

On Wednesday, he phoned back to tell me that Mrs. Frontiere was adamant: no women in the locker room. On Friday, Jerry Wilcox, the Rams' public relations director, called to say I would not be admitted to the locker room, but if I gave him a list of players I wanted to speak to, he would get them for me. As I recall, I mentioned this to my editor but said I would figure out a way to write a column somehow.

Friday night, I was at the Forum, waiting for the Lakers game to begin, when I was summoned to a phone in the front office. It was John Lindsey, the *Her-Ex* managing editor. He said the paper had filed a lawsuit against the Rams on my behalf, and he was putting Linda Breakstone, one of our best reporters, on the phone to "interview" me for a story that would run the next day.

Damn. The last thing I wanted was a lawsuit. I did not want the publicity, and I did not need the help. I would figure out how to get into the locker room myself. But the *Herald Examiner* obviously saw my situation as a boon for the paper, a move that surely would boost newsstand sales.

Saturday morning, I found the story about me on page one—naturally—below the fold, the headline reading, "Herald Examiner to sue Rams to allow Shah in the locker room."

The story quoted publisher Francis Dale saying, "We're going to fight this thing as a Neanderthal move against the 20th century. The timing is incredible. To think that a football organization headed by a woman would bar a prominent, superbly qualified sports columnist from doing her job, especially in the face of the court precedent just established with the San Francisco 49ers, the very team the Rams play Sunday afternoon."

Most of the article quoted sportswriter Michele Himmelberg who, only the week before, saw a federal judge declare the San Francisco 49ers had to provide equal access for all sports reporters.

Saturday afternoon, at an emergency session, a US court judge heard the *Herald*'s suit seeking a temporary restraining order to force the Rams to allow me into the postgame locker room. The judge ordered that male and female reporters covering the game will have access to Rams players—but not in their locker room.

This pleased nobody. The Rams' solution was to set up an interview room for all reporters, the idea being that several players would be dragged in for group questions. Apparently, before the ruling, the Rams' attorney announced in federal court that the team had just instituted a "change in policy" that would bar *all* reporters from the locker room.

My executive sports editor, Allan Malamud, was quoted in Sunday's paper saying, "They were discriminating against women. Now they're discriminating against men and women. They're equal in their discrimination."

Ironically, it was pointed out, I could interview 49ers in *their* locker room, but not Rams in theirs. Roy Firestone, a popular local television reporter, called the arrangement "unbelievable" and said the court was right in banning all reporters from the locker room. "If Diane isn't let in, nobody should be."

My phone started ringing. NBC Sports wanted an on-camera interview. Other reporters wanted my reaction to the ruling. Dammit, I thought, this was not what I wanted. I had always shied away from special attention. All that ever mattered to me was to prove I could do my job as well as—or better than—men. Normally, I only agreed to

TV or radio interviews if they were about upcoming games, not about me. I ignored pleas from publicists asking to represent me. "We'll make you famous!" they cried. I can't explain why I didn't want to be famous; maybe because it frightened me. I was taken aback one day while walking through a department store when a man hurried up to me saying how much he liked my column. *Like he recognized me.* Several times at movies or concerts, I would notice people staring at me. Once—and this was really wacky—I was driving along the Santa Monica Freeway when a guy in a green car pulled up next to me, held up the *Her-Ex* page with my column, and gave me a thumbs-up. How did he recognize me at 60 mph?

And now, without even consulting me, my paper had thrust me into the national limelight. I fretted. Finally, on Sunday, I called my parents to warn them they might see me splashed all over the news. Their proper young lady causing a fuss because she wanted to go into a locker room where *naked men* roamed. I figured they would not be happy. To my surprise, they sounded excited about seeing me on TV and had no qualms as to why.

At Anaheim Stadium where the Rams played, I was greeted by a guy from NBC, who led me to a table they had set up on a stretch of grass. After the on-camera interview, I went up to the press box, not knowing how I would be received. Most of the guys were friendly as usual, but some gazed at me silently, undoubtedly annoyed at what I had caused. As I set up my word processor, I heard my name called, and striding toward me, arms wide, was Tommy Lasorda. He gave me a big hug. I had never seen Lasorda at a Rams game, and I took his performance as a way of signaling to all in the press box that he supported me (and maybe to get his face on camera). I appreciated his gesture and settled in to watch the game—which the Rams lost 33–31.

Then the strangest thing happened: Georgia Frontiere came to my rescue.

After the game, all the reporters were herded into the makeshift interview room in the bowels of the stadium: concrete floor, folding chairs, a podium. And—*a bar*, two aluminum tables, covered with white cloths upon which stood bottles of liquor and wine, cans of beer, buckets of ice, glasses. Two bartenders stood ready to serve. Entering the room, the reporters stopped, gaped, shook their heads, and sat down. They were seething. Didn't Mrs. Frontiere understand this was not a party? We were working! We were on deadline! Not a single person took so much as a bottle of water. And as a result of this insult, any anger toward me ricocheted back to her. Thank you, Georgia!

The handling of the media improved at the next home game. Now there was carpeting and curtains and no bar. Each subsequent home game saw the interview room get new decorative touches as, one by one, reluctant Rams were carted in to be questioned.

In the meantime, Mrs. Frontiere garnered more bad press. Lawyers and players' agents told me of meetings where Dominic was always present—"Georgia isn't feeling well," he would say. He began replacing her board members with his friends; he brought in his own accountants and lawyers. He replaced the team comptroller and installed his personal secretary in the Frontiere house to answer the phone. "You're never quite sure who is making the decisions," one source told me. Nevertheless, Dominic vehemently denied he was involved with the Rams at all.

The next week, prior to the Rams taking off to play the Pittsburgh Steelers, Mrs. Frontiere addressed the team (in the locker room, I might add). "Everybody's out to get me," she declared. Then, urging them to play well, not for her sake or the Rams' sake, but their own, she said, "A lot of people will be looking at you as possible future coaches." Huh?

The bad press never stopped, but the locker room ban did. During the off season, someone got Georgia to concede that all reporters should be allowed into the locker room. The following September, I marched right in. Vince Ferragamo, the criminally handsome Rams quarterback, was talking to reporters, wearing nothing but a towel knotted at his waist. I sighed. And couldn't help thinking—naughty, naughty me—what if I ripped off the towel and threw him to the floor? Surely, I would set women's lib back 100 years.

Instead, I opened my notebook, asked questions, and behaved myself. While trying not to smile.

23

Dueling with the *New York Times*

I HADN'T BEEN AT THE *HERALD* LONG WHEN I GOT A CALL from Joe Vecchione, the sports editor of the *New York Times*. Would it be possible, he asked, for me to write a piece on Rams quarterback Pat Haden? (Ferragamo would replace him the next year.) I was thrilled. The *New York Times*! I said I would check with my editor, but I didn't see a problem. When did he need the story, how many words? He answered my questions, and then I asked, "How much do you pay?"

"Three hundred dollars," Vecchione replied.

I hesitated. Three hundred dollars? Seriously? I had never written anything for so little money. Of course, I wanted to write for the *New York Times*; what journalist didn't? But considering the time it would take to do the piece, the money was ridiculous. "I'm really sorry, Mr. Vecchione," I said. "I'd love to write for your paper, but what you're offering isn't enough."

"I realize we can't pay a lot, but that's our going rate."

"I'm sorry," I said again, "but . . ."

"Writing for the *New York Times* is something you can be proud of. It can only help your career."

"I know that. But I can't accept three hundred dollars."

He was silent for a moment. Then, "Well how much *do* you want?"

I took a deep breath. I wanted even more but finally squeaked, "One thousand."

This was followed by a loud sigh. "I don't know. I'll have to go down to the third floor and ask the managing editor. I'll get back to you." He hung up.

I doubted I would get what I'd requested, but how much would I agree to? I didn't think I was being discriminated against because I was a woman. I believed they paid both men and women this badly. Still, I couldn't help wondering if I had just screwed up a big opportunity.

A while later, Vecchione called back. "Well, you got it. One thousand dollars. It may be a first."

Surprised, I thanked him, and we chatted a bit longer. Then, before hanging up, I said, "Oh, by the way, I want to make sure you put my middle initial in my byline. Sometimes editors don't."

There followed a long silence. "We don't use bylines for stringer pieces."

"Wait a minute," I said. "You told me it would be an honor to write for the *Times*. But if I don't have a byline, how will anyone know?"

"You can tell them. Anyway, a byline is out of the question."

"Then I'm very sorry, Mr. Vecchione. I can't do the story. I've never written anything without a byline. And if I write for you, I would certainly want one."

An even louder sigh this time. "All right, I'll have to go *back down* to the third floor." He hung up.

Now what? If he said no, would it be wise to tell him I wouldn't write the story? Maybe I should anyway and try to get a byline the next time. If there was a next time. I continued to fret. He was gone a long time.

Then, "Okay, Diane K. Shah, you've got your byline. Another first. I look forward to seeing your piece."

After my self-congratulations faded, I began to worry. The *New York Times* was drearily matter-of-fact in its writing style, and I was not. I liked to have fun with stories; I was more of a feature writer than a strictly only-the-facts kind of person. So I was surprised and thrilled when my Pat Haden story ran with little, if any, editing.

I wrote many more bylined pieces for Joe Vecchione, which did not please my colleagues in the *Herald* sports department. Why me and not them? Once I was talking to Bob Kaiser, one of our best reporters, and I said, "You don't like me, do you?"

And he said, with a smile, "No, I don't. But I do respect you."

24

The Rednecks Come Calling

NOW IT IS FEBRUARY 1982. I AM SITTING BY THE ANGELS' DUGOUT, watching a meaningless spring training game. At the plate is Reggie Jackson, a man who lives in his own spotlight. A home-run hitter with an audacious flair for self-aggrandizement, he memorably proclaimed, in 1977, after being traded to the Yankees, "I'm the straw that stirs the drink." Which he then backed up by slugging three home runs in game 6 of the 1977 World Series. This performance, plus the postseason home runs he had previously hit with the Oakland A's, prompted sportswriters to anoint him Mr. October.

I had dealt with Reggie many times and had learned that to secure an interview, it was first necessary to perform what I called "a one-hour mating dance." This consisted of asking to speak with him, being rebuffed, following him out of the locker room and into the dugout, asking again, being rebuffed, following him onto the field, asking again, dogging him to the batting cage, asking *again*. Typically, after an hour of this kabuki, he would, for no apparent reason, plop down on the grass or sit in his cubicle—and talk my ear off.

In the summer of 1980, he was having his best season yet, but if that weren't enough, he made headlines off the field as well. One day he came upon a German woman lying in a Manhattan street, moments after she had been hit by a car. "Don't be afraid," he told her, as he shouted for an ambulance and applied damp towels to her forehead. "My name is Reggie Jackson, and everybody in this city knows me." Then there was the night that spring when he got into a fight over a traffic snarl and a stranger pulled out a gun and shot three bullets over his head. When I asked why these things always seemed to happen to him, Reggie Jackson said, with a nonchalant shrug, "It's not just me. It happens to Ali too."

But this spring rendered a new version of Reggie. Over the winter, he had been traded to the Angels (now called, for some incomprehensible reason, the Los Angeles Angels of Anaheim, or maybe just the Los Angeles Angels, who knows?), and he was determined to get off on the right foot. As a Yankee, he was famous for his spats with his manager, Billy Martin, and his catcher Thurman Munson, among others. But now he was cheerfully producing smiles for everybody.

One evening, he was dining alone at B.B.'s Steak-Out, an unglamorous roadside restaurant in Casa Grande. His back was to the door, and he was kind of scrunched over, nursing a bottle of beer, hoping no one would notice him. Looking up, he spotted me and another writer walking in, and he graciously invited us to join him. He seemed relaxed and of good humor. Soon his steak arrived; three and a half minutes later, so did the first town boor.

This was too good to pass up. I dug out my pen and notebook and took careful note.

The boor had a ten-gallon hat, jeans, a plaid shirt, a large belly, and a beer in his hand. He stared at Jackson with small, bright eyes. Hitching up his pants, he made his way over. He leaned his head close to Reggie's.

"Sorry to bother you," he said, without a trace of apology. "But I had to come over and shake your hand."

Reggie put down his fork and shook the man's hand. The man dug in. His head still inches from Reggie's, he embarked on a long, incoherent monologue that had something to do with "when I met John Wayne."

Reggie tried to eat his food, but the man would periodically slap him on the back or nudge him.

"I own a farm," he rambled on.

"Uh-huh," said Reggie, staring at the man with a frozen smile.

"Come down to my farm sometime."

"Okay."

"Tonight," the boor insisted. "You might want to buy one."

Eventually the creep left, and Reggie turned his attention to his salad. Suddenly, a woman in jeans with short, bleached-blonde hair perched on the arm of the empty chair beside him.

"Sorry to bother you," she sang. "But I just *had* to meet you." She sounded as if it were her birthright.

Reggie nodded pleasantly.

"I thought you might be interested in this." With that, she stuck a raffle ticket under his nose, and now, putting her face (and her smoldering cigarette) directly into his, she began making a low-toned sales pitch. Jackson jerked his head away from the smoke. The ash lengthened and threatened to spill onto his salad.

"Will you buy one?" she demanded.

"Maybe later."

"Here, all you have to do is fill this out." She shoved his salad bowl aside.

"I guess I was through with that anyway," said Reggie bleakly.

"Do you have a pen?"

"I told you," Reggie said, "I'll do it after I finish eating."

At this point, a yokel with a red beard appeared at Reggie's right. The blonde was at his left. It was a pincer movement as precise as any general had ever devised.

"Don't want to bother you, but I came to ask for your autograph," Red Beard said. As with the others, there was an edge of defiance in his voice. He had come not to beseech the superstar but to challenge him. It was high noon at the B.B. Steak-Out Corral.

Reggie signed the autograph. Neither the man nor the blonde seemed movable.

"Excuse me," Reggie said and got up. He fled to the men's room. When he returned, the rubes were gone.

A waitress came over with a round of unordered drinks. "From that table over there," she said, nodding to a group nearby. One of the men started to get up. Reggie called out thank you and quickly looked away. The man, cut off at the pass, slid back into his seat.

No matter. A fat woman in a tight red sweater appeared, demanding three autographs.

"How about one?" Reggie countered.

"Three," the woman said. "Right here. The first one you make out to Bill, this one here is for . . ."

The next man demanded—no one ever really asked—three auto-graphs, too. Then a large woman with a lit cigarette showed up. Then the blonde raffle ticket pusher reseated herself on the chair arm, *and* then the original ten-gallon boor stopped by. The waitress came over for the umpteenth time to apologize, "Mr. Jackson, for all the interruptions."

Reggie's attempt to eat dinner became a column. I ended the piece this way:

"Reggie once said that the difference between what he did and what I did was that 'anybody can do what you do.' Maybe he is right. But there is something I can do that he cannot. Like knock the table over and punch the people out. And the best part is, nobody would ever read about it in the papers."

25

"What on Earth Is the Matter with the Men in This Town?"

THE DAY THE REGGIE JACKSON COLUMN RAN, I WAS SITTING at my desk when the phone rang. "Yeah?" I said.

"Diane Shah?"

"Yeah." It was 10:15 in the morning. I was filling out an expense report, a chore that always made me cranky. Since I was never in the office at this hour, I figured whomever was calling wasn't anybody I wanted to talk to.

"This is Cary Grant."

"Uh-huh." *Had I eaten lunch on Monday, and if so, where was the receipt?*

"And I just wanted to tell you how much I enjoyed your column today."

I laughed. "Thank you." Whichever one of my friends was doing this had "The Voice" down remarkably well.

"Poor Reggie. I know exactly what he was going through."

At this point, the character on the other end of the line began talking about the perils of being a celebrity. Suddenly, I was pressing my ear against the phone. There was a loud banging, either my knees knocking together or my heart pounding. Then a faint voice was interrupting, whispering, "Excuse me . . . are you *really* Cary Grant?"

"Yes, yes. I don't know what happens to people sometimes, causing them to act the way they do."

And he kept on talking.

Soon I found myself so mesmerized by his voice that I started blurting out questions . . . anything to keep him on the line. *Cary Grant!* My God. Finally, after about 20 minutes, I came up with one more. "I've seen you sitting in Peter O'Malley's box at Dodger games. I know you're a big fan. Maybe we could do a column sometime . . ."

"No, no," Cary Grant said. "But I'll tell you what. The next time you see me there, come up. I'd very much like to meet you."

And so began one of the most unexpected—and surreal—storylines of my career.

We did meet at Dodger Stadium, about a month later. I spotted him sitting next to owner Peter O'Malley—both wearing suits and ties—in a box high above home plate, and I ratcheted up my courage and went up to meet him. He shook my hand and asked—his standard line, I am sure—if I had a boyfriend. When I said not at the moment, he gave me an appalled look and shook his head. "What on earth is the matter with the men in this town?"

From time to time after that, Mr. Grant (I could never quite utter the name Cary) would call me at home, usually to compliment me on something I had written. I never got over the shock of hearing his voice. At the time, in addition to my thrice-weekly sports column, I also wrote stories for GQ, most of them covers. One day the magazine's editor, Art Cooper, asked if I would do a story about a certain actor. I said sorry, but I wasn't interested. Art told me this actor was on his "wish list." I said, "Who else is on your wish list?"

"Did I ever tell you that the real reason I took this job was my desire to get Cary Grant on the cover?" he said. "We keep trying, and he keeps saying no."

"Hmm," I said. "Maybe I can help. I'll call you back."

But Mr. Grant said no. He assured me he would be happy to do a piece with me for any other publication, but apparently, twenty years earlier, GQ had written something he hadn't liked, and he refused to deal with the magazine ever again.

For a year, the editors at GQ drummed the steady beat of my telephone number onto their dialing pads. "Cary Grant!" they cried. "We must have Cary Grant!"

And I would hang up, and I would look at my calendar, and I would pick a day, maybe Thursday, put it off a little, and I would write carefully in ink, "Call C. Grant." Or maybe I would just sit there and stare at my phone for a while before lifting the receiver as if it were a piece of Limoges china and taking about an hour to push each of the digits and then taking a deep breath as someone at the Grant residence would put me on hold for a brief moment. Then—

"Hullo! How are you today!"

Just like that, over the line came the wonderful, lilting voice that could hearten the dead, that gravelly British-tinged voice that had impelled President Kennedy to call up from time to time and implore, "Say anything. I just want to hear your voice."

Now *that* voice was chatting amiably as if he had nothing better to do than sit there taking my call. And so it would go, month after month, until at last he finally agreed to let me chronicle a day at the races with him at Hollywood Park.

—⁓—

"How much are we betting today, darling?"

This was British-born Barbara Grant, his fifth wife and, in my opinion, a female clone of her husband. She was beautiful, impeccably dressed in a peach suit, charming, and had a dry wit that matched his. The query about how much to bet was a ritual because as Cary Grant had once explained over the phone, "I make $2 bets, you see, because they won't take a dollar-fifty. I've tried."

Barbara was bent over a card, marking entries. Cary studied the program and selected a horse named Safety Bank with 8-to-1 odds for the first race. He explained his handicapping system. First, he bet on jockey Chris McCarron, then on Laffit Pincay Jr., then he would alternate. Sometimes he'd bet on Gary Stevens. Asked if his system worked, he said, "Of course it doesn't work." Safety Bank plodded to a fourth-place finish.

But Pincay in the third race did place first, earning Mr. Grant a profit on his $5 bet.

Later, Barbara nudged him. "For the seventh race, we're going to bet this horse on your behalf," she said. "Lord of the Wind."

"I think I'm more Duke of the Wind," he said.

After the race, Barbara deadpanned, "Darling, did you notice? Lord of the Wind came from behind."

—⁓—

Two weeks after our day at the races, Mr. Grant left a message on my answering machine. He did not say his name; he never did, he once explained, because someone could give or sell the recording to a radio station. What the message said was, "Hullo, this is the fellow you were with at the racetrack. Please call me at your convenience."

I dialed him right away. "Now, look," Mr. Grant said, "it seems to me you might not have gotten everything you needed that day at the track. You were preoccupied, a love problem perhaps. Or maybe I was just a terrible bore. But somehow you were not there. So, if you still have some questions, and maybe you don't, we can continue if you like."

I was dumbstruck. In all my years of reporting, nobody had ever called up after an interview to suggest that maybe I was off my game. And the truth is we had not connected that day the way we always did on the phone. And he had sensed that. Cary Grant did. And now he was giving me another chance.

So, on a bright, beautiful day, I nervously set off for lunch with Cary Grant. Thinking, *please God, don't let me spill anything... just this once.*

His house was exactly the sort you might imagine Cary Grant would live in. It sat atop a hill overlooking Beverly Hills, plus the 16-acre estate of Harold Lloyd, Century City to the south, and the skyscrapers of downtown L.A. to the east. To the west, on a clear day, you could see all the way to the Pacific Ocean. He lived, as he should, on top of the world.

When I arrived, Mr. Grant was standing in the doorway. He had on a long-sleeve white shirt, tail out, white cotton slacks, and the kind of snowy-white socks seen only in detergent commercials; no shoes. There was a gold chain around his neck and a thin gold wedding band on his finger. His white hair glistened. The sun shone brightly, and he looked—with the blue sky and the San Gabriel Mountains in the background—like an angel descended from heaven. Surely Hitchcock was somewhere filming this.

"We are alone today," he said, explaining that the help wasn't there and his wife was away. "But she left us some lunch. I hope it will be okay."

Barbara Grant, who had taken on the chairmanship of a charity ball for the Princess Grace Foundation, a job that had turned into a 26-hour-a-day marathon, had, before dashing off to some meeting or other, left the kind of lunch that would have taken me a month to prepare—after a six-week crash course at the Cordon Bleu. Not only did she organize her husband's appointments (and handicapped his horses) but, knowing how much he liked wearing caftans at home in the evenings, once sewed him a closetful.

We sat at the table looking out the windows from which could be glimpsed the terrace, the lawn and, down the hill, the pool. I bit into the bread and awaited Hitchcock to come screaming "Cut!" and throw me off the set.

Mr. Grant, if you haven't already noticed, was an exact replica of the man who starred in 72 films—charming, debonair, and quick with one-liners. Despite his reputation for elegance, he was reluctant to talk about style. But he did drop one hint. He noticed long ago that powerful men always wore dark-blue suits.

"But you wear a lot of gray," I noted.

"I'll tell you a little secret," he said. And I waited for him to say how gray flatters white hair. But what Cary Grant said was, "If your hair falls out a bit, nobody will notice."

—◦◦◦—

I finished my story and turned it in . . . only to be confronted with an unexpected problem. Cary Grant, Art Cooper told me, refused to be photographed for the cover. He would supply one of his own photos. Art was practically apoplectic. GQ did not operate this way. Cary Grant, his dream cover, was turning into a nightmare.

I may have called Mr. Grant about this—I don't remember. But if I did, I was not successful. Neither was the GQ photo department. At last I urged Art to phone Mr. Grant himself. At the very least, he'd get to hear The Voice.

This phone call, as later reported by Art, was amazing. How charming, how funny, how nice, etc. "Finally, Cary said, 'Well if Diane wants this, then I will do it,'" Art Cooper reported.

He agreed to Mr. Grant's wish to use his own photographer, and Art promised to send Mr. Grant a choice of photos for the cover.

Not one to miss an opportunity, I said, "Well, well, well. So, Cary Grant agreed because of *me*. I think a bonus is in order, don't you?" Reluctantly Art agreed to pay me an extra $500.

The photo shoot date was set, and of course I planned to be there. But several days before, I received another distress call from GQ. Grant forbade anyone but his photographer to be present. No photo editor flown in from New York or anyone else. Apparently, not even me. I went anyway.

Clearly, he was in a bad mood when he opened the door to let me in. He was wearing a navy suit, white shirt, and tie, but he wasn't sure the suit was quite right. He excused himself and returned wearing a different suit. "There's no one here," he said bleakly. "My housekeeper had to return to Mexico because her mother is ill." Whatever other help he employed were also absent, and Barbara was away working on the charity ball.

He changed into one suit after another, posed wearing each one, then decided he needed help. He led me to his bedroom and ushered me down a hall with mirrored doors on either side. There was a secret spot; when he touched it, the doors popped open. This system was installed, he said, to stymie a potential suit thief.

On the left side of the hall, dozens of suits were neatly arranged by color; black, navy, medium blue, light blue, gray, beige, white. A collection of caftans followed. Mr. Grant began pulling out one suit after another, asking my opinion. Then he wondered if he should pose in a caftan, and if so, which one?

Next came an assembly of shirts. Which one looked best with which suit?

Needless to say, I had no idea, and the thought that I, *me*, should be advising Cary Grant on what to wear was preposterous.

I sat at a table near the living room where the shoot was underway. At one point, Mr. Grant went to his bedroom to change *again*, and when he returned, he was holding a white shirt, a spool of white thread, a package of needles, and a plastic pill vial filled with white buttons.

"I lost a button on this cuff," he said, showing me. "Would you mind sewing one on? Any one of these in the bottle. I save buttons, you know. When I get rid of shirts, I figure, why not keep the buttons?" Then he apologized that there was no staff to do this.

I knew how to sew on a button, but this was *Cary Grant's shirt*. As I held it in my hands, I realized I had never touched such fine, soft cotton, and all I could think was, *what if I prick my finger and bleed on it?*

A catastrophe was averted, the button was sewed on, and Mr. Grant was still changing clothes. He thought maybe the photographer should come back the next day to shoot his collection of caftans. I weakly murmured that *GQ* probably wanted a more formal shot, and eventually I left.

The magazine came out in January 1986, and the picture *GQ* selected showed Mr. Grant in a black suit jacket over a red-and-white-striped shirt, and a black tie with tiny red dots on it. His chin was resting on his hand, and the face, with that alluring smile and black-rimmed glasses, jumped off the page. Mr. Grant phoned numerous times to say how much he and Barbara loved the story and how they laughed and often read it again.

—⁊⁊⁊—

The last time I saw Cary Grant was on a hot August afternoon. The Los Angeles Raiders were playing a preseason game at the Coliseum, and I went to write about it. As I approached the media entrance, I spotted a tall man standing off to the right of the entrance. He was wearing a navy wool blazer and gray pants. His back was to me.

"Is that you?" I called out, still uncomfortable calling him by his first name.

Cary Grant turned around. "Diane! What brings you here?"

I told him I was working, and what was *he* doing here?

He explained that he and Barbara had become friendly with a couple in London, and they were visiting with their eight-year-old son who wanted to see a football game.

"The others are inside," Mr. Grant said. "I'm waiting for someone to take me up."

"I'll get someone right away," I said.

"Come up to our box and say hello," he said.

I didn't go up to his box. But after the game, I walked into the Raiders' locker room. The players were ripping off their jerseys, and the floor was littered with white bandages covered with yellow goo. As I picked my way in, I saw Mr. Grant. He was standing in one corner of the locker room, maybe 30 feet away. He looked at me, and I looked at him, and I could swear we were thinking exactly the same thing: "What are *you* doing in *here*?"

Three months later, before giving one of his talks to an audience in Davenport, Iowa, he collapsed in his hotel room and died of a massive stroke. He was 82.

I was saddened, of course. He had taken my career to a place I never could have imagined. Knowing Cary Grant—*receiving phone calls from him*—always seemed like somebody had slipped the wrong chapter into my biography. I thought of him more like an accidental friend than a real one. I wrote Barbara Grant a condolence note, and she replied with a beautifully written thank you.

My one regret—I never said thank you to Mr. Grant.

26

Inside Enemy Territory

LOCKER ROOMS, I DISCOVERED, ARE FILLED WITH COMPETITIVE-crazed athletes who like to give each other a hard time. They make fun of each other, pull outrageous pranks, and always test any newcomers. This includes reporters. If you can take it, and maybe even give it back, they leave you alone. If you appear fearful or angry, the provocation will continue.

An example. Ken Gurnick, our *Her-Ex* Dodgers beat writer, and one of the best in the country, is a little guy. For some reason, another reporter once referred to him as Mouse, and soon all the Dodgers called him Mouse. "Hey, Mouse," one would shout. And Kenny would trot over and pull out his notebook. He usually got the story first. "I don't think any of them even knew my name," he says, laughing.

I also learned not to take anything personally. Early on, there were three baseball players who refused to talk to me. The obvious reason was they didn't want women in their locker room. Only, at some point, I noticed these three refused to talk to men reporters, too. Lesson filed away.

To my surprise, I also discovered I could give it back. Hal McRae, a Kansas City Royals outfielder, had not done well for a couple of years, and it seemed he might be on his way out. Then he bounced back and was having a terrific season when I went to talk with him in the visitors' clubhouse in Anaheim. I got there early; only a few players had arrived. Hal was sitting at his locker, pulling on his socks. (It takes baseball players forever to get their uniforms on.) I dragged a stool over and began interviewing him, my back to the locker room. After a while, the rest of the team walked in and began changing into their uniforms. One Royal,

I couldn't tell who, said loudly to center fielder Willie Wilson, "Hey, Willie. Don't take your pants off. Diane's sitting right there."

The locker room fell silent.

Then Willie said, "Oh, you know what they say, you've seen one, you've seen 'em all."

Without looking up from my notebook, I said, "No, Willie, you're wrong. It's *always* a pleasure."

Everyone guffawed; end of story.

Another time—one September—the Angels had called up pitcher Doug Corbett from Triple A. He had pitched well early in the season, but then, in June, he pitched so badly they sent him down. "The Lord stopped walking with me," was how he explained it.

But now that he was back, I hoped I could squeeze a column out of him. I walked into the Angels' clubhouse and asked Rod Carew if Corbett was there. Carew nodded. Where? He pointed to the far side of the room. There were three lockers with a uniform hanging in each, but no players. "Which one?" I asked. "The one with his number on the uniform," the first baseman replied.

"I don't know his number," I said.

To which Carew, who usually couldn't have been nicer, growled, "We have media guides, you know. Why don't you read one?"

Silence in the locker room.

"Well, I've tried to," I said, "but it's so boring, I always fall asleep."

Laughter. End of story.

Okay, so these weren't big-deal situations, but I do think I was able to show that I could play, too.

27

Angels in the Locker Room

I WAS NEVER AFRAID OF LOCKER ROOMS.

Why, I cannot explain. Obviously, I should have been. I was often the first female sportswriter—or maybe the second or third—in a world of men, many of whom did not want me there. At *Newsweek*, my presence wasn't a major distraction. I wrote mainly profiles or features and had no need to deal with locker rooms. But when I was hired by the *Los Angeles Herald Examiner* as a sports columnist, I felt the laserlike beams of so many eyeballs zeroing in on my every move. Even in my daily life.

Although the *Her-Ex* was the number-two paper in town, most people thought our sports coverage was better than that of the *Los Angeles Times*. We had a huge following. We were especially well read by two groups of people with time on their hands: actors and cops. Early one Sunday morning, I was driving along a deserted Santa Monica Boulevard and made an illegal U-turn. From out of nowhere squealed up a black-and-white. The officer looked at my license and said, "Hey, you're the girl at the *Herald*. You think the Raiders will win today?"

Seeing an opportunity, I regaled him with Raider info. He laughed and asked more questions until, after a good 20 minutes, he said, "Sorry. Hope I haven't ruined your day," and handed me a ticket.

Another time I was leaving the Raiders' offices on draft day when I was stopped. After the cop identified me as *that* columnist, I told him I had just left the Raiders—this was years before the NFL made the draft a must-see TV event—and was heading back to the paper. He asked whom the Raiders had selected, and I told him what I knew. He handed back my license, asked to shake my hand, and sent me on my way—ticket free.

If some players begrudged my intrusion into their world, this, I decided, was their problem. For anytime I set foot on their sacred territory, I knew I had the law riding shotgun right beside me. This was the luck of timing. The women's movement was building strength, and the courts were there to back us up if necessary.

I also had another advantage—my comfort around men. Even as a young girl, I preferred the company of boys. With them, I could talk baseball or current events. And they were *funny*. Around girls, I was at a loss, self-conscious, awkward, unsure of what to say. With men, I felt an easy connection that I think helped me navigate their macho world.

This is how I remember those days, only now I realize my memory has glitches. Looking through my files, I dug out an interview I did with Roger Angell of the *New Yorker* for a story about women sports reporters. At one point I told him, "There's nothing I love more than baseball, but every time I walk out onto a baseball field, I feel a dread about being there."

Maybe those "dread" times have faded from memory, I don't know. But had I felt dread, I would not have told anyone. Because I was pushing my way into a man's world, I felt it important never to moan about a situation or to seek help. If a male reporter could get the job done, so would I. I did not think it wise to dump a load of girl-reporter problems on my editor's desk.

If there was a problem, I was determined to solve it myself.

—◦∿◦—

Labor Day 1982 was approaching, and the California Angels were fighting for a berth in the playoffs. That holiday weekend, they would play a five-game series with the Red Sox at Fenway. Although I had written many columns about the Angels, my usual strategy was to get to the ballpark early, interview a player, watch four or five innings from the press box, then listen to the rest of the game on the radio during my long drive home. But this series was important. I packed a bag and tagged along.

The Angels lost all five games. So into the locker room I strode.

First stop is always the manager's office. The Angels' manager, Gene Mauch, was already talking to four or five reporters when I stepped in.

As I opened my notebook, Mauch abruptly stopped speaking in the middle of a sentence and walked out. The other reporters looked at each other. What the heck?

I knew. It was me.

I drifted into the locker room and talked to the players I needed. I skirted Reggie Jackson, who made it a point to parade naked in front of me. I rolled my eyes and walked on. Sometime later, I went back into Mauch's office.

He was alone and had changed into his street clothes. His back was to me.

"Gene?"

He turned.

"Did you walk out because of me?"

He stared at me for a long moment. "Yes, I did."

Before I could ask why, he said, with surprising emotion, "I know you can be in here, but it makes me sick to my stomach to see you walking around in front of all these naked [he used the N word to finish the sentence]. You remind me of my daughter. I think about my daughter, and it makes me sick."

Then, to my utter astonishment, he began to cry. Gene Mauch, the 57-year-old, white-haired, highly respected manager of the Angels, was in tears. I was stunned.

I gave him a moment to compose himself, this crusty old manager who had broken into tears because of *me*. I shifted from one foot to the other; what were the rules for this? Yell at him? Hand him a Kleenex? As he brushed away a tear, I took a deep breath and said, "Gene, I know this is weird. Believe me, my mother did not raise me to do business with naked men." I gave him a small smile. "But here I am, and I have a job to do. And part of this job is talking to you."

"Fine. I'll talk to you in the hallway."

"That won't work."

"Tell someone to get me, and I'll come right out."

"I think you have a good chance of going to the playoffs," I said. "And I can't be out in the hall, waiting for you. I'll need to talk to players in both locker rooms."

He shook his head, picked up his bag, and walked out.

I was not angry. Nor did I feel defeated. If anything, I felt sorry for him. I was beginning to see how my presence could be difficult for all of us.

I flew home and didn't mention that bizarre incident to anyone. This was a challenge, and I intended to see what I could do about it. For some reason, it occurred to me that if I spent more time with Mauch, maybe he would get used to having me around and feel more comfortable.

So that September, I drove to Anaheim every chance I got. If Mauch was at the batting cage, I would walk over, stand beside him, and ask how so-and-so's bruised shin was or about a pitcher's strained elbow. If he was in the dugout, I would sit down on the bench next to him and just start talking.

October arrived, the Angels won the AL West and prepared to play Milwaukee for the division title, best-of-five series. The Angels won the first two games at home. Because I was on deadline, I didn't have time to go down to the locker rooms. The next day, the team traveled to Milwaukee. They needed only one win; it seemed like a lock.

The Angels lost all three games. Now I did need to question Mauch.

So . . . into the locker room I trekked. It was a large place and deathly silent. The players were on stools in front of their lockers, holding paper plates and shoveling forkfuls of spaghetti into their mouths. No one was talking. In the middle of this tomb, a circle of reporters and TV cameramen had formed around Mauch. He spotted me immediately.

"Okay, fellas, that's it," he said. And began walking toward me.

I took a deep breath. *Here we go,* I thought.

Mauch came right up to me, put his arm around my shoulders, and said, "Now, Diane, what can I do for you?"

28

"I Don't Need This Fucking Job"

MY NEXT CHALLENGE CAME TWO WEEKS LATER FROM THE meanest, scariest team on the planet—or so the Los Angeles Raiders liked to advertise themselves. Owner Al Davis had defied the NFL and whisked his team from Oakland to Los Angeles, even though his lawsuit against the NFL had ended in a mistrial. The Raiders, in their black-and-silver uniforms with the skeleton logo, had joyfully crafted an image as motorcycle-riding, chain-swinging hooligans who liked to warn cities they visited, "Pull down your shades! Lock your doors! Keep your women and children inside! The Raiders are coming!" Their ornery owner—the *bête noire* of Commissioner Pete Rozelle—was also a tactical genius who believed in the long ball and had won two Super Bowls, including one the year before.

I had never dealt with the Raiders, but I did hear they would not allow women in their locker room. I happened to run into Gene Upshaw, the recently retired Raider now serving as a member of the National Football League Players' Association. When I asked him about locker room access, he grunted, "Forget it."

That September, after playing two games, the NFL players staged a walkout, and the owners called a lockout that lasted 57 days (oddly, the same number of days as the baseball strike) and cut the season's schedule from 16 games to 9. The Raiders were on the road for the first two games, and I was too busy with pennant races to travel with them. But in late October—mid-strike—I arranged a phone interview with Raiders head coach Tom Flores. What was it like, I asked, to plan all week for a game that probably would not be played?

It was ten o'clock on a Tuesday morning. He and his coaches had arrived at their offices at eight thirty to begin looking at game film. They were scheduled to play Miami that Sunday, and they were studying all of Miami's defensive plays, their down-and-distance tendencies, formation tendencies, etc. In fact, they had been studying them since last Tuesday, after the game with the Broncos was called off. Flores admitted he was not used to going home for dinner during the season and wasn't quite sure what to do. "I'm bored," he said. "I'm not geared for this. I have all this extra energy to burn up. We look at films, but what's missing is the emotion and the adrenaline and the excitement that usually goes into these sessions. Now what we do at these meetings is drink a lot of coffee and go home early."

When I figured I had enough for a column, I asked if I could have a minute more to talk about something else: the locker room. I said I needed to get in and that I had been told I couldn't. "That's right," Flores said. "We don't allow women in the locker room."

I went into my now-standard pitch—my mother didn't raise me to do business with naked men; it's weird, but this is my job, etc. He tried the hall approach. I casually mentioned the lawsuits women were winning—including my own—and who wants to go through that? After a few minutes of this back-and-forth, Flores said, "Last year several Raiders dumped two *male* reporters in a garbage can. I can't imagine what they'll do to you."

I made a mental note: always wear slacks. Finally, I said, "Look, Coach, you need to let me in. If they're really, really mean to me, I'll cry, and I'll never come back. How's that?"

Flores went silent for a moment. Then, "Okay. But the first time you want to go in, tell our PR guy in the press box, and he'll call down to me on the field. Then I can warn the players."

Yes, I thought, *by all means warn them.*

———⌇———

I said I was never scared. But when the lockout ended and I went to the Raiders' first game back, I was nail-biting nervous. I figured it would be helpful if the Raiders won, which they finally did, beating San Diego 28–24. Whew.

After the game, I waited anxiously outside the locker room door until, at last, it was flung open. I didn't exactly march in—I sort of tiptoed. By now, the players had ripped off their jerseys and, as I frantically scanned the tops of their lockers for their names, I saw none. (The Raiders were the only team in any of the four major team sports who didn't bother to put their names on their lockers.) Since I had never met any of them, and since their jerseys were balled up on the floor, I was already in trouble.

"Can I help you?"

I looked up at the very large, thickly muscled, sweaty man towering over me. I swallowed. "Uh, yes. I'm looking for Ray Guy."

Guy, by far the best punter in the league, was going to be the subject of my column—if I could find him.

The behemoth pointed down a row of lockers. "Last one," he said and turned away.

Oh sure, I thought. *He's probably sending me to the water boy.* But when I reached the last locker, there was a tall, skinny guy. "Ray?" I said.

He smiled. "Yep."

Ray Guy couldn't have been more cooperative, and I wrote my column. So much for the scary, garbage-can-dumping Raiders. In fact, the Raiders became my favorite team to deal with. They were smart—tight end Todd Christensen often sent me scurrying to a dictionary to fathom the meaning of five or six of the words he threw at me—they were funny, and they were *nice.* The next time I went into their locker room, Al Davis yelled out, "Diane, good to see you!"

I don't know why I didn't have problems in the locker room. Was it because players didn't want to mess around with a well-known columnist? Or was it because—and this is my favorite reason—of the way I was perceived? As my friend, the talented *Washington Post* columnist Sally Jenkins once noted, "Diane would saunter through the locker room wearing Armani and a gold wristwatch, and she just radiated *I don't need this fucking job.*"

At any rate, the mean, scowling Raiders never gave me a hard time. Here are some of the moments with them I remember.

———

The large man who had greeted me when I first entered the locker room was six-foot-four, 272-pound offensive tackle Henry Lawrence. One

Sunday, I was in the locker room after a game, and I told the team doctor my right leg had buckled as I was crossing Broadway downtown and I had crumpled to the street. It also hurt. The doctor drew me into the trainer's room and had me lie flat on my stomach. He poked around then told me to come to his office the next morning.

I did. He X-rayed my back and determined I had a herniated disk and would need surgery. Later that morning, Henry Lawrence called me at home. I have no idea how he got my number, but he wanted to know what was wrong with me. Many of the players had seen me prostrate in the trainer's room, and nothing fascinates an athlete more than someone else's injury. I told him the doctor's prognosis. "Listen to me," Henry said urgently. "First, you don't let that man touch you. He's a quack. Second, don't have surgery. If some doctor put a knife in my perfectly healthy knee and immediately pulled the knife out, my knee would never be the same. Let me give you the names of some really good chiropractors."

An hour later, another Raider called with the same message. I got a second opinion from a doctor who worked with the Lakers and who specialized in backs. He took one look at my X-ray and shook his head. "You don't have a herniated disk. You have back spasms. I'll prescribe some muscle relaxants. You'll be fine." And I was.

—⁓—

Then there was a promising rookie who'd grown up five miles from the L.A. Coliseum and still slept in his boyhood bedroom. He was playing well, and I often spoke with him after a game. He was shy but always willing to talk. The strange thing was he would sit on his stool, stark naked, his legs spread. And every single time, one of the veteran players would walk over, drop a towel on his lap, and say, "Cover up."

—⁓—

From time to time, I liked to give it back. One day, again in the Raiders' locker room, a player was telling me that he and his wife had been talking about me the night before. "She said if you have legitimate credentials, you should be allowed in here." Then, looking quite proud of himself, he added, "And I said, yeah, she's just one of the guys."

I said, "Oh, no I'm not. I dress better than they do, I smell better than they do, and if you're really, really mean to me, I'll cry." His eyes popped open. I smiled and walked away.

—⁓—

There were only two times I can remember that a Raider was mad at me. Once, when I referred to quarterback Marc Wilson as having a concave chest. (He wasn't very good, unless you like interceptions.) The other time proved far more serious.

After the Raiders won the 1983 Super Bowl, the team began to slip. In 1986, when they were 5–3, I wrote a column midseason making fun of them. I noted that the Hell's Angels from Oakland had bought beach houses and had grown comfortably laid back. I carefully did not use the word "wimps," believing that would go too far. I turned in my column and went home.

The next morning, I picked up the paper in my driveway and thought *Oh, no!* The sports editor had used "wimps" in the headline. (Editors write the headlines, not the writers.)

That morning, cornerback Lester Hayes phoned me. He had grown up with a bad stutter, but during the time I had known him, he had worked hard to overcome it. Carefully enunciating his words, he said the guys were furious about my column. That it had been posted on their bulletin board. "Look," he said, "you've always been fair to me, so I want to warn you. Don't come into the locker room after the game on Sunday."

When I became a columnist, my friend David Israel, referring to his days as a sports columnist for the *Chicago Tribune*, gave me a piece of advice: "If you write something critical about a player, show up as soon as possible. Let him yell at you. The longer you wait, the angrier he will get."

I didn't have a chance that week to drop by a Raiders practice, so as I sat in the press box on Sunday, I wondered, *would this be my garbage can moment?* The game against Denver seesawed. Into the fourth quarter they went, the Raiders down by a touchdown. I *really* needed a win here. Suddenly I wished I had brought a pillow to stuff inside my clothes; they wouldn't hit a pregnant woman, right?

Then, with the clock ticking down, Marc Wilson fell across the goal line to tie the score 28–28. The game went into overtime. I was biting my lip, until blessedly, a field goal secured a Raiders win.

I crept into their locker room. Center Don Mosebar spotted me immediately and grinned. "So, Diane, you still think we're wimps?"

No one else mentioned the column and, mercifully, that was that.

29

Marcus, Slow Down!

THE STAR OF THE TEAM WAS RUNNING BACK MARCUS ALLEN. He was already a local celebrity, having set all kinds of records at USC, and he was drafted by the Raiders in the spring of 1982. Now it was December, and I needed to finally write about him.

I called him. "When can we get together for an interview?"

He laughed. Marcus Allen, as I was about to learn, laughed all the time. When he wasn't laughing, he was smiling. Maybe that was because he had made the transition from USC tailback to Raiders running back better than many expected. Of the Raiders' 15 touchdowns, he had scored seven.

"I'm on my way out to have breakfast," he replied. "Why don't you meet me."

He gave me the name of the restaurant, and then he uttered a word that made me gulp: "Hurry."

I flew into a panic. *Hurry?* When normal people tell you to hurry, you make a mild attempt to get your arms and legs working a bit faster. But when Marcus Allen tells you . . .

Deciding to have a little fun, this is what I wrote:

I leapt into my turbocharged Saab and blasted off. I was at least a half-hour away. It was hard to hurry though. All along Santa Monica Boulevard, cars stood in a frozen tableau.

No problem. I jumped out of my car, strapped on a pair of roller skates, and tore off down the sidewalk. I felt bad about the man with the cane and the two children I bowled over, but I was in a *hurry.*

Five minutes from the restaurant, one of my wheels fell off. No problem. I wrenched off the skates and jammed my feet into a pair of running shoes. Seven minutes and 49 seconds after I left home, I lurched into the restaurant.

—◦◦◦—

Allen was sitting at a table by the door, leaning back in his chair and smiling lazily. Already he was halfway through three platefuls of food, including an enormous ham-and-cheese omelet, potatoes, french toast, and an apple.

"I couldn't wait for you," he said.

As I began taking notes, he talked about the process of becoming a Raider. "At first I was very quiet. I didn't want to be cocky," he said. "I just want to go quietly and unnoticed into the record books. Like I don't want to say anything about gaining two thousand yards."

"And someday you will?" I asked.

He laughed. "When I was ten years old, I started playing football, and I knew I was better than anybody else. But my father told me, 'Always remember there is going to be somebody better than you.'"

Suddenly, Allen remembered the time. He had to go see his lawyer in West Hollywood. He climbed into his gray Mercedes 380SL and told me to follow.

By the time I got my car started, Marcus was gone in a cloud of dust. I wrote:

Flooring it, I tried to keep pace. Suddenly there was this frightening boom. No problem. We had just broken the sound barrier. Marcus was definitely going for daylight. I glanced at my dashboard clock. It was now tomorrow in time. There was another sonic boom, and I landed in a parking lot.

Marcus Allen was leaning against the side of his car, laughing. "I thought you said you could drive fast," he commented. Then he dashed across the street and was gone.

The doctor said I would be fine. If only I could learn to slow down.

—◦◦◦—

Now it was the off season of 1984. Someone, a reader I think, called me at the *Herald Examiner*. "I just heard Marcus Allen was arrested," the man said breathlessly. "Something about a stolen car?"

I immediately called Ed Hookstratten, Allen's agent/attorney and, I will confess, my Deep Throat on many columns. Ed knew everyone—or at least everyone who might be of importance to me—and he would pass along spicy tidbits from time to time. Only now he seemed reluctant. "Marcus won't talk to you," he said.

But Hookstratten did. With his help and a contentious conversation with the LAPD, I was able to piece together what happened. Allen, the Most Valuable Player in the Raiders' Super Bowl victory over the Washington Redskins five months earlier, had been driving along Melrose Avenue in Los Angeles between eleven thirty and noon on a Friday in June. He was at the wheel of his new black Ferrari. A car sure to catch the eye.

It caught the eye of Officer Steve Watson, Hollywood Division, LAPD.

According to Lieutenant Dan Cooke, an LAPD spokesman, "The officer observes this vehicle being driven by a"—he paused—"man." Officer Watson next observed that the license plate on the front of the Ferrari was missing. "Always a good sign of auto theft," Lieutenant Cooke told me over the phone.

A license plate was in place on the rear of the car, however. Which Officer Watson also observed. He called in the license plate number on his radio, and the word came back that the plate belonged to a 1984 Pontiac. Another good sign of auto theft. Officer Watson immediately called for a backup unit.

Allen turned onto the 700 block of Formosa, a residential street, and pulled into a driveway. Officer Watson was right behind him.

Officer Watson jumped out of his car, approached the Ferrari, and pulled out his gun. The police would insist the officer was just doing his job when he hauled Allen out of his car and held him at gunpoint. He did this because it was conceivable, after all, that Marcus Allen, who is six feet, two inches, 210 pounds (and African American) was an *auto thief.*

He then ordered Allen to drop to the ground into what is known as a "felony kneeling position." He did not ask Allen for his driver's license. Just pointed the gun at the Raiders' running back. And waited for reinforcements.

According to Lieutenant Dan Cooke and Hookstratten, people started running out of their houses. Adults and children. Yelling, "It's Marcus Allen! It's Marcus Allen!"

Also according to Lieutenant Dan Cooke, who didn't want to discuss the hours-old incident, calling it "history," Officer Watson later commented, "I wasn't a football fan, but I recognized that name right away." Then, as if to hammer home the credibility of the officer, Cooke added, "Watson learned his lessons from Sherlock Holmes."

Officer Watson also supposedly said that as soon as "I realized he was celebrity and not a car thief, I let him go."

In fact, according to Lieutenant Dan Cooke, Officer Watson did not put his gun away and let Marcus Allen go until the backup unit arrived and the officer in that car confirmed the identity of the football player.

The gun had been pointed at Allen for only a matter of minutes, it should be noted. And the mix-up about the license plates should also be noted. According to Hookstratten, Hollywood Sports Car, where Marcus had purchased his Ferrari, mistakenly sent the wrong plates to him. Just one of those things.

No, I thought. Not *just* one of those things.

I said to Lieutenant Dan Cooke, "If it were me in the Ferrari, a white woman, would the officer have pulled a gun and yanked me out of the car?"

"Do you want to talk to a deceased officer who stopped a motorist?" Lieutenant Dan Cooke shouted into the phone. "You tell me the right way to stop someone. Seven officers have been killed in the line of duty, and you question how we make a felony stop?"

"I was just asking."

"And I'm just telling you. Goodbye!"

Lieutenant Dan Cooke slammed down the receiver.

I was writing my column when John Lindsey, the editor of the *Herald Examiner*, walked over. "I just got a call from a Lieutenant Dan Cooke. He insisted that we not run this story."

"Really? Well, I'm writing it."

Lindsey smiled. "Good."

My column ran. And Marcus? Why he was hurrying to his next assignment. Flying to Miami to be a judge in the Miss Universe pageant.

30

Pass-Rushing Houseplants?

ONE OF THE FIRST THINGS HOWIE LONG SAID TO ME WAS, "I explode in my sleep instead of exploding socially. I think I'm a time bomb."

Anyone watching Fox Sports NFL coverage would hardly consider the handsome analyst with the bookkeeper's glasses a time bomb. Certainly, I didn't back in the eighties, when he played defensive end for the Los Angeles Raiders. Sure, I had watched him explode off the line and mow down every offensive player he could. But the guy, at six foot five, 270 pounds, was an All-Pro, maybe even the best defensive end in the National Football League and a Hall of Famer for sure. So when *GQ* asked me to write a cover story about Long, I thought, why not? I had never had a problem with him, and I was happy to accept the assignment.

Until I actually did the assignment.

This was when I learned that Mr. Nice Guy in the locker room could be a terror off the field too. He had *demons*.

"First time I roomed with him, I wake up in the middle of the night, Howie's screaming and yelling he's going to kill somebody," said nose tackle Bill Pickel. "He gets out of bed. He starts moving around the room. I don't know what he he's going to do. And I can't wake him up. So I made the sign of the cross.

"Once, up in New England, he picks up the room-service tray, throws it across the room. I mean, it's one of those heavy silver things. In the morning, he looks at all the glasses and dishes and stuff scattered around and goes, 'Jeez, what happened?'"

Diane Long, Howie's wife, who had witnessed a sleepwalking Howie sacking imaginary rats and pass-rushing houseplants, shrugged and smiled prettily. "I make sure the shotgun is not in his hands, and then I just ignore him."

I used these quotes to start my story after this lead sentence: *Howie Long does not go softly into the night.* Only then I thought, was this the way to begin writing about Howie Long? Someone might think he was, well, unbalanced. Besides, he did point out, "I don't leave the house now. So the neighborhood's safe."

New lead. Howie Long does not go softly into battle. (Yes, this was better.)

During a Thursday afternoon practice last season (I wrote), Bill Lewis, a backup offensive lineman, challenged Howie, held him out, blocked him. This, coming from a rookie, set Howie off. He punched Lewis. Then, as Lewis fell to his knees, Howie kicked him in the face. Drove a tooth right through his bottom lip. Split the lip in half, seven stitches on the inside, six on the outside.

"I felt terrible for weeks," Long said. "That's not me. You ask ten guys on the team, and they'll say don't set Howie off. But I don't see myself that way. Really, I'm not like that." Earlier, in training camp, he beat up Raiders guard Mickey Marvin.

—⁓—

No, no, no, I thought, stopping my fingers on the keyboard. What kind of story was this? After all, here was a gifted athlete. Beautifully spoken, a handsome charmer, quiet neighbor, doting father of a two-year-old. This was an intelligent, highly motivated 27-year-old who was considered by most of his peers to be the best defensive end in the game and in 1985 was voted defensive lineman of the year. Opponents described Long as a fair, clean player; normally quiet.

So, I thought, let's roll it again. Take three. The body.

"The first time I saw him," said Sean Jones, the Raiders' right end, "I thought this is the best-put-together white guy I've ever seen. He's a white guy with a black guy's body."

Long brings to the position an uncommon mixture of herculean strength and tactical finesse. Then, of course, there is the angelic smile set across that strong jaw, making him handsome enough to remind some of a young Marlon Brando, especially when he is wearing a T-shirt. Which is most of the time.

And so, were a child to draw a picture of Howie Long, he would crayon that large square body and the pretty smile, and he would put in a white picket fence. At which point Long would grab the crayon and sketch onto the sky a big black cloud.

—⁘—

For all the praise heaped upon Long, it hasn't made a dent in the way he regards himself. "You look at Howie, and you think here's a guy who's got everything," said former teammate Lyle Alzado. "Most guys that big aren't good-looking. He walks into a place, people look at him. Now, here's the key to Howie. Howie's thinking, 'The fuck they looking at? Hey, mister, you got a problem, or what?' Because no matter what he seems to have, Howie's very hurt. That hurt makes him insecure. Insecurity makes him afraid of failing."

"I never think I look good enough," Long says. "I always think I look too big, too heavy. I'm not good-looking. I mean it's tough walking into a restaurant, everybody stopping eating and staring and seeing what I order. I hear comments about my size. 'That Howie Long. Watch out. He'll tear the restaurant apart.' I hate that. That's why I come to places like this."

We are sitting in a nearly deserted Mexican restaurant in Marina del Rey at two o'clock on a Saturday afternoon. Several men sit at the bar watching a sporting event on TV. They shake Long's hand when he enters and again when he leaves. Other than that, only the owner comes over to speak with him. "I go where I'm comfortable. I'll go out of my way to drive to a movie theater that isn't crowded, no matter what's playing. I feel real uncomfortable in a crowd."

So far, my sessions with Long have gone well. Then—oops—I crossed a line. Sheila Gillis, assistant to Long's agent, Greg Campbell, phoned and began speaking insistently. "Howie must not be asked about his childhood. *Under no circumstances* can the subject be raised. The past is the past, and Howie wants to get on with his life."

Okay, fine. Only present tense. Except hardly a single topic of conversation flows without Howie-inserted references to "how I grew up." "One of the driving forces in Howie," observes Sean Jones, "is that he knows what it's like to be at the bottom."

—⁓—

The blue-collar section of Boston known as Charlestown was a place where good people struggled simply to hang on. Howie Long Sr. worked back-breaking hours loading milk for a dairy, and Howie's mother was often bedridden, suffering from epilepsy. The family, including Howie's sister, lived with his grandmother, Elizabeth Hilton Mullan, and one of his uncles in a small two-story row house. When Howie was 12, his parents divorced. Although his mother was awarded custody, his grandmother took him in.

"She is a great woman," Long says of the person he calls Ma. "If she walked down to that school once, she walked down to that school ten times. 'Mrs. Mullan, could you please come down to the school, Howie's been suspended again.' And she used to say when she got home, 'Not my Howie.' I could be standing over the body with the gun in my hand, powder burns on my fingers, and she'd deny the whole thing."

But Mrs. Mullan couldn't help Howie on the streets. When he started school, he was younger than the other kids, but bigger. "Here was a six-year-old kid, but he was the size of a nine-year-old, hanging around with nine-year-olds,' Howie says. "I think that had a lot to do with my insecurity. I didn't go out for Little League baseball because I didn't think I'd do well. The fear of being embarrassed. I've always had that fear, for some reason."

The neighborhood was dangerous. Bigger kids beat him up and took his lunch money. "Then it was almost like I opened up the window and said, I'm not going to take this shit anymore. At age 13, I just stood up."

He went to a gym and learned how to throw a punch. "I still remember the first punch I threw," he says. "Someone approached me on the street, getting ready to take my lunch money, and I took care of it." Howie laughs. "Two days later, his older cousin came by and beat me up."

Charlestown was not exactly known for high teas and debutante balls. Social occasions, such as they were, consisted of a ride on the subway to the Jordan Marsh department store. "We'd have one kid on the platform, one kid in the door, and he would signal the kid inside, who would grab all the stuff he could. He'd run out the door just as the train was pulling up." Long paused. "We stole milk too."

When forced busing was declared in Boston, and Charlestown High was the recipient of busloads of new black faces, Long cut classes for 45 straight days. "The school was surrounded by mounted police and riot patrols, and I didn't want anything to do with it," he says. "Also, you really weren't looked upon highly if you buckled under to Judge [Arthur] Garrity [who ordered the busing]. There was so much tension."

The Mullans did not know what to do with the troubled 13-year-old. The four uncles were all struggling with their own responsibilities. Although Howie felt his family's love, he had been jockeyed from house to house. *Bedroom* meant somebody's sofa. *Meals* meant fending for himself.

"Howie was the kind of kid, if he had to go to a banquet or something, there would be no one there for him," said Bill Pickel. "He'd say, 'Gee, my whole family has the measles and they're in quarantine.' I remember when he made All-Pro the first time. He was so excited. He called his grandmother. All she said was, 'I hope they're not hurting you out there.' Finally, my dad called. I think that meant a lot to him."

Long's uncle Billy, who was stretching to pay the bills for four children, eventually took Howie in. From the streets of Charlestown, he was transported to the grassy suburb of Milford, 20 miles to the southwest. At Milford High, he began playing football, although, despite the military-like atmosphere in Uncle Billy's house, playing hooky was a sport he still often engaged in.

—◊◊◊—

Rereading these pages now, decades later, I still can't determine what got Howie so angry with me. But maybe it was something in the pages that followed. So let us continue.

—◊◊◊—

Diane Addonizio first encountered Long walking across the Villanova campus. She was a freshman, a classical-studies major from Red Bank, New Jersey, thinking of becoming a lawyer. Long was an uncommunicative sophomore jock who had grown up accustomed to, as he put it, "the men getting up after dinner and going into the parlor to watch TV." It was the *Love Connection* at its worst. "He was such an angry young man," says Diane. "He had a ten-foot outer shell that had to be penetrated. But there was just a glimmer of the great person he is."

Their first Valentine's Day, Howie didn't even send a card. Diane was hurt. When he phoned for their regular good-night call, he could tell something was wrong. When she told him, he said, "We never celebrated holidays in my house."

Despite being on a football scholarship, Long felt embarrassed. He had no idea how to write a term paper; he had barely read anything. He decided one thing he could teach himself was how to speak. He eliminated the Boston accent and the "ain'ts." Although he did not graduate on time, he went back and earned his degree in communications.

His football future was hardly assured. Villanova was not a football power, and Howie wasn't impressing anybody anyway. "I looked at some game films from his senior year, and he was terrible, just terrible," Earl Leggett, the Raiders' defensive line coach recalls. But Long, a last-minute fill-in for the annual Blue-Gray all-star game, played with such energy that he was named defensive MVP. Leggett decided to check him out, and not only did he like Long's strength, speed, and agility, he liked that Howie had been kicked off the team for fighting. "Seems he went into a frat house one night and sort of cleared it out. I liked that."

It wasn't a frat house. Long busted into an apartment when a friend banged on his door at two in the morning saying he'd been beaten up by 50 guys. Long rounded up a posse and had taken out four guys when the police arrived. He wasn't charged, but he was suspended two games.

He was taken by the Raiders in the second round of the 1981 draft and became, as Leggett puts it, "the greenest player I'd ever had to coach."

—⁓—

Long's travels from the tired, broken streets of Charlestown to the sunny two-story house in Redondo Beach, with its Porsche and Mercedes and the beach only steps away, are one measure of his success. His endorsements are another. But if he possesses the looks, wit, and charm of a future marquee attraction, he has mastered in advance one state of the art: the prickliness of a star.

Miller Lite created a Lineman of the Year award and named Long and Jim Covert of the Chicago Bears as its first recipients. According to one Miller source, Long demanded royal treatment. Three weeks later, Miller asked him to appear at a cocktail reception in Anaheim for media covering the upcoming Super Bowl. Long demanded to be paid. "He was a colossal pain in the ass," the source said.

One newspaper reporter who covered the Raiders on a regular basis noticed a gradual change in Long. "At first, he was like a little kid, excited, genuinely glad to be here," the reporter said. "But the last couple of years he's become harder, less friendly. Maybe he's gone Hollywood."

Teammates too have noticed a change. "Because he's such a great player and has gotten so much publicity, he's treated like a god, sometimes even by opponents," offered one Raider. "The trouble is, he acts like a god."

—·—

Early on a bright Tuesday morning, the Longs, all three of them, are sitting around their breakfast table. Howie gets up and slides four pieces of bread into the toaster. House rule: count on Diane for dinner only. Howie recalls good-naturedly when she was studying law at USC, three years earlier: "There was this hamburger joint, they'd see me coming in the door, they'd start the order. I mean, I went there every night. That's what happens when you marry a liberated woman."

Diane shoots him a look.

"Hey, I'm grateful for the little bit of home cooking that I get," says Howie, rolling his eyes. "The way I grew up, it doesn't take much to make *me* happy."

Once she passes the Bar, Diane will work for a law firm in Long Beach, creating the couple of the eighties: the Litigator and the Terminator. But despite his relentless teasing, Long concedes, "I need someone to argue with. When I turn on the light, I need someone to talk to. Besides," he says with a smile, "she goes over all my contracts."

Says Diane, "I've learned a lot about street smarts from Howie. From me, he's learned diplomacy—he's still working on that—and what the sorbet's for."

"You have your Type A people, well, I'm like Triple A," he says. "I mean, stress is my middle name. I lie in bed for an hour and a half at night before I can get to sleep, thinking about football, wife, everything; worrying. But I'll tell you one thing. I've always thought insecurity was a hidden ally. It pushes me to be better."

Most nights, he does not lie in bed though, worrying. Most nights, he slips downstairs to that nice sofa in the den. There, he eventually drifts off, only to go one more round with the demons in the night.

Old habits die hard.

—✺—

That was a big chunk of the story that appeared in *GQ*. I wasn't trying to present Long in a good light or a bad light. I simply tried to incorporate my reporting into what I hoped was an accurate snapshot. But Howie did not see it that way. He was furious with me for reasons I only learned months later when he wrote me a letter contesting critical comments from three of my sources. Why hadn't I consulted him? I trusted those sources, had I been wrong to? When the magazine hit the newsstands, September 1987, *GQ* threw a party in L.A. Howie, not happily, did show up. We said hello, nothing more, and went our separate ways.

31

I Always Feel Like . . . Somebody's Watching Me

WHEN ROCKWELL RECORDED HIS HIT SONG, "SOMEBODY'S Watching Me," football writers across America immediately assumed the song had been written for them. That's because all of us who write about football are paranoid. We're dead sure somebody is watching us.

That somebody is the National Football League.

And I had proof.

Using a well-entrenched and somewhat mysterious network, the NFL receives every newspaper and magazine article in literary captivity that refers to league activities or any activities that might have bearing on the league. It is not known precisely how this is accomplished, just as one does not know how the KGB knows what it knows.

All we know is that the NFL knows.

I offer into evidence two items from my files.

Last November I wrote a column about New Jersey Generals' owner Donald Trump. It appeared in the *Los Angeles Herald Examiner* on a Thursday. The following Monday I was on the phone with Dallas Cowboys' president Tex Schramm. He said he had read the Trump piece.

"You saw it in Dallas?" I asked.

Schramm chuckled. "I see everything you write," he answered enigmatically.

More recently, I was typing a column about owners in the NFL who were dissatisfied with Commissioner Pete Rozelle. An NFL PR man called me. After chattering on for 30 minutes, he idly wondered if I had seen an article from a Boston paper suggesting that some owners were unhappy with Rozelle. "Do you believe that nonsense?" he said.

Gathering information makes up only half of the crack NFL intelligence operation. The other half: it disseminates it.

Once every six weeks or so, football writers receive large packets of articles from the NFL. It doesn't take a seasoned cryptologist to figure out that all the articles relate to certain pet issues—the USFL is one; the Raiders are a staple—and that the articles just happen to reflect the NFL point of view.

Again from my files:

During the (1982) football strike, I wrote a column posing two solutions for the impasse. One came from a San Francisco prostitute. The second one came from me and suggested that the commissioner himself might take some action, seeing as how he had been instrumental in settling such matters in the past.

The packet of articles that was sent contained only the first half of my column, the second half—about Rozelle—having mysteriously disappeared.

32

The Accidental Invitation

THE INVITATION WAS PRINTED ON THE LETTERHEAD OF Solters/Roskin/Friedman, Inc., the well-known public relations firm:

The Los Angeles Friars Club

Would Like to Invite You to a

Stag "Toast & Roast" Dinner of

Super Bowl Champion

THE LOS ANGELES RAIDERS!

My first thought was, *what fun! It could be hilarious to hear the Raiders roasted.* My second thought was . . . *Stag?*

"Is that still a word?" I asked someone in the office.

I checked a two-year-old dictionary. Way down at the bottom of all the definitions it said, "a social gathering attended by men only."

Still? After all these years, I was again being invited to something I was not allowed to attend?

I looked at the name on the envelope. Diane Shah. Apparently, I was welcome to attend. As long as I didn't attend.

Confused, I put through a call to Solters/Roskin.

"You got an invitation?" gasped a publicist.

"Yes," I said.

"Friars' roasts are always stag," she informed me. "That's their policy. But why don't you check with the Raiders?"

I called the Raiders. Al LoCasale, the executive assistant, was not in. I left a message and got another executive on the phone. "I'm sorry," he said. "You can't come. Everyone wants to feel they can let down their hair. Besides, the humor . . . you'd be embarrassed."

"I think I should be the judge of that," I said.

Then, as if suspecting a ruse, he warned me. "The waiters are trained to detect women disguised as men."

Sometime later, a woman who worked for the Raiders phoned me and spoke in a low tone. "We're all rooting for you," she said. "I mean the women here are. We're pretty annoyed that we're not invited either. Well, except for the Raiderettes."

"The cheerleaders are invited?"

"Yes. The whole squad. They're supposed to entertain for ten minutes. Then they're going to eat dinner in a separate room."

"A separate room? Like for the *help*?"

"Some of the players are going to boycott."

"Really?"

"Well, so far [defensive back] Kenny Hill. Anyway, we wish you luck."

I wasn't sure why I needed luck. I was simply a person who had been invited to a dinner, only to be uninvited three words later. What I probably needed was a glass slipper. I was beginning to feel like Cinderella.

In the next two hours, both the Solters/Roskin publicist and the Raider executive phoned back with the same message. In delighted voices, they said I was invited to attend . . . the cocktail hour. "But you can't stay for the dinner."

Then Al LoCasale called. "All I can say is that this is their roast. You know we allow women writers into our locker room and to all our functions. If this were a club function, you'd be invited. I'll pursue it, though."

Two days later, I received a letter from the publicist at Solters/Roskin. "We do not set the policy for who may or may not attend the stag roast. As a matter of fact, it was our recommendation that all working female press be invited and that any four-letter words that might offend them would not be our responsibility."

The letter concluded, "If you would be willing to come to the affair disguised as a man, Lee [Solters] would get you into the dinner—he feels it would make a great story."

Disguised as a man? Had they lost their minds? That would mean I would have to cut my long, red-polished fingernails. I had been warned this was a tough job, but this was too much.

All I wanted was to go to the roast, preferably as a female, which is the way I generally showed up at things. Or, at the very least, I wanted to make up my own mind not to go. I mean, I do get to vote; the US government even lets me write checks to the IRS.

I called the Friars.

"Why do you want to sit with 1,100 men and listen to filth?" the event chairman yelled by way of opening the conversation.

For the same reason, I supposed, that 1,100 men would want to sit with each other and listen to filth. What I said was, "I received an invitation."

"It was obviously accidental," he said. "The Raiders *accidentally* put you on the mailing list." He paused. "Tell you what. How about if I send you a tape? Then you can hear the whole thing."

Ah. So it was okay for me to hear the "filth." As long as I heard it in private.

I wasn't sure what to make of that. I decided to think it over.

In the end, I did not go, nor did I request a tape. I decided my delicately pierced ears might be irreparably damaged.

33

Up Yours, Steve!

STEVE CARLTON WAS A MASTERFUL PITCHER WITH THE Philadelphia Phillies. When his career ended in 1988, he had recorded the fourth-most strikeouts in baseball history, his lifetime ERA was 3.22, and four times he had won the Cy Young Award. His first year, this left-hander—with his biting slider and killer fastball—won 27 of the team's 59 wins. So, yeah, he was a phenomenal pitcher.

He was also a Class A jerk—to be polite.

He was especially a jerk around sportswriters, whom he treated like annoying panhandlers.

For example. In 1980, after beating the Kansas City Royals in game two of the World Series, he was, of course, the one player we all wanted to talk to. We crowded into the locker room and finally caught sight of him hiding behind a closed glass door to an office. I was standing with a Hall of Fame team of our own—Red Smith of the *New York Times*, Roger Angel of the *New Yorker*, and Pete Axthelm of *Newsweek*. We stood there, a mere eight feet away from this hero—and waited.

Suddenly, the door flew open, and one of Carlton's stooges, pitcher Dickie Noles, stepped out and threw a bucket of water on us as Carlton scurried across the locker room to the trainer's room and slammed the door. We stared at each other in disbelief. Pete was wearing a beautiful beige suede jacket—drenched.

Time marched on, and so did Carlton, who had recorded his 300th win at the end of the 1983 season. Now it was October, and the Phillies were in town to face the Dodgers in the playoffs. The day before the first game of the series, I sharpened my pencil and went to work. This is what I wrote:

Having recently passed a statistical benchmark, that is having just written my 300th column, I find I am besieged by athletes begging me to interview them. I know that only 15 other sports columnists in the history of journalism have reached this plateau, but I must say the constant round of interviews does grow wearisome. Every time a new team comes to town, it's the same thing. You'd think all the athletes could just get together and agree to one mass interview.

To make matters worse, I once again find myself covering the playoffs. So now the requests for interviews have intensified all the more. Yesterday morning, no sooner had I reached my office than the phone rang.

"Yeah," I said.

"Er, Miss Shah? This is Steve Carlton with the Philadelphia Phillies. I was wondering—"

"I haven't even had my coffee yet," I grumbled. "Don't you guys ever sleep?"

"I'm sorry," said Carlton. "It's just that I was, er, wondering if you would have time today to interview me."

"What team did you say you were from?"

"The Phillies. I'm a pitcher."

"Oh, right, I remember. But haven't I interviewed you before? When the Phillies won the 1980 World Series or after you got your 300th win? I'm sure I did."

"Actually, you didn't," Carlton said. "I was rather hoping you would, but you always walk right past me. I've even sent you notes requesting interviews, but you never reply."

"You know how many games there are in a season?" I said.

"Yes," said Carlton meekly. "But I felt I had to give it a shot."

"So what is it you want me to interview you about?" I said, trying not to sound bored.

"Well you could ask me about my tough conditioning program," he said. "The kung fu and pushing my arm into a tub of rice. Or how many more years I'm going to pitch. Or what I think about the playoffs."

"Same old stuff," I said, stifling a yawn. "You'd think occasionally one of you guys would come up with something new to say."

"Perhaps you could ask me about being an oenophile," Carlton suggested.

"Don't try to impress me with big words," I snapped. "I hate looking things up in the dictionary."

"Oh," said Carlton deflatedly. "Well, er, I did lead the league in strike-outs. With 275."

"Are you a Cy Young candidate then?"

"No," he said sadly. "That would be John Denny. He pitches Wednesday night."

"Don't take this personally," I said, "but readers would probably be interested in finding out what he has to say."

"I wouldn't need much time," Carlton pleaded. "Although I usually like as much time with the writer as possible."

"I've heard that before," I sighed. "You athletes think the longer the interview, the better the story. Only I'm not getting paid to shoot the breeze with you guys. I get paid to write a column. I know it's important to your line of work to get interviewed, so I try to accommodate you when I can. But it's not in my contract here at the paper to just sit around doing interviews all day."

"I'll try to be as brief as possible," said Carlton. "Perhaps we could have lunch or a cup of coffee before the game."

"Absolutely not," I shouted. "You want me to talk to you, we'll talk at the ballpark. I hate when athletes try to interfere with my private life."

"Fine," said Carlton. "What time should I meet you?"

"Well, let's see. I'll get to Dodger Stadium about 2½ hours before game time. Then I go up to the press box and set up my word-processing machine. I have to find a plug and take the machine out of its case and make sure it works. This is a special time for me. I don't like to be rushed."

"How about after you finish word-processing practice?"

"No. 'Cause then I like to stroll around the batting cage, chatting with my colleagues from the other papers. It's really annoying when an athlete comes over and interrupts. Some of the best jokes I hear are at the batting cage."

"After that?" said Carlton hopefully.

"No," I went on. "Next I have to stop in Tom Lasorda's office. I need to check out the food and which celebrities have come by. And then I have to run through the Dodger clubhouse and say hello to everyone 'cause they expect hometown writers to be friendly to them."

"Gee," said Carlton. "This is really important to me. It's the playoffs."

"Tell you what," I said. "I'll send an intermediary. I'll get Vin Scully to interview you. He'll give the tape to Steve Brener, the Dodger publicist, and he'll screen the best answers out."

"I really appreciate this," said Carlton.

"Sure," I said. "By the way, what did you say your name was?"

—— 〰 ——

Naturally, I got no response from Carlton. But I was rewarded 17 years later when David Halberstam chose this column to include in his book, *The Best American Sports Writing of the Century.*

34

The Bully of Baseball

I STARED AT MY BLANK COMPUTER SCREEN AS DEADLINE approached. How, I wondered, to describe Yankees owner George Steinbrenner?

I was not the only one at a loss. A writer for *Time* magazine invoked no fewer than 11 literary references or other phrases in his attempt. Among them: "He was the celebrity despot who runs his team the way Don Vito Corleone ran the rackets. He did away with managers the way Bluebeard ditched wives. He was the archetypal father; the family tyrant; the Great Santini. He has the qualities of a local Aztec volcano."

Surely, had the writer been given more space, he could have come up with still others. But he could have saved his thesaurus and his library undue wear if he had merely stated the obvious: George M. Steinbrenner III is a bully.

I went on to explain the classic definition of a bully is a person who hurts, frightens, or tyrannizes those who are smaller or weaker. This was what Steinbrenner did, sometimes outrageously, sometimes with charm, but always with the dead certainty that he was right. Clearly, he was baseball's most famous owner, a headline grabber who hired and fired employees at will. He also criticized his players and pretty much made everyone working for him miserable. Still, during his 37 years as owner, he won 7 World Series and 11 pennants. Obviously, he could not be ignored.

In 1982, the baseball owners were meeting in San Diego to decide if they should fire Commissioner Bowie Kuhn. Predictably, they hemmed and hawed and tabled the decision for another time. But Steinbrenner was there, outspoken as always, and I asked if I could interview him. He agreed.

I met him in his hotel room. His eyes sparkling and his tone forceful, he carried on like a politician trying to sell his platform to the lone voter who had turned out to hear him. But when asked about his modus operandi, he resorted to his bullying charm.

"The owner in today's game has to assume an assertive role," he said. "Managers can't do it; they're not paid enough to get the respect of the players." He could also have said that his managers aren't around long enough to earn that respect. Like Billy Martin, whom he hired and fired *five* times. "Sure, I let managers go. But I hire back the same guys. And look how well my alumni have done."

He then ranted about the use of corked bats. He was absolutely, positively certain that cork was in vogue, especially in California (where, coincidentally, Reggie Jackson, whom Steinbrenner traded to the Angels, was knocking them out of the park). Steinbrenner insisted he had unimpeachable corked bat sources. And he was going to be proven right, no doubt about it.

Then he made a comment that caught me by surprise. I was wearing a long cotton print dress and sandals, my legs properly crossed. "You have nice ankles," he said with a sudden smile.

Huh? In my whole life, my bony ankles had never been praised or perhaps even noticed. I thanked him and asked my next question. At some point, I apparently mentioned that when I was hired by the *Herald Examiner*, I had kept my New York apartment and returned every two months, "To get my brain jump-started," I said.

"Let me know when you're in town," he responded. I said I would.

And I did. I'm not sure why—was I hoping he'd tell me stuff that would make a good column? The man was always in the news—firing and rehiring managers and other front-office people; throwing loud, angry tantrums in the Yankees' locker room; and of course, his corked bats accusations.

My next trip in, I called Yankee Stadium and left word with Steinbrenner's secretary. I was out most of the day. When I returned to my apartment at around six thirty, I found two panicky messages on my answering machine. They were from Ken Nigro, the Yankees' public relations director.

"Thank God!" he said when I returned his call. "Mr. Steinbrenner wants you to come out to the stadium and watch the game with him."

"Now?" I said, checking my watch. The game started at 7. It was already 6:40.

"Yes, now. Please hurry. I've got to tell him you're coming."

"Kenny, I'm not doing this. It's cold and rainy, and I'm tired."

"No, no, listen. You have to come. Mr. Steinbrenner insists."

Before Kenny had been given (or was punished with) this job, Mickey Morabito was the team's PR director, and I knew how terrified he was of displeasing The Boss. Mickey had told me that no matter how late a game went, he was expected to be in his office at 9 a.m. sharp and that Steinbrenner often called to make sure he was. I could hear the same note of fear in Kenny's voice.

"I'm sorry," I said. "I am not going to the game."

"You have to. He'll kill me."

"Look, why don't you tell him you tried to reach me, that you left several voicemails, and that you never heard back."

"I don't know," Kenny said miserably.

Had I believed this would be a "legitimate" meeting with Steinbrenner, I would have jumped in a cab and sped to the stadium. But this sounded more like something else.

"Tell him how hard you tried," I said. "I'm really sorry, Kenny. Good luck."

Nigro was let go after working for Steinbrenner only that one season. Not because he couldn't lasso me into the stadium but because of the infamous pine tar incident. Kansas City's George Brett had hit a ninth-inning home run to take a 5–4 lead over the Yankees, using a bat thick with pine tar. Manager Billy Martin went nuts. The game was halted. Appeals were issued, along with a lawsuit claiming Brett had used too much pine tar. Baseball and the courts decided the homer was legitimate, but with only two outs in that inning, the teams had to meet to finish the ninth inning. Nigro was canned for passing out I SURVIVED THE PINE TAR GAME T-shirts in the press box.

From then on, I steered clear of The Boss.

35

Breaking and Entering

I HAD NO CHOICE BUT TO BREAK INTO THE WHITE HOUSE.

In broad daylight.

No one even tried to stop me. I am that good.

It all started when the Los Angeles Lakers defeated the Boston Celtics for the NBA championship, despite the cranked-up heat in the Boston *Gahden* and the hotel fire alarm that rattled the Lakers at some ungodly hour of the night.

The morning after the victory, the Lakers were bound for the White House, having been summoned by President Ronald Reagan for a Rose Garden ceremony.

Deplaning at National Airport, the Lakers were ushered onto one bus, the media another. Our bus pulled up to the first White House gate. After consulting his clipboard, the guard announced our names were not on it. Several writers jumped off the bus to protest. I stepped off too—and took off! Full speed toward the second gate on Pennsylvania Avenue. I had covered events at the White House, and I assumed the driver had pulled up to the wrong gate.

At my approach, the guard at the second gate reached for his clipboard. Waving my press pass—which he couldn't read—I yelled, "I'm with the Lakers!" and kept running. Next thing I knew, I was tugging open a door and stepping into the White House. I raced from room to room—by myself!—no people anywhere, searching for the Lakers.

No other reporter got the story I did. Here are some excerpts:

—⁓—

Washington—Fewer than 24 hours after they conquered Boston, here were the Lakers drifting through the White House, looking a bit dazed over what had befallen them. Twenty-four hours ago, they were scrapping for loose balls on a parquet floor in a sweaty, overheated gym. Four hours ago, they were walking through the airport in Boston to the warm applause of passengers who set down their hand baggage to honor them as they hurried to their gates. *In Boston.*

Now, the president of the United States was summoning Pat Riley, General Manager Bill Sharman, and Kareem Abdul-Jabbar into the Oval Office. *At the White House.*

What did he say, what did he say, the other Lakers cried out . You were in there for a minute and a half!

"We made small talk, mainly," Kareem said. "He congratulated us." He paused. "He said he hadn't watched the game."

And later, after Kareem had presented him with a Lakers jersey bearing number 1 and saying, "I'm not a member of your party, but I do know who is number one around here," and after Magic Johnson had given him a basketball autographed by the team and Pat Riley had given him a Lakers world champions cap and T-shirt, saying, "You can wear this when you come to California where it's a little more casual." The president again moved to the mike. "I want to apologize for the height of the microphone," he said. "We could only set it at one height. If we set it for you, I'd never be heard. And I knew you could all bend over."

Now the Lakers were inside. *The White House.* For their own private tour. When the public tours come through, they roll up the priceless oriental rugs, store them away. For the Lakers, the rugs were down.

"We'll just step through here to the China Room," a Secret Service-man said.

Inside the small, ornate room, place settings of official White House china from every administration were on display in beautiful, lighted breakfronts.

"Ooh, this is what I want for our dining room," Angela Worthy said to James, clutching his arm and pointing to one of the cabinets.

"What's that?" said Kurt Rambis, standing in front of the shelf with the Reagan china and pointing to a thimble-size silver bowl and spoon.

"That's for salt," someone whispered. Rambis rolled his eyes.

They liked the East Room. FDR had a pony in there once and roller skating for the kids and a boxing match one time. "And you'll like this," the Secret Serviceman said. "President Eisenhower once had the Harlem Globetrotters play in here." He paused and gazed up at three enormous chandeliers. "And they didn't even the take the chandeliers down."

The Secret Serviceman continued to rattle off names, dates, and historical anecdotes as if he were a talking encyclopedia. "How does he bark out names like that?" asked broadcaster Chick Hearn in awe. "I have trouble with the starting five."

"Listen," said Riley to the Secret Serviceman, as the tour wound down, "anytime you need a job, you can be Chick Hearn's color man."

The Secret Serviceman smiled politely.

The Lakers were ushered out onto the South Portico overlooking the South Lawn. Rambis took a picture of the Washington Monument, off in the distance, and the team photographer made everybody pose for a shot for the Lakers family album. (I snuck in.)

Then it was over. They were on the bus to the airport, quiet now, letting it all soak in. From the Boston Garden to the Rose Garden, America's number-one basketball team meeting America's number-one man, one captain greeting another, all done now.

The White House disappeared through the rear window.

The monuments fell away.

The bus driver said, "And to your right, Watergate."

Coach Pat Riley gazed at the famous apartment complex and said, "It's just like the Celtics. Covert behavior."

36

Coach Fashionista

LAST JUNE, THE DAY AFTER THE LOS ANGELES LAKERS WON their second consecutive world championship—like repeated—40,000 jubilant fans gridlocked their way downtown to cheer their gigantic conquering heroes.

Still, this was L.A., a town that drifts in and out of sporting events as if they were cocktail parties—and still believes a moving pick is *Gone with the Wind*.

So, it was highly unusual that on into the following week, the Lakers were still the talk of the town—well, at least Pat Riley was. Riley had boldly, most thought stupidly, promised a year before that the Lakers would repeat, even though no team had done so in nineteen years.

And it was the coach's name, not Magic Johnson's or Kareem Abdul-Jabbar's, that fell from the lips of the Lakers' faithful.

They chorused, "What was that horrible shirt, that purplish *thing* that Riley wore in the victory parade?"

Of all the gym joints in all the NBA towns, the Lakers had to walk into this one.

—∿∿—

So began my *GQ* cover story on Pat Riley. When I was given the assignment, I assumed it would be filled with glowing tributes from players and coaches and maybe even the Forum janitor. Here was a man who had clawed his way from barely hanging on as a player, then—with no more basketball in his future—became a *carpenter*—and then, insanely was named the coach of the Los Angeles Lakers. During the seven years he has held that position, he has not only become a highly respected coach who has led his team to the finals six times and won four of them—three in the past four years—and has, at age 43, more wins than any coach in NBA history—but this man has become *a fashionista.* There he is, prowling the sidelines in his Armani suits and carefully coiffed, slicked-back hair, looking for all the world as if he were waiting for his Maserati to be brought round. So, yes, it would surely be an ode to Coach Pat Riley.

Only it wasn't.

Riley and I had both come to the Lakers in the fall of 1981, I as a recently created columnist and he from the radio booth—more or less. And while it was true that Riley took an unusual path to coachdom, his athletic life had surely portended a distinguished career. He had been recruited by both the legendary basketball coach Adolph Rupp at Kentucky and by Alabama's Bear Bryant to play *football.* He went to Kentucky as a short six-foot-three center and was named the team's MVP each of his three varsity years. Although he had never touched a football in college, the Dallas Cowboys drafted him anyway. Still, he chose to play for the then San Diego Rockets as the seventh pick in the NBA draft.

Three years later, he packed everything he had—including a plastic plant and his new bride, Chris—into his Corvette and headed north to Portland. Back surgery, ankle and knee injuries, switching from center to guard, and a college talent that hadn't translated well into the pros had kept him on the bench much of that time. The Portland Trail Blazers had taken him in the expansion draft.

When the Lakers flew in for a preseason game, Chick Hearn, the team's revered broadcaster, remembered, "I went out to get on the team bus. It was pouring rain, and there was Pat and his wife huddled under an umbrella, waiting at the bus. He said, 'Mr. Hearn, I was thinking the Lakers might need an extra guard. If there's anything you could do for me, I would really appreciate it.'"

And indeed, a few days later, Portland sold Riley to L.A. for $1,000. For the next six seasons, Riley played a supporting role for the Lakers. An aggressive banger, he kept himself in perfect condition, his stomach a washboard. But then he was traded to Phoenix, and one year later, he failed the team physical. His knees were finished, and so were his NBA dreams. At 31, he had nowhere to go. He fell into a deep depression.

He spent the next year furiously hammering away at 18-hour-a-day household carpentry projects and wrote a 400-page book about basketball life that he never published. At which point Chick Hearn again rescued Riley. He asked him to audition as his color man.

He won the job and began to transform himself into a polished broadcaster. Thorough as always, he spent time with voice and acting coaches and took a production course at USC. Then, in the fall of 1979, Lakers coach Jack McKinney suffered a freak bicycle accident and had to step down, and the newly appointed Paul Westhead asked Riley to be his assistant coach.

Two years later, on November 19, 1981, in a kind of bizarre transfer of power that only Abbott and Costello could have scripted, Riley was named head coach of the Lakers—sort of.

A hastily called press conference broke the news that Westhead had been fired and *who?* had been named to replace him.

"Jerry West has been appointed offensive coach of the Lakers," owner Jerry Buss began. "Pat Riley will stay with the Lakers as coach."

"Well, who do we talk to after a game?" one reporter asked.

"In basketball, typically, the coach," Buss said.

"Right," said the reporter. "Who's that?"

At which point West took the podium and flatly announced, "I'm going to be working for Pat Riley. I feel in my heart he is head coach."

Only years later, when I was reporting this story for GQ, did West confide that he was Buss's overwhelming choice for the top job, but he turned it down.

Like an orphan dropped at the church door, Riley began his Lakers coaching career.

—⁓—

In the beginning, he was easy to deal with. He was charming, available, seemingly forthcoming, and friendly enough with reporters that on the road he often joined us for dinner. Sometimes he welcomed me into the locker room—"Diane, good to see you!"—and once he wrote me this note:

Diane,

Just a note to let you know that a touch of class was added when you began to cover the playoffs. Your stories were always different and not just because of the substance but because of the idea. Your mind seems to work in many different ways and the variety makes for good reading. Like finishing up the last chapter of a great novel.

Best Regards,
Pat Riley

I might add the note was handwritten on a yellow Lakers card with purple ink—the Laker colors.

In many ways, Riley was a perfect fit for the Showtime Lakers, with their dancing girls and the TV camera shots of movie stars—notably Jack Nicholson—cheering in the stands. But as time went on, Riley became obsessed—possessed?—scribbling plays on a pad of paper on bus and airplane trips then ripping out the page, crumpling it, and starting anew. No more dinners with reporters. And even some practices were closed. The cool, unflappable image of Riley pacing the sidelines did not tell the story. He simply didn't let the sweat show. (He had his shirts custom made—oxford cloth for game days because they absorb perspiration better than regular cotton.)

A native of Schenectady, New York, he transformed himself into the perfect laid-back Californian, moving fluidly, his speech relaxed. I caught up with him in Honolulu, where the Lakers were holding their training camp. Every afternoon, following an intense four-hour practice, Riley could be found poolside, sprawled on a lounge chair, in swimming trunks and shades, sipping an iced drink: a man at his leisure. Except that on the table beside him were thick books of offensive and defensive strategies and in his hand a felt-tipped pen with which he was scribbling on large (specially ordered) powder-blue sheets of paper.

"I was still up at 3 a.m., working on today's practice plan," he noted the second afternoon of training camp. "I looked at the videotapes and . . ."

"Wait. Videotapes . . . already?"

"Sure."

"You tape *preseason practice?*"

"Well, I can't watch everybody. And what I like to know is how guys move onto the court and go off it. That tells you a lot."

Even before training camp, Riley was in prep mode. As he always did, he wrote a letter to each Laker to set the tone for the coming season. "You can't come into training camp every fall and tell players they have to win a championship," he said. "That gets old fast. You have to give them a reason above and beyond the natural motivations of just trying to win."

He cited as an example the fall two years before, in 1986. That May, the Lakers had been knocked out of the playoffs by the Houston Rockets and their two seven-footers, Ralph Sampson and Hakeem Olajuwon. Seemingly, the era of the Twin Towers had arrived, and the not tall enough Lakers were finished .

Riley's brainstorm: The Year of the Career Best Effort. Each Laker was given a complete statistical breakdown of his career, from which Riley had selected five key categories, circled a player's best year in each, then demanded he improve by 1 percent.

The Lakers ran away with the season and beat the Celtics for the title. The champagne barely uncorked, Riley dropped his famous bombshell: "We will repeat." Which they did, squeaking by Detroit, four games to three.

But now he knew he couldn't use that gambit again for the '88–'89 season. By early summer, he was mulling over motivational strategies for the coming season. This was what he was best known for, his creative approaches to motivating the Lakers. He had read accordingly: Shakespeare, the Bible, the campaigns of Patton and MacArthur, and *Character: America's Search for Leadership* by Gail Sheehy. He'd steal from anybody. Selected passages were combined with memories of his NBA playing days, mulled over, spliced, and finally dispensed to his team at strategic moments of the season. But here at training camp, he was feeling some trepidation because he hadn't solidified his concept. "I'm thinking about transformation," he said. "To go above and beyond your form. To reinvent yourself. To be something more than you were."

But Riley went further than that. Before any other basketball coach did, he was plying the Lakers with personal videotapes of their opponents and reams of esoteric computer data measuring their performances, not to mention their effort expended. He spent three hours mapping out a three-hour practice, remembered to send each Laker a present at Christmas, and to boost spirits on dreary midseason trips to the east, made sure baskets of fruit arrived in each player's hotel room.

Players testified that Riley did push them harder than any other head coach would and that no team was better prepared. Although on the sidelines he may have looked nonchalant, he was, underneath that cool, unwrinkled exterior, a man possessed. "Listen to this," said Lakers trainer Gary Vitti. "I get to training camp here the day after Pat does, and already there is a stack of messages. He has been to the gym, and he thinks the rims of the baskets should be painted Day-Glo orange, and wouldn't it be nice to get shiny new bolts to replace the ones on the backboards? I mean, I've got better things to do."

The next day, when the Lakers arrived at the University of Hawaii gym for their first practice, the rims were freshly painted. The bolts stayed the same.

—⁓—

His first year as coach, Riley recalled, he suffered stomach pains so severe he turned to an acupuncturist. "Once a week, I'd go in, and she'd put one of the needles in the top of my head. She said, 'You're always thinking, thinking, thinking.' I was all cluttered up."

Despite winning a championship against Philadelphia that first year, Riley continued to receive zero credit. He has never been named coach of the year. For doing what? With Magic Johnson and Kareem Abdul-Jabbar, combined with the talents of James Worthy, Michael Cooper, and Byron Scott, why, heck, an amoeba could coach that team. Is what critics said.

Publicly, Riley maintained his humor. "We have total discipline in our locker room," he often quipped. "It's yes, sir, Kareem,' 'No, sir, Magic.' 'James, sir, what would you like to do today?'"

But privately, he was not so sanguine. "I'm always judged for style, flair, the slicked-back hair look," he said ruefully. "Then it is said that to coach the Lakers, all you have to do is roll the ball out—you know, Robo-coach."

What surprised me while reporting this story were the negative comments from Laker players and personnel. The motivational stuff Riley worked so hard on was considered a joke. "Those letters he sends out in August," noted two people in the Lakers' hierarchy, "are tossed right into the garbage."

"In no way does the Lakers' success reflect on Riley," said one man. "Moe from the Three Stooges could have coached this team, Xs-and-Os wise. I mean, if all else fails, you throw it in to Kareem, right? Riley's asset is that he doesn't coach. He lets the greatness of the team shine through."

———

Riley's homelife appeared as painstakingly arranged and elegant as his on-court persona. He is married to a pretty, vivacious woman named Chris, has two adopted toddlers, one nanny, and a former schoolteacher who comes in mornings to keep track of the Rileys' appointment calendars. He lives in a fashionably decorated home in upscale Brentwood, complete with his own detached study that has French windows facing the pool and the tennis court. The shirts, which he designed himself, are made in Hong Kong. The art is exquisite: Ed Ruscha, a young artist named Steven Heino, and other up-and-coming California painters. He drives an immaculately cared-for charcoal Mercedes sedan.

This is where the story veered unexpectedly. Not only had Lakers personnel downplayed Riley's coaching, but they also had it in for his wife.

Chris, I was told, was known to meddle. During the Lakers-Celtics battle of 1984, Riley became furious with the calls made by the referee. On the flight home from Boston, Chris surveyed writers as to whether Riley should go public with his complaint. He did. And was fined heavily by the league.

Then, last September, a story blazed through the Forum, igniting tongues for days. Chris Riley went to see Claire Rothman, president and general manager of the Forum. Chris wasn't happy with the piped-in music during Laker games; here was a list of songs she would like to have played instead.

Incensed, Rothman ordered Chris out of her office, out of the arena, fuming, "I don't care who the hell your husband is. Get out."

———

Needless to say, my story did not go over well in the Riley household. Nevertheless, GQ editor Art Cooper decided to hold a cocktail party to honor his cover boy. I heard that Pat and Chris were debating whether to show up, though in the end they did. As, of course, did I. For most of the evening, I moved in and out of clusters of guests, hoping to avoid the Rileys.

As the party began to wind down, I stopped in the ladies' room. When I came out, there was Pat walking toward me. "Hi," I said. He smiled, hugged me, and thanked me for writing a very nice story. Then he walked away.

I never said the man didn't have class.

37

A Word about David Letterman

THE PITCHER LOUNGING IN THE VISITORS' DUGOUT DID NOT look like a fat tub of goo. He did not resemble a silo. He was neither pizza-shaped nor circus tent–like. What he looked like, this pitcher lounging in the dugout, was your typical pitcher lounging in the dugout with a balloon under his uniform shirt.

This was how I started a column one day when the Atlanta Braves visited Dodger Stadium. The pitcher was Terry Forster, formerly of the Dodgers. "I don't know why he's getting on me like this," said Terry gloomily.

For weeks, the not-quite-svelte Braves pitcher had to endure unrelenting attacks from David Letterman regarding his generous girth. The week before, for example, Letterman held up a bubble-gum card with a picture of a considerably thinner Forster on it and declared, "If this is Terry Forster, he must have been 12."

He then scanned the theoretical information on the back of the card.

"Aah, here it is," Letterman sang. "Favorite food, Mexican. And plenty of it. And here it says Terry plans to travel the world. Well, those plans have changed. Terry plans to *eat* the world."

So it went for about three weeks. Letterman had supposedly glimpsed the six-foot-three Forster in a game on TV and decided he was "somewhat larger than your average ballplayer." Three hundred pounds, Letterman figured.

Forster quickly had his fill of this. He said maybe his stomach was big, but that Letterman's mouth was bigger. He called Dave a jackass. He called him "Johnny Carson's janitor."

161

At last, the talk-show host invited the pitcher to appear on his show. Forster accepted. But that wasn't going to happen for three weeks, and I wanted the story *now*.

Sitting in the dugout, his famous stomach under a warm-up jacket, Forster manfully defended his weight. "I weigh 240," he said. "But the last two years I weighed 250 pounds."

Then he leaned closer and said in a confidential voice, "I retain a lot of liquids."

Ah. Well, you can't get on a guy for that, Dave, retaining a lot of liquids. Geez.

"I know why he's doing this," Forster went on, aggrieved. "Five, six years ago when I was with the Dodgers, I went to the Comedy Store, and he was performing. I guess we got on him a little, and after a while, he said, 'Who are you guys?' Someone in the audience said, 'That's Terry Forster.'"

The pitcher paused. "He's just trying to get back at me."

Perhaps. But, as I wrote in my column, it should be noted that Forster was not exactly having a slim season. In 26 relief appearances, he had given up only five earned runs for an ERA of 1.25. "I'm getting everybody out," he said proudly.

He was also getting famous. In Atlanta, a deal awaited him. Someone wanted to make a "fat video song," and said Forster, "They told me I can sing it myself."

Imagine that, I thought. *Forster as the Jane Fonda of the beer-gut set.*

Obviously, I had to talk to Letterman. A phone call to his NBC office in New York elicited the suspicious information that the show was on vacation for the next two weeks. Bulking up, are you Dave?

"Right," said Letterman, when I eventually hunted him down, in Los Angeles of all places. "Every morning I eat two or three tubes of frozen cookie dough. Then I eat more, all day. I envy a guy who's 310."

Letterman said the first time he saw Forster on the mound this season, he wondered if he was looking at a hallucination. Could anyone be that large? "And I thought what are the kids of America going to think? Pass the potatoes, Mom, I want to grow up to be huge like Terry Forster? So I knew I had to champion the cause. And now, thank God the hostage crisis is over and we can turn our attention to something really important."

He paused. "The good news is we found out we can sue Terry for millions of dollars. We just don't know why yet."

In truth, Letterman confessed he had started to feel guilty after calling Forster a "big tub of goo."

"I was prepared to make an apology," he said. "Then the next day, a reporter from Atlanta called and said he talked to Forster's wife. 'Oh,' she said, 'I've called Terry much worse.' It's impossible to insult anybody anymore."

To think this thing was blown up out of all proportion (the incident, not the stomach) was to totally miss its significance. For while Forster's appetite was threatening to *make* his reputation, it was threatening to destroy Tommy Lasorda's.

"Let me tell you something," the rotund Dodgers manager said to me, his voice rising in anger. "Terry Forster may think he can eat. But I'm now down to a three-pronged fork and he's still using a four-pronged fork."

Lasorda became really worked up. "Letterman has reason to get on Terry," he said. "He's the only guy I ever had on this team that we had to take to the truck scales to weigh."

Then, fearing he was being too harsh, Lasorda softened his tone.

"He's really a nice guy," the manager said. "The only time I ever saw him get mad was when they made a mistake and painted Goodyear on him."

Forster seemed to be taking all this abuse in stride. Of his upcoming appearance on Letterman's show, he said, "He can dog me if he wants. I've got a surprise or two in store. But I won't get malicious or vicious." He paused. "Plus, he'd bury me."

"You're being awfully good-natured about this," I offered.

The pitcher shrugged. "I always said someday everybody is gonna know me," he added with a small sad smile. "I just didn't know it was going to be for this."

He sighed and stared bleakly at his stomach.

—*◊*—

This was the second time I had turned to Letterman to help me with a column. The first time had been 2½ years earlier, when he was carrying on about how he alone was supporting the Jamaican bobsled team for the upcoming 1984 Winter Olympics. The team, of course, did not exist, although possibly because of his antics, Jamaica did enter a bobsled team in the 1988 Winter Games.

The first time I tried to reach Letterman at his New York office, I was told he was unavailable but to leave my number. I left both my office and home numbers, not really expecting him to call. But to my surprise, he rang me at home, and we chatted for quite a bit. After I had what I needed, I did something I had never done in an interview: I complimented him. I said for some reason, I watched his show more often when I was in New York than I did in L.A. But I couldn't explain why.

"I get that a lot," Letterman said. "And there's a reason. People in New York stay up later because they're afraid of getting murdered."

After I wrote my final column for the *Herald Examiner*, I received a lovely note from Letterman saying he would miss seeing my byline. The next time I was in New York, he added, I should call, and we could meet for coffee. Wow. I wondered what Letterman would be like in person. When I was next in New York, I did call his office—he was unavailable—and left my number. I believe I did this twice. I never heard from him again.

38

Wherefore Art?

I DOUBTED ART BUCHWALD KNEW WHO I WAS. WHY WOULD he? He was the best-known humor columnist in the country—his column, written for the *Washington Post*, was carried in hundreds of newspapers. But late one December, as the Rams were getting ready to play the Redskins in DC, I thought, *who better to give some perspective to my L.A. readers?* Because it was easy to reach people back then—no voice recordings prompting you to push this button or that—and because phone numbers were listed and breathing human beings answered calls, I dialed the *Post* and asked for Buchwald.

I was immediately put through.

"Yeah?" came a gravelly voice.

I introduced myself and told him what I needed. That is, in anticipation of the important Rams-Redskins divisional playoff game, what were fans saying?

Buchwald cleared his throat. "There doesn't seem to be any hate for the L.A. Rams," he replied. "Nobody ever heard of the L.A. Rams," Buchwald continued between loud yawns.

Obviously, this was a geography problem. As I pointed out in my column, DC was quite provincial, being located somewhere in the Far East, but sort of heading to the South. One of its closest neighbors was Dallas, which explained the great rivalry between those two rather obscure locales. Buchwald confirmed this. "The reason you don't find people are up for this game is that we used up all our frenzy during the Dallas game," he admitted.

Then continued, "We're very confused in Washington. The Raiders are from Oakland, or were, and the Rams are an Anaheim team. We're not too clear about who we're playing. But we're definitely convinced we're not playing an L.A. team."

I asked if he would give me a rundown of the Redskins. At the time, Buchwald was taking a breather from promoting his new book of collected columns, *While Reagan Slept*. Apparently, the title was catching, for as I was speaking to him, suddenly, all I could hear were more yawns, followed by a noise that sounded suspiciously snoozy.

Art?

"Yeah. If we can stop Dickerson, we can win," he said drowsily, speaking of Eric Dickerson, the Rams' terrific running back.

Anything else?

"Sure. We have a fairly good line, you know. We did stop Dorsett."

Tony Dorsett, the Cowboys' running back. Well, so did the Rams, less than a week ago, but it takes time for news to travel this far east. "Who are the guys the Rams need to look out for?" I asked.

"We're really a team with no stars to speak of," Buchwald said.

"So how does it look to you, Art? How will the Rams fare?"

"They'll get a good opportunity to see Washington," Buchwald said. "And since they live so close to Disneyland, they'll get a chance to compare the two."

"What's the difference?"

Said Buchwald, "Not much."

I thanked him and said maybe I'd see him at the game.

"You kidding? In that cold? I'm going to watch on TV," Buchwald grunted.

One more phone call remained before my editor stopped walking by and snapping his fingers. It seemed a matter of national importance to get a fix on whom President Ronald Reagan, the California resident who lived in the White House, would be rooting for.

A man named Robin Gray answered the phone in the press secretary's office. The urgent question was posed. After what sounded like, yes, another yawn, Mr. Gray reported the following: "The president expressed no preference."

What? None at all? This isn't yams or sweet potatoes for Thanksgiving we're talking about; this is *football*.

"The president, being neutral, sees himself as being the president of all the people," Mr. Gray declared unwaveringly.

I hung up wondering if the president would have said the same thing had the Redskins been playing the Cowboys.

—⁓—

The game was not memorable; the Redskins thrashed the Rams 51–7. What was memorable was the night before, New Year's Eve. That day, I had flown to DC with four of my *Her-Ex* colleagues. Realizing that it would be New Year's Eve, I had packed a dress with the intention of going out somewhere to celebrate. Although I had been an Angeleno for 2½ years, I clearly hadn't acclimated very well.

As I boarded the plane, I passed our young photographer, who was wearing a yellow windbreaker. I asked if he had brought a warmer jacket. He asked why. I said, "It's seventeen degrees there."

He said, "Oh."

At the hotel, we went upstairs to check out the press room. No one else was there. "I guess they'll have some food later, so we can eat here," one of my colleagues said.

And I said, "Uh-uh, guys. You don't mess with a girl with a dress. We're going out!"

But where? I remembered Duke Zeibert's legendary restaurant, where even presidents ate, and I called. They had two seatings, but only the later one was available. I told the guys we had a 9:30 reservation and that we should meet in the lobby at 9:15.

When we were assembled, I saw that only one man was wearing a jacket and tie. The others wore pullover sweaters. I wondered if jackets and ties would be required and if so, what then? As we were about to enter the restaurant, a couple emerged, she in a long mink coat. *Uh-oh,* I thought. But to my surprise, we were warmly welcomed and shown to our table. It turned out to be a delightful evening.

The clash of our cultures ended in a draw.

39

The Dreaded Balcony

IT'S A HOT LOS ANGELES AFTERNOON, SUN BURNING THROUGH the thick blanket of brown smog lying on top of the basin. But here on Sunset Plaza Drive, where Jim Brown's house sits at the highest point of the rise, the air is clear. This house—with its 180-degree view of the downtown skyscrapers to the east, the beaches of Santa Monica to the west—is a common note in articles about Jim Brown. Interviews are often conducted right here. "You are in my house," he says. "That puts you at a disadvantage."

Even now, 21 years later, still looking for the edge.

As was I.

I don't know why *Sport* magazine asked me to write about Brown for its 40th anniversary issue devoted to "The 40 Who Changed Sports," but of course I accepted. I had never seen Brown play running back for the Cleveland Browns—from 1957 to 1965, when he abruptly retired—but now, in 1986, he was still considered the best who ever played in the NFL. He was a headline-maker—even after all these years—though rarely did the headlines glorify him.

A housekeeper lets me in. Jim, she says, will arrive shortly.

For nine seasons, Brown played football exactly how he wanted to. If he disagreed with the calisthenics his coaches prescribed, he didn't do them. If he believed he knew the game better than his head coach, he gave his linemen his own set of instructions. "If I score a touchdown," he would tell them, "nobody will care. If I don't, I'll take the heat."

No other running back has come close to duplicating his accomplishments. Certainly nobody has matched his 5.2 yards per carry, or his average 104.3 yards per game. And though the Bears' Walter Payton surpassed Brown's career yardage (12,312), it took him 18 more games to do so.

When Brown unexpectedly left the game, that too was on his own terms—at age 30—to become a movie star. "I don't want you to think I didn't enjoy the sport," he would say. "I just understood it for what it was."

At last he arrives, late, hurrying in the front door with a pretty, doll-like girl trailing behind. Both look slightly damp. He is wearing black nylon shorts and a matching windbreaker zipped halfway up. There is no shirt underneath. The two have just finished their daily workout at the Sports Connection in West Hollywood, where Brown first encountered her months before when she was working as the club receptionist.

"Meet Debra," he says and disappears.

Debra Clark in her tights, all 90 pounds of her, looks like a stick figure. Her long, thick, black hair is pulled back in a ponytail to show off a startlingly beautiful face. She will turn 22 the following week but looks no more than 15. She leaves, Brown returns, and leads me onto the infamous balcony.

Yes, infamous. Along with his amazing football career, he is known for, as one example, supposedly tossing a girlfriend off this balcony. Nervously, I sneak a peek. It's a long way down.

At age 50, Brown still has a foreboding presence, that at any moment his mood could darken. Though he will deny that he was, or is, an angry man, the sight of him as a player fueled that belief. Six-feet-two, 230 pounds, a body of rolled steel, a dark and expressionless face, chiseled to show the hard edges, his features seem to proclaim that no matter what, this man stands alone.

The size and the muscle are still there. And when you greet him and reach for his outstretched hand, glimpse the polite smile, you are aware of a deep sense of disquiet. Seemingly, he has played his postgame life much the way he played football, calling his own shots as much as any man can. "I have an option," he says in a rather long-winded speech. "I've always had an option. If I became a pawn of society and said the things I was supposed to say, as most of your superstars do today, I would be rich, and I would be given false popularity.

"But when history comes down, that ain't nothing. I am a free man within a society. I love that. I love that over money, over being popular.

I don't want to be Michael Jackson. Whew, I wouldn't trade places with Michael for a million dollars. I don't think Michael Jackson knows what he's doing. I think he's lost. I don't think he has a point of view, you know? I think you have to have a point of view."

It is an odd remark, but figuring out Brown's mind is like trying to figure out his next move with the ball. "What I'm saying," he concludes, "is I just want to be normal."

Debra reappears, speaks softly to Brown, then exits. Brown gruffly concedes he will probably marry her "in the next few months," praising her as "extremely bright and sensitive." When I ask how she spells her first name, he shrugs and yells, "Hey, Deb! How do you spell your name?"

<hr/>

Ten days later, Debra's name is spelled out in newspapers across the country. In the middle of the night, she phoned the police for help, having locked herself in a bedroom at Brown's home, armed with a .44-caliber revolver. According to Clark, Brown had been drinking and accused her of having paid too much attention to male patrons at the Sports Connection earlier that day. She said Brown had pummeled and kicked her in a jealous rage.

Clark, who wound up with a scratch under one eye, a bruised arm, and a possible cracked rib, identified herself as Brown's fiancée and said they had planned to be married the following day, her birthday. Brown was arrested at his home and spent three hours in jail until he was able to post $5,000 bail and was released. Three days later, Clark walked into the Hollywood police station and said she did not want to press charges.

All this happened as I was writing my story. Now I would have to go back to hear Brown's account. To confront him with questions about beating up his fiancée made me squirm. I thought about his temper and his bulging muscles. I reached for the phone.

"Being who I am, one telephone call creates a thing across the country," Brown said in soft, mellow tones. "As a people event, it was nothing. As a media event, it was something else."

But surely, I said, something happened; Debra had called the police. "It's the fear that goes on in minds because of me," Brown insisted. "I am not going to give a defense. We are still living our lives."

With that, he put Debra on the phone. "Hello," she said in a small voice. Brown took the phone back and laughed. "I don't know what that proved," he said. "That voice could have been anybody's."

I asked if he had a quick temper. "I'm probably a very patient person in most cases."

Brown had been in the news frequently since he left football. In 1965, he was accused by an 18-year-old female of slapping her and forcing her to have sex. He was found not guilty.

Four years later, he was accused of assaulting a West Hollywood man after a minor traffic accident. He was acquitted. He was not acquitted of beating up a golf partner during an argument over placement of a ball on the green. He was fined $500 and served one day in jail.

Then, 22 months ago, a schoolteacher who was a friend claimed Brown beat and raped her when she refused to have sex with him and another woman.

I had brought this up when I interviewed him at his house. "What exactly happened in that case?" I asked, sounding braver than I felt.

"You must have read about it in the papers," he replied, looking amused, "or I don't think you would have come here."

Although the woman had clearly been beaten, the charges of rape, sexual battery, and assault were dismissed after she gave confused and inconsistent testimony.

"I'm very vulnerable and I don't have much chance if someone wants to get me," Jim Brown said.

—⁓—

Brown presents himself as hardened to the realities of life, but he seems as sensitive as a wallflower to any perceived slight. "It's very simple," he notes. "I don't like inequities. I don't like being a second-class citizen. I want to be a full part of any society I live in. So that's always going to drive me. The fact that I'm black in a white society."

Only Brown, of course, knows the racial trouble he's experienced. But more than most black youngsters, he was offered the advantages of privileged white society. He spent the first eight years of his life in St. Simons, Georgia, under the care of his great-grandmother and his grandmother. His mother sent for him then, and brought him to the well-to-do community of Manhasset, Long Island, New York, where she worked as a cleaning woman.

Brown offers conflicting views on life in Manhasset. On the one hand, "I had to deal with racism ever since I was born. Sports was an area that was more progressive than others. You never could have been a nuclear scientist because grade-school teachers would say don't even bother taking those kind of courses 'cause they're not going to do you any good anyway. So what I had to do was set a standard that was a little higher."

On the other hand, "At Manhasset, everything was done for me is why I'm here now. I was taught about education, I was taught about fairness, given a chance to excel, encouraged to run for student-body president. I was given a confidence that I ordinarily wouldn't have had. These people were the finest people I ever met in my life."

Brown so excelled that he received 40 scholarship offers from colleges. And here he ran into problems. At Manhasset he had come under the paternal eye of a group of local boosters, including a lawyer named Ken Molloy. Molloy wanted Brown to go to his alma mater, Syracuse, but Syracuse had no interest in Brown. So Molloy, unbeknownst to Brown, raised enough money to finance his first year at Syracuse after securing the school's unenthusiastic word that, yes, if Brown were *that* good, a scholarship might later be made available.

"At the time, Syracuse didn't want any black athletes," said Molloy, now a New York State Supreme Court justice. "But I didn't know that. I put the kid in the mouth of a cannon."

Brown vividly remembers that first year. "They tried everything they could to discourage me. I had to just fight. Hard. Probably an observer would see that and say this guy is angry. But all I was doing was fighting to overcome the cynicism and the doubts and the tests and intimidation that were put on me."

Brown wanted to quit. But Ray Collins, the superintendent from Manhasset High, drove to Syracuse and persuaded him to stay. "It was the only time I doubted myself in my life," Brown says. "And they almost had me. But when I stayed, and went from fifth-string to All-American, I said to myself never again in my life will I let anybody tell me what I can't do. And that was the start of a certain attitude. But it was close."

On the field, Brown kept a steely hold on his emotions.

"He was always a gentleman," says Sam Huff, the fabled New York Giants linebacker. "No matter how hard I hit him. In fact, on an especially good tackle, he would often compliment me."

Molloy remembers a lacrosse game at Syracuse during which an opposing player baited Brown with racial epithets. Brown did not respond. "A lot of teams tried to get Jimmy enraged, hoping to provoke a fight as a ploy to get him thrown out of the game," Molloy said. "I never once saw him lose his cool."

But off the field, he was not so predictable. When I reached one of Brown's longtime friends for an interview, he told me, "I don't know. It would make me nervous. I might say something that would offend Jim, without my meaning to. Frankly, I've always had this insecurity with him."

—∿∿—

"Daddy, will you fix my bike?"

Four-year-old Kimberly snuggles up to her dad. Brown's only marriage produced three children, none of whom he is close to. Kimberly came along when he was living with her mother, Kim Jones, a young woman whom he met roller skating at Venice Beach. Brown says that after the split with Kim, he was not allowed to see his daughter for two years. Then last December, she was brought to the house; she has been there ever since.

"Her mother's now filing for custody or something," Brown says. "She said I took Kim out of school. She lied and said I stole Kim. But how can you steal someone when your phone number hasn't changed since 1968, the address is the same, and she's here?" He pauses. "My front door is generally open."

"What stands out about Jim is his highly tuned sense of fairness," Ken Molloy said. "He's made a fine art of it. And this, I think, is what precipitates a lot of other things. He's like a cat in a jungle, always looking for things."

Jim Brown's vision of how things must be was also violated by his former close friend, actor-comedian Richard Pryor. "Richard fooled me," Brown says. "I'd known him as a person who would come into my life usually when he was in trouble. I was foolish enough to think he really cared about me."

Brown says he was trying to help Pryor, who had been freebasing cocaine, had hired detectives to report what his wife was doing, and had guns lying around. The comedian accidentally set himself on fire while freebasing. He called Brown from the hospital.

Brown says he took over Pryor's affairs. "People wanted the combination to his safe, I kept that from happening. With his feeble hand, I got him to write a check so his family could have money for the house. I worked closely with the doctors. I kept one of his daughters at my house. I dealt with all the ex-wives, I mean everything you could think of."

Not long after his recovery, Pryor started a film company, Indigo Productions, funded by Columbia Pictures, and Pryor asked Brown to run it. They made one film, *Richard Pryor: Here and Now*, and then, according to Brown, Pryor went to Africa. "When he came back, he said he wanted his company back. He said, 'If you're here, I won't be here.' He wrote me a strange letter. Said something about 'differences of opinion, but if you ever need me . . .'" Brown's voice trails off, and he laughs.

"I feel sadness. There's no animosity. See, I never depend on anybody anyway. I thought Richard cared about me. But he didn't care about anybody. I knew he didn't care about his kids. I knew he didn't care about his wife. I knew he didn't care about anybody. But, shit, he suckered me."

When I contacted Pryor, he would only issue this statement: "Jim Brown without a doubt was the greatest football player ever in life. Other than that, I do not wish to comment on anything he said about me or Indigo."

But in an interview with *Essence* magazine last spring, Pryor said, "He was a bully. And there was a point when I had to say, 'All you can do is kill me, but you can't be the president of my company because I'm not going to take any more of this shit.'"

The complexity of Jim Brown is compounded by a side of him that receives far less publicity than his run-ins with the law. "Most of my work through the years has been related to the economic development of black people," he says.

Once, long ago, according to Ken Molloy, Brown asked him, "What can I ever do to repay you?" Molloy said he replied, "Help a kid like I helped you."

Years later, the two were playing tennis at the Port Washington Tennis Academy. Molloy was surprised to find that Brown knew the head pro, Bob Binns, a black man. "How do you know each other?" Molloy later asked Binns.

"I grew up in Cleveland, and Jim was of help to me," Binns said.

—⁓—

Football hardly figures in Brown's life anymore. His house, modestly furnished, has no memorabilia. Sometimes he'll turn on a football game, but rarely will he stick around for the finish. "I like performances, not games," he said.

But those performances never compare to his own. "I never think of myself as the best," he says. "I think of myself as someone who *performed* the best in history. It's not even close."

Fifty years old and Brown has already walked out on two careers. When he was 30, he simply failed to report to training camp. "Although it was a good life," he says. "I couldn't take it too seriously. And I definitely did not want to get to a point where an owner didn't want me anymore. That would take my self-esteem away."

By then he was an actor in *The Dirty Dozen* and launching a film career. But that eventually ended too. "I went out in style," is how he explains that one. In today's films, he adds, "Blacks only seem to be able to sing, dance, tell jokes, and be in poverty."

Jim Brown, once the man who so masterfully zigzagged across a field of play, leaving everyone in his wake, now seems—if Cervantes will forgive me—a somewhat askew Don Quixote, forever tilting at the windmills of injustice in his own life.

40

And Then I Was Gone

I CAN'T EXPLAIN WHY I LEFT THE *HERALD EXAMINER*. NOTH-
ing bad happened. Nothing, in fact, had changed. And who with a
functioning brain would leave such a prominent position? No one. As
I looked around the press box, I could see many guys who had been
doing their jobs for decades. Why not me? I could only point to one of
my inconvenient faults: I was easily bored.

My first Super Bowl was exciting to attend—even though it was the
NFL's brilliant idea to stick it in Detroit. But a press credential hanging
around my neck made me feel important. Same with my first World
Series. But each subsequent one became less thrilling and more routine.
I remember my last World Series—the Red Sox vs. the Mets in 1986.
Old Fenway Park was cramped, and I found myself sitting on the floor
of the press room, eating dinner out of a cardboard box before one of
the games—with reporters stepping over each other. At that moment,
I desperately wished to watch the World Series sitting on my bed, surrounded by Chinese food cartons.

It wasn't the games that bored me. To this day, I watch a brain-
damaging amount of sports on TV. Often, when I am out to dinner,
friends groan as I keep checking my phone for scores. I guess it was the
routine that I grew tired of. I had told Jim Bellows I wanted to write
magazine articles and mystery novels when he offered me the columnist's job. I am so glad I accepted, but now I was ready to move on. And
so, after a wonderful six-year span, I left the *Her-Ex*.

41

The Man Every Man Wants to Be

I BEGAN WORK ON A MYSTERY NOVEL, *AS CRIME GOES BY*, SET in 1947 Los Angeles. Since it was now 1987, this meant research. This meant the UCLA library. But because I had a 45-minute library attention span, I recruited my friend Marsha Robertson to babysit me for at least two hours at a time in the reading room as I pored over 1947 magazines. (Why the hell hadn't Google been invented yet?) Still, I had to admit it was fun seeing the prices (houses for $7,000!) and cigarette ads featuring a doctor smoking.

At home, I felt like a stranger. What was I doing here *now*? I wandered from my office (a converted second bedroom) past the laundry room into the kitchen for another cup of coffee, then back to my desk, where I stared at my computer screen with no idea what to put on it. So I was relieved when *GQ* editor Art Cooper called.

As I mentioned, I often wrote cover stories for the magazine. The choice of which male to put on the cover depended on three factors: He typically had to be an athlete or actor, and he had to be very good-looking. Also, he had to be younger than 40—unless he was Cary Grant. None of this was official policy, but these seemed to be the ironclad criteria. And although the editors often approved my choice of cover subjects, the one I really, *really* wanted to do—Sean Connery—always got a resounding *no!*

For one thing, Connery was old. Like 58. And he hadn't made a James Bond film since *Diamonds Are Forever* in 1971, unless you count *Never Say Never Again*, which I'll get to later. And worse—the man was bald! Not cool bald—shaved heads hadn't come into fashion yet—but *old* bald.

(Did you know he wore a toupee as James Bond?) Still, to the amazement of many, he had successfully transitioned from Bond to playing other roles magnificently. Recently, he had starred in *The Untouchables* and had won an Academy Award for best supporting actor. That was 1988. In 1989, *People* magazine named him the Sexiest Man Alive. At which point, my phone *finally* rang.

"I am calling to tell you that I have granted your wish," sang Art Cooper. "Go do Connery."

—⁓—

Right. *Go interview the acting legend and come back with something sparkling.* I was both thrilled and terrified. Would this be his 1,000th interview, his 2,000th? What on earth could I ask him? He wasn't making a movie, so I couldn't collect color from the set or revealing quotes from his fellow cast members. He did play golf . . . would he let me traipse around the course with him? I did my usual homework—reading dozens of previous articles, talking to people like Steven Spielberg, Kevin Costner, and Harrison Ford and watching several movies I hadn't seen before.

—⁓—

Sean Connery, I would write, is wearing a light-blue caftan, which he keeps fussing with, and sitting at the end of a long pastel-print couch, here at his house in the Bahamas. There is a second home in Marbella, Spain, and a condo in West Los Angeles, but it is to this one, in the exclusive, gated community of Lyford Cay in Nassau, that Connery repaired to earlier this year. You see, the house is located on Lyford's eighth green. He is here to recuperate from throat surgery and to play golf, not necessarily in that order. The surgery, to remove benign polyps from his vocal cords, was hysterically reported in the British press as cancer of the worst kind, which Connery did not bother to refute. "In three weeks, I'll go back to the Academy Awards," he says sardonically, "which will signify that I'm not dead."

Dead? At 58, the man looks as if he could plow the north forty, throw back a couple of beers, then, checking the sun, say, "Well. Time to go dam up the river."

It is on screen that he has aged, choosing as he has, to play older than he is. In *Indiana Jones and the Last Crusade*, he is father to 46-year-old

Harrison Ford, and in the forthcoming *Family Business*, to 51-year-old Dustin Hoffman. In *The Untouchables*, playing the Chicago cop Jimmy Malone and running after a Capone bootlegger at the Canadian border, Connery, looking heavy, huffing and puffing, finally catches the guy, panting, "Enough of this shit!"

But here in the living room, high-ceilinged and airy, with peach-colored walls, adorned with canvases painted by his wife, the furniture overstuffed and pastel, the old screen image is much intact. Standing in the doorway, he fills it totally, as if he were a portrait fitted into a wooden frame. He is six feet two, 215 pounds, but his large face, with its clean, chiseled features, makes him seem bigger somehow. He moves with the lightness of a dancer.

Connery clears his throat. "Before I had the surgery, a specialist suggested I try thirty days of silence to cure the problem," he relates. "Well, that was a pill. I had this pen, which I wore around my neck, and every time I wanted to say something, I wrote it down on the back of old scripts. I wrote hundreds of pages, and I should have kept them, because it was so crazy. It was lots of non sequiturs, because you never knew the question. Like there would be, 'How the fuck do I know?'"

A housekeeper enters bearing freshly squeezed grapefruit juice. Through a large picture window, Micheline, Connery's second wife, whom he married fourteen years ago, can be glimpsed in a bikini, sunning herself on a chaise longue.

"Anyway," says Connery, "I printed up cards saying, 'I'M SORRY I CANNOT SPEAK. I HAVE A PROBLEM WITH MY THROAT. THANK YOU.' And ten out of ten would look at the card and say, 'Why? What's the matter?'"

He rolls his eyes. "And when I would write out what I wanted to say, half the people would take the pen and write their answers back. You realize very quickly that the world is full of idiots."

—◦◦◦—

Connery is fussing with his caftan and looking straight ahead as he speaks. I am fastened down at the other end of the couch, slightly turned toward him. Occasionally, he glances at me, but mostly he doesn't make eye contact. I find this a bit unnerving, but at the same time I feel relief.

I may not have come with killer questions, but Connery seems happy to unload anecdote after anecdote. I begin to relax.

But then, Connery is known to take control, an ability that has served him well. As James Bond, he took what could have been a cold, humorless character and made him a heart-stealing rogue, with his charm, his wit, and that devilish arched eyebrow. But like something of a Cary Grant with a Beretta, he was given little credit for the skill the role demanded or for turning what might have been a one-night stand into a twenty-year love affair. Just as Grant never received an acting award, so Connery never received one for playing Bond. "I suppose people feel you made enough money," Connery is saying. "That's your award." It's only now that he is beginning to be appreciated as one of the most gifted actors of his time.

"There are seven genuine movie stars in the world today," says Steven Spielberg, who directed him in *Indiana Jones and the Last Crusade,* "and Sean is one of them. I won't name the others because some of my best friends wouldn't be among them."

At a time when most actors go round unshaven and T-shirted, tilting at garden-variety woes, cutting movies down to people-size, Connery ennobles his characters with a toughness and romanticism you rarely find on screen anymore.

"If you were casting *High Noon* today," said *Family Business* producer Larry Gordon, "who could leave Grace Kelly behind and walk down the street like Gary Cooper did? I think only Sean Connery could."

It is said that Connery is worshipped for being the man other men want to be. Comparisons to Cooper and Grant, Spencer Tracy and Clark Gable ring true. In many ways, the Scottish-born Connery seems a throwback to the American man of the past, the tough individualist who lives by his own set of ethics and his wits, a man who will fight for what he believes in, a dreamer who is never deluded by what is not possible.

"He's the kind of guy you want by your side," Gordon said, "even though you know he'll probably steal your girl."

If his celebrity peaked during the sixties, when, as 007, he shared the world spotlight with the Beatles ("and there were four of them to kick around," he once pointed out), he is now more in demand than ever. In the past three years, he has made six movies, and this May he will begin filming a lead role in the adaptation of Tom Clancy's *The Hunt for Red October*, playing Marko Ramius, captain of Russia's most advanced submarine.

Top billing or not, Connery grabs your attention. In *The Untouchables*, he stole the film from Kevin Costner and Robert De Niro to win his Academy Award. In *Indiana Jones*, he took over the whole movie. In their first meeting with Connery, Spielberg and producer George Lucas talked only in general about the role of Professor Henry Jones, refusing to hand over a script. Connery went away feeling "there was a reluctance on the part of George for me to play the part."

Which was true. "George wasn't thinking in terms of such a powerful presence," Spielberg says. "His idea was for a doting, scholarly person, an older British character actor. But I had always seen Sean Connery. Without a strong, illuminating presence, I was afraid Harrison would eradicate the father from the movie. I wanted to challenge him. And who could be the equal of Indiana Jones but James Bond?"

In the original script, Henry did not appear until page seventy. Then, there he was on page fifty. Before long, Connery had four additional scenes written for him. Of course, in the finished product, his endearing, witty portrayal of Harrison Ford's estranged father provided more pyrotechnics than motorcycle chases, exploding planes, thousands of dead Nazis, and even Indy himself could.

While filming *Family Business*, Connery made it known he would not tolerate any foolishness on the set. According to Matthew Broderick, who played Connery's grandson, "He just kind of let you know he didn't want some smart-ass kid in his face all the time." Nevertheless, Broderick often performed overblown impressions of Connery as Bond behind the actor's back. When an assistant told Connery what was going on, he said, "Well, why doesn't Matthew do it for me?" Informed that Broderick was afraid to, Connery replied, "Good. He should be afraid."

A few years ago, in what may have been his best performance to date, he went mano-a-mano with Barbara Walters, when she tried to accuse him of being a male chauvinist on national TV. Citing a 20-year-old *Playboy* quote in which Connery had said, "It's not the worst thing to slap a woman now and then," and thinking she was doing women a favor, Walters righteously declared, "You are a male chauvinist, aren't you?"

Connery, unflappable, had answered, "Am I? And what is a male chauvinist?" Sending it back into her court. Only Walters, unable to volley, to have some fun with it, ended up sounding tongue-tied and banal. Later, as the interview wound down, Connery, not letting her off the hook, got in the final shot.

"Finish this for me," said Barbara sweetly. "Sean Connery is . . ."

And he, grinning, replied, "Almost a male chauvinist pig."

He couldn't believe the reaction the next day, as he drove down Pico Boulevard to Paramount, the way men would raise their fists, *right on!* and the woman at the stoplight who gave him the finger.

Now Connery shrugs. "I'm talking about a slap on the face and that you could do much, much worse damage to a woman, or a man, by totally demoralizing them, by taking away their whole identity," he says. "I'm saying if one of the couple is intent on having a physical confrontation, it's impossible for it to be avoided. It's emotional, it's passion. And passion lacks thinking. Therefore, it will explode. And that's all I'm saying, without getting into a three-act play."

A question immediately pops into mind, but I hesitate. Had he ever hit his wife? But before I can open my mouth, the doorbell rings, and in walks a repairman, come to fix the satellite dish.

"How was church?" inquires Connery pleasantly.

"Fine," says the man. "I prayed for all the sinners."

"Did you?" says Connery. "I'm surprised you're not still there."

I laughed and put away my questions, though in retrospect, I feel I failed.

—◦◦◦—

Contrary to what some might imagine, Connery is a true student of the craft.

His use of body movement, which he has indeed spent hours perfecting, is one quality that distinguishes him as an actor. Although naturally athletic, Connery, at the urging of his first wife, actress Diane Cilento, took an intensive course in movement from a ballet dancer named Yar Malgrem in London. He still refers to his dog-eared copy of Malgrem's textbook.

"Look, if this were a set," says Connery, getting up from the couch and walking toward the center of the room, "and suppose you had a glass curtain, you should be able to follow something of the drama by the walk and the body language without having to understand what the people are saying."

He then walks out of the room.

A moment later, he strides back in purposefully. He leaves, comes back, this time a bit slouchily. He makes two more entrances then sits down. "Surely, you've seen someone sitting with their legs crossed, arms folded across their chest, perhaps a bit slumped over," he says. "That demonstrates the person is insecure."

It takes a moment to sink in—for me to realize this is exactly how I am sitting. Embarrassed, I uncross my legs and straighten up. I hope my face hasn't turned red. "The body," Connery continues, "is our first impression, and it's what makes people respond or not respond."

It certainly was what the producers of *Dr. No* responded to when Connery burst into their London office in 1961, determined to be Bond. At the time, producers Harry Saltzman and Albert Broccoli were considering more polished contenders—Roger Moore among them—when in came Connery with that walk of his, a kind of fluid swagger once described as "the threatening grace of a panther on the prowl." Poorly dressed and with his thick Scottish burr, he delivered his theory of Bond, pounded the desk to make his points, then swaggered out, leaving the two men dumbstruck.

"I used strong and commanding movements," he says, "not with weight, but to show how Bond is always in control of a scene."

At every level of filmmaking, Connery is there, offering his thoughts. The scene in *The Untouchables* in which he and Kevin Costner (as Eliot Ness) take a blood oath was originally set in the street. "But I thought it should be done in a church," Connery says. "When you're making that kind of declaration about the Chicago way—you know, 'Capone puts one of yours in the hospital, you put one of his in the morgue,' all this kind of dialogue—if you put it in a church, it suddenly becomes something different."

The scene—shot in a church—became one of the film's most memorable.

Connery also believes that if tensions exist between characters in front of the camera, they should exist off camera as well. "I kept them very much on a wire by snide little remarks, digs at America, what have you," Connery says.

"I remember one night when he really got me," Kevin Costner says. "I was talking about my favorite movie in the whole world, *Hombre*, and I was doing it to the nth detail, doing all the parts, all the voices, and finally I say, 'Then this bitch gets in front of Paul Newman, and she won't move. This bitch ends up getting him killed.' And Sean just looks at me and says, 'That bitch was my first wife.'"

—◆—

For the man who would one day play the debonair 007, Connery came out of a most unlikely background. Industrial Fountainbridge is Edinburgh's hopeless side of town, and the hardworking people who live there rarely find a way out. The older of two sons of a rubber-factory worker, he was driving a milk wagon at 13, making deliveries before school. When the schools closed due to World War II, Connery went to work full time, helping to support his parents and younger brother. "There was no question I wanted to get out," he says. "The problem was what equipment one had to get out. The navy seemed almost like an inspiration."

At 16, he signed up for twelve years, but after three, developed ulcers and was discharged. "I went back to driving a horse." He also trained as a tailor, an upholsterer, a carpenter, a barber, a furniture craftsman.

Persuaded by a friend to enter the Mr. Universe bodybuilding contest, Connery took off for London in 1950. He didn't win any prizes, but someone suggested a good-looking guy like him might get a job in the theater. Connery wound up in the chorus of *South Pacific*, where someone else brought up the idea of acting. "I said, 'Acting? What do I know about acting?'" Connery recalls. "I told him, 'I can sing "Nothin' Like a Dame," I can do handsprings on the stage.' Frankly, I was happy just to get my 14 pounds a week and drive around."

But eventually Connery bought a tape recorder, and every day, as *South Pacific* was touring, he'd work on his voice, trying to get rid of that thick Scottish accent. In the afternoons, he would visit the local library. He read Dostoevsky, Turgenev, all of Shakespeare, all of Shaw, and Thomas Wolfe. He read Proust and Oscar Wilde. He bought a dictionary and read that too. Then he pored over Hemingway and Stephen

Crane. He also went to repertory theater and met the actors. "I always felt they were so clever, so erudite, so world-wise," Connery says. He grins. "Of course, I've learned differently."

Connery has barely moved from the couch. Except for fussing with his caftan, shifting the material this way and that, he rarely gestures. Nor does his voice ever seem to carry dramatic overtones. He still makes eye contact only intermittently. He occasionally flashes that nasty little Connery smile, but it always comes a beat too late, as if he has stopped to replay what he just said and found it suddenly amusing.

Despite his soaring popularity with each Bond picture, Connery was conflicted. There was constant battling with the producers. And the role, he says, became a straitjacket. The films often did not start shooting when they were supposed to, and it was impossible to get a finish date, so Connery never knew when he might be free to make a non-Bond movie. And he desperately wanted to. "If you were his friend during those days," notes Michael Caine, "you didn't raise the subject of Bond, ever."

Says Connery, "The problem was that Bond was so popular, the public only wanted to see me doing that. All I can do now is what's interesting and rewarding for me. To try to erase the image of Bond is almost impossible."

After *Diamonds Are Forever*, he gave splendid performances in such films at *The Great Train Robbery*, Sidney Lumet's *The Offence*, considered by some to be his finest, and perhaps his favorite movie, *The Man Who Would Be King*, directed by John Huston and costarring his good friend Michael Caine. Fond memories of that experience still linger. "We were in this little town at the edge of the Sahara, and there was nothing to do at night except go to this disco," Caine recalls . "But it was men dancing with men because women weren't allowed out at night. So we're standing at the bar watching all these guys dancing, when Sean leans over and says to me, 'Do you mind if I dance with your driver? Mine's too ugly.'"

In 1982, after three straight box-office duds (*Time Bandits*, *Outland*, and *Wrong Is Right*), Connery began reading of Roger Moore's contract problems as the new Bond, as well as reports that a producer named Jack Schwartzman had secured the film rights to an Ian Fleming story—*Never*

Say Never Again—and was interested in casting Connery. If Roger could get the $5 million he was asking to play Bond, Connery figured he was worth more.

So, at 52, and for a reported $5 million (Moore got $4 million), Connery became 007 for the seventh time. But the experience was enough for Connery to finally say never again. "Schwartzman was totally incompetent," he says, "a real ass. In the middle of everything, he moved to the Bahamas with an unlisted number. It was like working in a toilet." Connery was so upset, he didn't work again for nearly three years. "I should have killed him," Connery says.

Micheline, 53, still shapely in her bikini, comes in from the patio. Watching her husband leave the room, she says, "Sean is always shocked by people. He has such high ideals; he's a totally genuine man. I have tried to teach him cynicism. 'Don't be shocked,' I say. 'The world is like that.'"

It is noon now, and Connery wants to hit the links. And no— *absolutely not*—can I go with him.

But there is one last question before he leaves, one last question for the man, the hero—hell, the icon—who both on screen and off, through his dash, wit, sophistication, and grace, set the standard for a generation of men. And by his response, you would think it's a question he's never considered.

"Do you have, um, any flaws?"

For a frighteningly long moment, Connery is silent. "I, have a flaw?" he says, sounding baffled. "Hmm . . . a flaw."

More silence. Then, "You mean, what is my worst flaw? Well, I could be more organized."

More *organized*? That's it?

"Yeah, I could be more organized," Sean Connery says.

———

After I turned in the story, Art Cooper called. He liked it well enough, but he had two problems. First, he wanted me to cut out the part where I describe Connery demonstrating how physicality helps shape a character. To me, that was the best part of the story. An acting lesson played out in real time; I had been mesmerized. I argued. Finally, Cooper asked me to shorten that passage, which I did, reluctantly.

His second problem: did I ask Connery if it was true his first wife ran around on him? No, I hadn't heard that.

Nor would I have cared. Anybody can cheat on their spouse. How ordinary is that? But how many people can be Sean Connery? How many folks can climb to the top of their profession? How can someone growing up in the poorest of conditions rise to become a worldwide superstar? That is what captivates me—not their sex lives but how they have accomplished so much. How did they overcome the times they failed? But in the dawning age of gossip magazines, my interests seemed not to resonate with editors.

Well, said Cooper, would I call him and ask? No, I said. I would not.

Even without that scintillating detail, my cover story ran. "Sean Connery, The Last Real Man in America," was the title.

42

Quick! Hide Your Hand!

I HAD NEVER MET MICHAEL CAINE.

When I interviewed him for the Sean Connery story, it was on the phone. Often, I would see him in Tommy Lasorda's office before Dodger games, always wearing a black leather jacket and ignoring the reporters who drifted in.

Then I did meet him. Quite unexpectedly.

At some point, my column had caught the attention of Irving "Swifty" Lazar, a legendary Hollywood literary agent. One morning, I picked up the phone, and in his squeaky voice, he said we must have lunch. We met at Ma Maison, *the* restaurant at the time, and there he was at table 1. He stood to greet me then laughed. I am five-nine-and-a-half, barefoot. He looked to be five-two or five-three, and he wore large, round, black-framed glasses. He extended his hand. "And I thought you were a little girl!" he exclaimed and sat down. The point of the lunch was his insistence that he be my agent. I tried to explain that I had a wonderful agent. After that, he would call me from time to time to remind me I was making a big mistake and that he should represent me.

Late one afternoon, on a gray December day, he phoned again. December 23, 1992, to be exact.

"Are you married?" is how he began the conversation.

"Not at the moment," I replied.

"Then you should marry me."

"Well," I said, "I'm kind of old-fashioned and think we should have a date first."

"Then come with me to Frank Sinatra's Christmas Eve dinner tomorrow night."

After I pulled myself up off the floor, he told me to be at his house at six o'clock. *Good god*, I thought. *Really? Sinatra?* I adored Sinatra. Of course, it would be a big bash, and maybe I'd get to shake his hand. But . . . Sinatra?

I don't remember if my first call was to my mother—who swooned— or to the saleswoman at a department store who often waited on me. Suzanne rattled off everything in my closet that she had sold to me then settled on a navy silk pants and jacket outfit. "Do I need navy shoes?" I asked, panicking.

"Definitely," Suzanne said.

The next day, I bought shoes, had a manicure, and studied my jewelry box. I chose my two best pieces, a one-carat emerald ring and a narrow diamond tennis bracelet, jumped into my red Saab convertible, and headed to Swifty Lazar's house. (Please note: Swifty was never to be called Swifty to his face; it was Irving. Supposedly he got the name Swifty for the speed with which he could make a deal.)

As I drove into Beverly Hills, I thought about Mary, Swifty's lovely wife. She was suffering from cancer, and thus I had become his date. After I rang the doorbell, he invited me in and said, "Why don't you go say hello to Mary?" and he led me into a den.

Mary was lying on a sofa, her head bolstered by pillows. She was wearing a black velvet track suit with a chemo pack belted around her waist. Even in this condition she looked beautiful. I squeezed her hand and sat down at the end of the sofa. We had met several times, but I was at a loss as what to say. After a few minutes, Swifty came in and led me away. (Mary passed away a few months later.)

Now we were sitting in his living room with a big fireplace and dozens of framed photos of him with famous people on the mantel. We just sat there, and I wondered what we were waiting for.

"Hello, hello, hello!" boomed a familiar cockney voice, and then into the room burst Michael Caine and his stunning wife, Shakira.

I was introduced, a few pleasantries were exchanged, then Caine suggested we go. Shakira drove her husband, and I drove Swifty. A valet took my car in Sinatra's driveway, and as we were walking up to the front door, Swifty mentioned that he had told Barbara Sinatra I was coming, that I was a reporter but that I wouldn't write about the evening. "Understood?" he said.

"Of course," I said. (I didn't say I wouldn't mention it in a book someday.)

Swifty rang the bell, and the door was immediately opened. No mob scene inside, as I had figured, only Frank Sinatra, smiling, extending his hand to me. I did not expect him to be so tall, my height, or to have such riveting, big blue eyes. "Thank you for having me," was all I could think to say.

"May I get you something to drink?" Sinatra said. "A glass of wine?"

"Yes, white wine, please. Thank you." Sinatra, waiting on me? I was flabbergasted.

I found myself standing in a large living room, some of the furniture pushed back to accommodate three round tables of eight seats each. On the far side of the room was a grand piano and a man bent over the keys playing softly. Nearby was a sofa with film director Billy Wilder sitting alone. After Sinatra handed me my wine, I walked over and sat down. Wilder had fled Nazi Germany, and although English was his second language, he had a razor-sharp wit that he often displayed in his screenplays, such as *Sunset Boulevard*, *Some Like it Hot*, and *Sabrina*.

I was writing my next mystery novel, *Dying Cheek to Cheek*—also set in 1947 Los Angeles—and, knowing that Wilder was working in Hollywood then and was a sports fan, I asked him questions about the pre-Dodgers Pacific Coast League days. I could have spent the entire evening in his company, but soon we were called to dinner.

I was seated at Barbara Sinatra's table. Michael Caine was to my left, Swifty to my right, and Barbara next to him. Caine, who had always ignored me in Lasorda's office, proved to be a chatty, funny dinner companion. At one point, I was turned to my right, listening to Barbara Sinatra talking, gesturing, when I realized that—on her right hand—she wore the same emerald ring as mine, only many, many carats larger, and her right wrist was covered with eight or ten tennis bracelets—similar to my lonely one.

Noticing me looking at Barbara, Caine leaned over and said, "Maybe you should keep your hand under the table."

43

The Enigma

FOR MOST OF THE EVENING, DENZEL WASHINGTON HAS BARELY spoken, sitting there, gloomily, in his own private funk. Dining at Daphne's in London, the actor has picked at his food, listened uninterestedly to the conversation at his table, contributing polite comments when called for, and generally avoiding eye contact with his wife and two companions. "I think he's tired," Pauletta Washington apologizes.

But as the hour grows late and the diners thin out, Denzel suddenly perks up. From a distant table in the back come the loud, querulous voices of two men in a fierce argument. Some kind of business deal, going sour fast. One voice is relatively restrained and British, the other loud and possibly from Baltimore. The voices draw nearer. Denzel winces. And nearer! Stopping suddenly to renew hostilities several feet away.

Putting a hand to the side of his face like a barrier, Denzel starts to laugh.

"Here it comes," he says. "The American's gonna say, 'You want money? Listen, I got money. How much you want? Hundred and fifty grand? No problem, man. I got it. You think I don't got it? Hey, count me in.' God, just listen to him. Trying to impress the guy with all his money. In another minute he's gonna be opening a suitcase with two million bucks in it. The good old ugly American."

The voices rage on, the American's louder and clearly drunk, putting on a show for the elegant restaurant. Denzel scrunches down in his chair, dying. On the way out, he pulls the maître d' aside, taking his elbow. "Please let me assure you, sir. Not *all* Americans are like that."

It is 1988, and I am writing a *GQ* cover story on Washington. We first noticed him as Dr. Philip Chandler on the TV series *St. Elsewhere*, and now he is drawing raves for his big-screen roles. Although the Academy Awards have not been presented yet, he will win an Oscar for best supporting actor in *Glory*, in which he played a slave turned soldier in the Civil War. And as time went on, he would win another Oscar for best actor in *Training Day*, three Golden Globes, and one Tony. But now he is in London to introduce one act in a concert that is being held at Wembley Stadium in honor of imprisoned South African activist Nelson Mandela's 70th birthday. I flew with Denzel and his family from L.A. to London—first class, of course—because what better way to interview him than on a long plane ride? Also, back then—ah, the good old days— expense accounts seemed to have no cap, and many of us journalists lived better on the road than at home.

I had first met Denzel during a halftime break at a Lakers game. We arranged to meet for lunch the following week.

The lunch went well. He was going to London, he explained, because having played the martyred South African activist Stephen Biko in *Cry Freedom*, a critically acclaimed movie that was largely ignored in Britain and the United States, he was an obvious candidate to introduce one of the acts.

Then, he said, another invitation arrived. Several days before the concert, a celebrity tennis tournament was to be held at Windsor Green to raise money for the Prince's Trust; would Denzel play? Sure, why not?

Two days before his flight, he was in New York attending the Mandela-inspired Broadway musical *Sarafina!* Despite what he had learned about South Africa while making *Cry Freedom*, he was stunned by what he saw on stage. "I felt guilty," he says. "It was like, how dare we try to tell the Biko story? Although I know [director Richard] Attenborough's heart was in the right place, there was a girl up there with burns on her arms and on her legs. What do I know about what she suffered? I never suffered anything like that."

After the show, he went backstage. "They all hugged me and called me Steve Biko, and man, I almost cried. And that's when it hit me. At the tennis tournament, I would have to meet all those lords and ladies and ministers who had refused to attend the premiere of *Cry Freedom* and who refuse to support anti-apartheid. I said the hell with that. I ain't going."

—ᴧᴧᴧ—

For Washington, the question of who he is and what he should be is one he must grapple with constantly in pursuit of a career. "It's not a coincidence that the last three pictures I've made, I've had to go out of the country to do," he says, referring to *Cry Freedom* (Zimbabwe and London), *For Queen and Country* (London), and *Finding Maubee* (Jamaica), the latter two scheduled for release early next year.

The complexity of the issue is mirrored by the complexity of the man. Despite a number of meetings with Washington, in London and Los Angeles, I was never certain which Denzel to expect. Evasive or reticent one minute, he becomes expansive the next. Subjects he refused to discuss yesterday he expounds upon today.

Once the plane is airborne, Washington walks a few rows back to where I am seated and sits down in the empty seat beside me. We speak for a while, and then I ask if race still affects his career. Sipping a glass of wine, he replies, "Isn't that a racist question? I don't want to talk about being black. Why do I always have to talk about it?"

With that, he stands and goes back to his seat to help Pauletta with John David, 4, and Katia, 1, during dinner. And I'm thinking, *oh god, did I just kill the rest of the story?* I am surprised by his reaction to a subject he has discussed so openly in all the stories I have read. What did I say to anger him? It is awful the subject must be raised at all, but it seems to be a major factor affecting his career.

I slump back and try to figure out how to fix this.

But then, returning two hours later, and not even being asked, he says, "One of the curses about being black in this industry is having someone to blame. I have white friends who don't work. Who do they blame?"

—ᴧᴧᴧ—

Denzel's neat little two-step here suggests his acceptance, at least on a political level, of the black actor's plight, but it does not reflect reality. For example, actor Roy Scheider casually remarked recently, "Denzel

Washington is one of the finest young black actors around. Maybe the finest. He's just terrific."

Which is how Washington is perceived. Adjective first. But if, on the one hand, this means his opportunities are limited—"There's never been a black actor who's saved America yet in a movie," says his friend Robert Townsend, the writer, actor, director. "The black guy's always the one who gets injured, saying to the white hero, 'Go without me!' The white guy going, 'I'll come back for you later'"—it has also meant he has seized those opportunities and turned in some sterling performances.

Still, after an Oscar nomination for *Cry Freedom* and the promise of two forthcoming movies and the Broadway play *Checkmates*, Denzel spent the early part of this summer sitting in his new house in Toluca Lake, a Valley suburb north of Los Angeles, wondering where his next part would come from.

—⁓—

In London, the Washingtons are met at the airport by an imposing Daimler-Benz limousine, sent to fetch them by the concert organizers. Which is where the glamour ends.

Washington is hardly a prepossessing figure. He is of that certain size—barely six feet tall and slender—typical of most leading men today, wearing the requisite jeans or warm-up knits, although there is, in the luggage, a mink-lined leather jacket, but it ends up more often on the shoulders of Pauletta. Furthermore, he never seems to raise his voice, even when imparting strongly held views, of which he has many, his words deliberate with the barest hint of his native New York in them.

Soon after arriving at the hotel, Washington is whisked to the London Hilton to tape a segment for the *Today* show. Later, he takes John David to a cast-and-crew screening of *For Queen and Country*. He plays an ex-paratrooper who, after returning from the Falklands War, tries to adjust to civilian life in strife-torn inner-city London. As of that moment, Washington has yet to see the movie, although he was cheered by an uncommonly glowing review in *Variety* following a showing at Cannes. "I'm just going to make an appearance, watch a few minutes," he tells Pauletta. "I'll be back by seven."

—⁓—

Pauletta Washington, wearing an elegant pantsuit, is sitting in the hotel lobby, waiting. It is now eight thirty.

A nanny has been engaged and is upstairs with Katia. "I can't understand what happened to him," she says. "I mean, he's got John David" (who all these years later starred and acted brilliantly in Spike Lee's movie *BlacKKKlansman*). "The child must be exhausted by now."

At nine o'clock, Washington appears at last. He is wearing a suit, a handsome black-and-white tweed coat, soft black Italian loafers, and a pinched look. He collapses into a chair.

"How did it go?" asks Pauletta.

"All right."

"You stayed for the whole movie?"

"Yeah. I sort of felt I had to."

Silence.

Pauletta asks, "What did you think, Denzel?"

"I don't know. It wasn't what I thought it would be." A frown. "I think it needs to be recut. The music wasn't right either."

"How was John David?"

"He fell asleep."

Denzel, looking uncomfortable, stands up. "Tomorrow, I'm going to make a lot of notes, then I'm going to meet with the director. I think the movie needs a lot of work."

"It's probably better than you think," says Pauletta solicitously.

Denzel forces a smile. "John David had it right. After five minutes, he said, 'Daddy, let's go.'"

—◦◦◦—

Like most successful actors, Washington is a hard worker who is hardest on himself. He dislikes looking at his films, for instance. "You've got to see yourself about twenty times before you get anything out of it," he notes. "The first nineteen you're too busy noticing your nose is too big or your hair is funny on one side. About the twentieth time, you get around to analyzing what you did."

He fanatically researches each role. In *Checkmates*, he played a yuppie liquor distributor. The character has worked his way up from salesman, and although this is only alluded to in the script, Washington made the rounds selling liquor to better understand how his character would think. Years ago, when he played Malcolm X off Broadway, he dug up all the black militant's books and taped speeches. "He played them so often, I knew them by heart," Pauletta says.

"Some of the scripts he gets are such garbage," Pauletta adds, "he throws them into the fireplace. He says his main concern is his children. That he will never do anything to embarrass them. Before the children, he said he never wanted to do anything that would make his father hang his head down. But really, I think it's Denzel. He doesn't want to embarrass himself."

Two years ago, she recalls, a studio begged him to do a movie. "They finally offered him a million dollars, and he still wouldn't do it. I said, 'I agree with your decision, Denzel. But . . . *the money*.' He just shook his head. It's all about principle with him."

—◆◆◆—

A limo arrives to transport Denzel and Pauletta to Wembley Stadium, at two fifteen on a chilly, overcast day. Washington has dressed for the occasion, wearing a white shirt, buttoned at the collar, under a black sweater jacket, an arty black beret and glasses—his Malcolm X look.

He is nervous. Word has come down from the British government warning the BBC, which is carrying the concert live, to dispense with political speechmaking and get on with the music. Furthermore, Denzel worries that if he says the wrong thing, Fox Broadcasting, which is showing the concert to America on tape delay, will cut out his remarks. (Fox ended up excising virtually all politically oriented statements.)

Shortly before he is to go on, someone hands him a slip of paper with the words he is supposed to speak. Denzel crumples it up and throws it away. What he will do, he has decided, is to get the 75,000 attendees to say "happy birthday" to Nelson Mandela.

At last his moment arrives.

He walks on stage, accompanied by Emily Lloyd, the teenage star of the movie *Wish You Were Here*.

The ovation is resounding. It is hard to tell, though, whether it is for Lloyd or Washington or perhaps for Washington's Stephen Biko. Washington decides it's for one of the latter two. And now, the crowd quieting down, he is speaking at last. He is saying—having traveled 5,000 miles for this moment: "I wish you were here, Nelson Mandela!"

Hurrying it, not stretching the moment one bit, saying, "But we're going to put a group on now that definitely belongs here today. Put your hands together for . . . *Simple Minds!*"

And that is it.

The moment is over. He is off the stage. No matter. He is aglow. "That was a rush," he gushes backstage. "*Seventy-five thousand people.*"

He walks over to Gregory Hines. The entertainer hugs him. Denzel's eyes shine brightly.

Hines asks him how it's going.

"Fuck acting," Denzel Washington says. "I want to be a rock star."

—◦—

"Denzel hated your story," the actor's agent reported to me. "But Pauletta thought you captured him perfectly."

Why Denzel hated the story I wasn't told. But apparently, he really did hate it. Some ten years later—maybe more—an editor from a movie magazine called. Denzel was promoting his latest film, and she wondered if I would interview him. It wouldn't be much of an interview or a story. The way these things worked, a star would be imprisoned in a hotel suite, and a bunch of reporters would be cooling their heels outside, each waiting to be ushered in, one at a time, for about 15 minutes. It was certainly not the kind of story I would ever do, but I liked Denzel, saw all his movies, and thought he was an amazing actor.

"Sure," I said.

The next day, the editor called back. "Denzel won't talk to you," she said. "Sorry."

44

How to Fly an Airplane: Step 1

UNLIKE DENZEL WASHINGTON, DENNIS QUAID COULD NOT have been more amiable. It is a Saturday. I had gone to his house at 10 a.m., as arranged, and possibly woken him up. He smiled and apologized. After years of struggle, he has finally hit the big time with three movies: *Innerspace*, *The Big Easy*, and *Suspect*. Which is why *GQ* called me. After reading articles about the actor, I concluded that he liked to show reporters a good time. But now, as I nervously look out of the airplane window, I am thinking—*this is a good time?*

"My first time out with passengers, I took a couple of friends to Vegas," Quaid is saying. "This was three, four years ago. We gambled for a while. Then we went back to the airport."

Uh-huh.

"So the guy at the airport said there's a big storm coming in, but if we could leave in the next thirty minutes, we'd be okay." He pauses. "You watching for traffic?"

I glance out the side window. "Yes," I say.

"Anyway, we take off, and suddenly we're in the storm, and the plane's shaking so badly, I'm fighting for control. I'm scared out of my mind. But I'm the pilot, right? So I tell my friends, 'Just a little turbulence, no problem.' Real cool. But deep inside, I know it's all over. I'm going to die."

I scan the horizon for thunderclouds. But the sky is pure turquoise and improbably clear for a late-summer day in smog-blanketed Los Angeles. Forty-five hundred feet below us are the famed multimillion-dollar beach cottages of Malibu, little matchstick houses all set in a row. Nearby, tanned stick figures lie scattered about the sand like abandoned dolls.

Only an hour and a half earlier, Quaid had driven his black BMW into Hollywood to dub some lines for *D.O.A.*, his forthcoming movie, and, either to remind himself of the chore or merely to be polite, had dressed in a black T-shirt with "D.O.A." printed across the front. Then, somewhere along the Hollywood Freeway, driving back to his house, Quaid had suddenly gotten an urge: "Let's go flying!"

We are heading north, up the coast. The plane, a single-engine Piper Archer II, has a cabin the size of a sports car's. When you step onto the wing to shoehorn into the plane, if you rap your knuckles against the metal fuselage, the tinny responding ring is enough to make your stomach somersault. Tentatively, I settled into the copilot's seat, behind a duplicate set of controls.

"So," he says, leaning toward me, "you put your hands on the wheel, like this. Your pedals are your rudders, remember that. Now we want to turn right, like this. Okay?"

"Uh . . ."

"That's it, a little more, use your pedal now, the right one."

I stare at him. He is leaning back in the seat, watching me. I say, "Dennis, what are you doing?"

He grins. You know, that grin from the movies. That sweet smile with the little feathers sticking to the edges . . . canary feathers. And says, "I am watching you fly the plane."

Oh, Jesus.

"Are you going to let her land too?" comes the accusatory voice of 12-year-old Buddy Quaid, Dennis's half-brother, from the back seat.

Land?

I shoot a look at Quaid. Still grinning. Then, ignoring his brother, he says calmly, encouragingly, "Remember now. Just try to keep it steady."

O-kay. Thankfully, I did not land the plane; Dennis did.

And I—lived happily ever after.

45

Newman Again, Really?

IT WAS THE WINTER OF 2000, WHEN AN EDITOR FROM *MODERN Maturity*, a magazine I had never heard of (it's now the AARP monthly magazine) phoned to offer me a cover story assignment. Paul Newman. The actor was turning 75 and starring in a new movie.

I replied that of course I would be happy to accept the assignment but, "I'm not sure he will deal with me," and I explained Newman's reaction to the *Newsweek* article 22 years ago.

The editor suggested I call Warren Cowan, a legendary publicist—Newman's—and a man I had dealt with before. After I explained the situation to Cowan—how I had mentioned Scott's death and Newman's anger—he said, "Let me call Paul. I'll get back to you."

Several hours later, he did. "Paul said if you don't bring it up, he won't bring it up."

Surprised, I boarded a plane and flew to New York.

———

Paul Newman is slumped in a wheelchair. His head lolls, his jaw is slack, the vivid blue eyes stare vacantly into space. A determined nurse tries gamely to cajole, then sweet-talk, and finally intimidate him to snap out of it. But he is totally unresponsive. We squirm, not really wanting to watch this. Not Paul Newman. And still it goes on, for a good half hour more, the guy all but dead.

So began my story. I was describing a scene from Newman's latest film, *Where the Money Is*, and the image he presented was shocking. For although the youthful Newman with the sneer on his lips and the devil in his eyes had long ago faded from the celluloid, watching one of the handsomest and most spirited and playful actors of our time loll and drool as a stroke victim was, well, unnerving.

Thus, it was a relief to find the actor sitting quite undamaged in the sunroom of his Manhattan penthouse, which overlooked Central Park. "I tried Novocain injections so my whole face would fall," he said merrily. "But considering how often I'd need them, the doctor was afraid there'd be some damage."

Looking suspiciously as if he were playing himself as an older man, Newman wore a sweatshirt, cotton slacks, athletic shoes, and a pair of turquoise-framed reading glasses perched low on his nose. At times his words were halting, and he was so slow to answer a question that I wondered if he would. "People often think I'm terribly brooding," he said, as if reading my mind. Then, when he did speak, it was often with humor or mischievousness.

He was sipping a glass of lemonade (his brand, Newman's Own). His longtime prop, a bottle of Bud, was nowhere in sight. "I've cut back," he deadpanned, "from four six-packs a day to two."

Two themes ran through Newman's life and movies—luck and the big con—the two closely intertwined. "People always ask me why I wear a Timex," he said, displaying his $49 watch. "I do it because when I go to auto races, it's marvelous to a hundredth of a second. But also, you can really hustle people. I say I'm prepared to bet right now that this Timex is not more than a second off, probably *right* to the second." He smiled with satisfaction. "I make a couple hundred bucks a year off it."

Newman traced his good luck starting with being born in America. During World War II, he enlisted in the navy for pilot training. This time his luck landed big time. He was assigned as a radioman/gunner in a torpedo bomber in the South Pacific. One morning his crew was grounded when the pilot had an earache. Five other planes went out. They were attacked by Japanese fighters, and two of the American planes went down. "And that was just an earache," Newman said.

Luck followed him into his movie career. After graduating Yale Drama School and turning down several scripts, he finally took the role of a Greek slave in *The Silver Chalice*, possibly one of the worst movies ever made. "There I was in that short cocktail skirt with skinny legs—and went straight from that to Graziano (*Somebody Up There Likes Me*) to *The Rack* and two years later to *The Long Hot Summer*." By avoiding traditional leading-man roles, he said, "I got to do the other stuff, which I always felt more comfortable doing." He paused. "That was good fortune."

—◆◆◆—

My second meeting with Newman was at his house—a converted farm house—in Westport, Connecticut. He gave me a tour, leading me outside to a barn converted into a screening room, and pointed to the stream that cut through the back of his property. Inside the house, he led me down a few stairs into a large, comfortable den filled with bookshelves containing many of the classics. Family photos lined one wall, and commanding the middle of the room was—what else?—a pool table.

He sat down behind a large desk and pointed to an armchair next to it for me. As we were talking, he leaned over and opened a desk drawer. "Do you like chocolate?" I nodded. Inside were several bars, one partially eaten. He broke off a piece of the chocolate and handed it to me. "You know it has to be good if I pay retail for it."

It was good, although I was half-expecting something creepy to crawl out of the chocolate, given that Newman was a famous practical joker. "I was the master," he declared and recounted the havoc he wrought while making *Buffalo Bill and the Indians* in 1976. Director Robert Altman started it, Newman claimed, by setting off an explosion that left Newman in an eight-foot heap of popcorn. He told Altman, "You shouldn't have done that, Bob. I'm richer than you, and I've got more time."

First, Newman stole a pair of Altman's expensive deerskin gloves and had them "breaded, deep-fried, and served to him—little wizened fingers—as garnish on his lunch plate." Another day he filled Altman's trailer with 400 live chickens. Then he jacked up Altman's Mercedes eight feet into the air. Finally, Newman sent Altman a bogus message that he had fallen off a horse and broken his shoulder. "Altman goes running out to his golf cart," Newman related gleefully, "and an explosion under it put him seven feet in the air."

I began to squirm, wondering what he might have in store for me.

Newman, perhaps thinking the same thing, said, "But that's in the past. I've reformed." His eyes wandered to the window where Joanne

Woodward, his wife and one-time film star, was walking by, unaware that she was being observed. A small smile played on Newman's lips. "I'd like to make one more film, then retire," he said. "A film with Joanne."

The pool table invited the obvious: was he any good?

He flashed his famous sly grin. "Good enough to hustle. A guy'll come up to me and say, 'I got a pool table in the back. Want to shoot some?' I say no. He'll say, 'Oh, come on, we can play straight or eight ball; what do you like?' I say, I don't think so. He'll say, 'Aw, come on. Let's have a game. What do you bet?'

"And then I look him straight in the eye. 'How about your house?'"

I had arranged for a ride back to the train station, but Newman insisted on driving me. I don't remember the make of the car, nothing expensive, but it housed a super-powerful engine. He slipped on his sunglasses. "Don't worry. I'll get you there." I tightly fastened my seat belt anyway.

———

His film, *Where the Money Is*, hadn't opened, but a screening in Manhattan was arranged for me. It was terrible, but I could see why Newman wanted to do it. It was caper movie in which he, a con, comes up with a new way to break out of prison: fake a stroke and get transferred to a nursing home, only to have his plan foiled. But the script was bad. When I returned to my apartment, there was a message on my answering machine from Newman. He asked that I call him and tell him what I thought of the movie.

I lied; I had to. He sounded so hopeful on the phone. "I really liked it. Fun plot. You come across awfully well."

"Do you think a lot of people will go see it?"

I sighed inwardly. "That I can't say. Even producers never know how the public will react. But," I bit my lip, "I think it will do well."

Feeling sad, I hung up.

The movie bombed.

46

Lose Your Gun, Chief!

WHEN I MOVED TO LOS ANGELES TO WRITE A SPORTS COLUMN, I knew little about the city. There was an ocean, and there was Disneyland—somewhere—and that was about it.

No, wait. One other thing I knew with absolute certainty: the Los Angeles Police were a bunch of shoot-em-first rednecks, and their top cop, Daryl Gates, was the most racist of them all, if not an outright Nazi.

Unlike New York City, where you can spend a lifetime and never interact with a cop, in L.A., it is only a matter of time. That's because in L.A. you must drive to get anywhere, and at some point, one of these well-toned cops in his perfectly ironed uniform will pull you over and cite you for something. Being nice was not in their instruction manual.

Steve Randall, the editor who oversaw the *Playboy* magazine interviews, asked me if I would do one with Lee Brown, then the New York City police commissioner. This was November 1990, and crime was rampant, especially in New York, so Steve thought it would be interesting to hear from Brown. At the time, *Playboy*'s Q-and-A was considered the very best of its kind and often made news. Well, I said, why not Daryl Gates? He was always issuing highly charged statements and frequently made headlines either with his words or the actions of his department. Steve liked the idea, and I put in a call to the LAPD. To my astonishment, Gates agreed. I scheduled four two-hour sessions with him beginning in February.

———

Tall, tan, and obsessively fit, Gates, 65, seemed to think his natural place was in the eye of a storm. From the moment he took over as L.A.'s chief of police in 1978, he repeatedly managed to stun vast subgroups of the city's population with his seemingly thoughtless remarks. Latinos, he joked, rose slowly through the ranks of the LAPD, possibly because they were "lazy." Women had their place, but not as officers. As far as recruiting gays—who'd want to work with one? And—worst of all—the reason black suspects were dying from vigorous applications of the choke hold, Gates once volunteered, might be that "veins or arteries of blacks do not open as fast as they do in normal people."

Whatever he meant by his perceived slurs—he often claimed his nemesis, the *L.A. Times*, had misquoted, misunderstood or bamboozled him—his actions generally did not match his words. Following a court dictum, he drastically changed the complexion of the police department, hiring thousands of women, Latinos, and blacks— then defended them, if need be, in the same paternalistic way he defended any of his officers who came under attack. And he continued to run a department widely considered the finest in the country. His officers adored him, conservatives made him their hero, and the police commission, which hired him, gave him consistently high marks. Popularity polls named him the most respected Republican in Los Angeles.

He was also an innovator. He developed the concept for SWAT teams, which quickly became used around the world as an offense against hostage situations. He also persuaded the board of education to devise a drug-education program that his officers could teach in schools. Called *DARE*, the program was soon offered throughout the United States.

Having no idea what to expect, I arrived at police headquarters downtown and discovered a press conference underway. The day before, Tina Kerbrat became the first LAPD female police officer killed in the line of duty. Gates angrily attacked the shooter, calling him, "an El Salvadoran asshole." But later, as we talked, he seemed visibly shaken by Kerbrat's death, and after our three-hour interview, he thanked me for taking his mind off the tragedy. He gave no hint that he had been up all night at the hospital, comforting Kerbrat's husband and her distraught partner. Nor did he mention it.

Gates came across as soft-spoken, somewhat shy, self-deprecating, and able to poke fun at himself. But his manner could, at times, belie his words. When I looked over the transcripts of our conversations, the printed words often sounded like the ravings of a narrow-minded, stub-born, unenlightened despot. It was those words, appearing in print, that caused him so much grief.

One other thing struck me that first day. Although I barely knew the difference between a sergeant and a lieutenant, Gates never made me feel I had asked a silly question.

—◦◦◦—

During one of our talks, I raised the subject of his most controversial statement, that blacks were more susceptible to the choke hold than "nor-mal people." He admitted he'd used very poor language but that doctors had written him saying there was a sudden-death syndrome in blacks that no one understood and that research was still being conducted by the military. But his department did not use the choke hold. It used a modified carotid hold that involved placing pressure on the carotid arter-ies that supply blood to the brain.

Can you show me? I stupidly asked.

In a flash, Gates was on his feet, standing behind my chair. He put his forearm across my throat and pressed. And pressed. *Oh god,* I thought . . . and at the very moment I was sure I would pass out—or die—he pulled away.

—◦◦◦—

It was after our third session that motorist Rodney King was videotaped being beaten by four LAPD officers, and Gates agreed to see me two days later. He had been en route from the Kennedy School in Boston when it happened. When he got off the plane, he was told, and he had a chance to look at the videotape. It had physically sickened him. But as I kept asking questions, he seemed of two minds. Instinctively, he defended his department and its 8,000 officers, while admitting that the incident had horrified him. But he was also deeply troubled that the media and civil libertarians were sympathetic to King.

> **GATES**: I think the vast majority of people are outraged. And they have a right to be. But I think a lot of people are also saying, you know, this wasn't the nicest guy in the world. He's a parolee. Armed

robber. Arrested several times for assaulting people. Driving one hundred fifteen miles an hour, in two thousand pounds of metal, menacing every single person on the street. And what did we hear about him? He had a job. On Monday. And this prevented him from going to his job. How touching. And he has two fine children. I hear those things and I'm amazed, amazed that people won't put this in a proper perspective.

Because the Rodney King story wouldn't go away—and there were fresh headlines every day—I came back to see Gates two more times. Public outrage over the sadistic beating had only begun to heat up. It was questionable whether Gates fully understood the impact the incident would have, including calls for him to resign. At our final session I asked how the controversy had affected him personally.

GATES: I don't even know how to answer that. It's certainly no fun. I would much rather be back where I was, in a position where the majority of people said I was more believable than any other public official in this city. The president was saying nice things about me. That's a pretty long way to fall in a couple of days.

As I was about to leave, Gates told me he had signed a deal with Bantam Books for a memoir, but his coauthor had turned in the first 100 pages, and Bantam found them unacceptable. "I think they want me to fire him," he said. "But I'm very loyal. Could you read the pages and tell me what you think?"

Sure, I said. I'll take them home and . . .

"No," said Gates. "Read them here." With that, his secretary walked in and placed the manuscript in front of me. Gates stayed at the conference table as I quickly read the first 30 pages. I said, "I think if he does a rewrite, leading off either with you finding about Rodney King or behind closed doors with Mayor Bradley, it should be okay."

In fact, I could see why Bantam didn't like it; it sounded like an omniscient narrator talking, not like Gates at all. By chance, I was just finishing my second mystery novel for Bantam. I called my agent as soon as I got home. "Keep an eye on this, okay? If they fire the writer, I want in."

I wanted a behind-the-curtain view of what certainly would be a chapter of Los Angeles history. And I had come to like Gates, though

I often disagreed with him. Sometimes I would ask him about a police shooting, and he always convinced me it had been necessary—until I went home and thought about it again. I also believed the charges of racism and sexism in the department were, if not untrue, at least overblown. I believed Gates measured his officers strictly by how well they did their jobs. I also decided he was probably the smartest official in Los Angeles. But he had two big problems. One, he was arrogant and believed if you heard him out, you would agree. Unfortunately, he had not learned to talk in sound bites. I would ask a question. He would seemingly begin to answer then go off on a tangent before circling back to complete the question. TV news was not going to give him that much time and often only used a headline-grabbing sound bite. The *L.A. Times* was not much better.

Even worse, he sometimes said things that would definitely get him in trouble. Such as, speaking of pot users, he once declared, "I'd like to take them out back and shoot them." When that quote blew up, he chuckled and tried to explain, "It's a phrase we all use sometimes, you know, to a misbehaving child, 'I'd like to take you out back and shoot you'." But the controversy did not go away.

Bantam fired the writer, and I was told to forward some of my articles to Gates. I heard that two male writers were flying in from New York to meet with him. But Gates chose me.

Some of my friends stopped speaking to me.

———✠———

Aside from wanting that front-row seat, I saw another advantage working with Gates: personal safety. Should I be captured or imprisoned in a foreign country (I often daydreamed such scenarios) or get into trouble at home, I now had two protectors. The other? Tommy Lasorda.

Yes, that Lasorda. The manager of the L.A. Dodgers. I had barely started working at the *L.A. Herald Examiner* when I heard this story. One of my colleagues, Lyle Spencer, who often covered the Dodgers, had traveled to Europe and was on an overnight train through Spain. His car was empty. A 12-year-old boy stuck his head in and left. Lyle went to sleep in his seat, his coat covering him, his knapsack on the floor. When he awoke, he discovered his knapsack was gone and so was his wallet. He had no money, no traveler's checks, only his passport, which he found floating in a toilet.

When he arrived at his destination, Algeciras, he didn't know what to do. While he was explaining his plight to an agent at American Express, a man pulled him aside. He could help. If Lyle would act as a mule and carry hash to an appointed place, the man would pay him $500. "It was the stupidest thing I ever did," he says.

After the man taped dozens of bags to Lyle's body, Lyle took off. But when he arrived at his destination, a policeman grabbed him from behind and arrested him. The law was clear: one year in prison.

He wrote apologetic letters to his parents. His mom contacted Lasorda. Lasorda called Frank Sinatra. Sinatra wrote a letter to King Juan Carlos of Spain, pleading with him to let Lyle go. But since Lyle had already served half of his reduced eight-month sentence, he was forced to stay.

Years later, Lyle and Lasorda were having lunch. Lyle thanked him again.

"I didn't do it for you," Lasorda said. "I did it for your mother. I felt sorry for her. You really fucked up."

So you can see why I felt safe. Spoiler alert: I never did need Lasorda. Once, I did need Gates. I called him in a panic. "I have rats! And one just got caught in a trap. In my kitchen! Can you come over and get rid of it? *Please?*"

Gates said sorry, he was on his way to give a speech in Malibu. "But I'll send SWAT," he chuckled and hung up.

—∿∿∿—

Other than *that*, Gates proved easy to work with as I wrote the book. Whenever I needed to see him, he made time. His office responded quickly to supply me with old police records. My editor, however, made me want to scream (which I often did after we hung up). Bantam had brought in a tough editor, Gene Young, who made it clear over the phone she found Gates deplorable. I would send her pages, and she would disagree with things he had said and want me to delete them. But, I would argue, shouldn't he be able to say what he wants to? And she would demand more context. I never told Gates what I was dealing with, and as the deadline drew near, I began to wonder if I should quit. I felt I was trapped halfway up a mountain, too tired to press on but reluctant to go back down. Finally, a few days before Christmas, I turned in the finished manuscript, and a week later, Gene called and said she was thrilled. There were several things she still would like to go over with Gates and planned to come out to see us early in January. We arranged to meet at his house in the beach community of Dana Point.

During our conference, I had to keep from smiling. Gene melted—*absolutely melted*—as Daryl answered her questions.

—————

The book, *Chief: My Life in the LAPD,* was to go on sale in late May 1992. In the meantime, I often got together with some of the police officers I had come to know, men and women who worked closely with Gates. Sometimes they came to my house and scolded me for not having a shotgun—"You live in the Hollywood Hills by yourself, you need a gun!"—but I hated guns and refused even to allow any into my house. One evening, Gates joined several of us and proudly showed off his new ankle holster. I pulled him aside and asked if he would please leave his gun out on my doorstep. (My house was surrounded by a wall with a locked gate.) He refused, but he did find a safe place for it in my kitchen.

For the next three months, the trial of the four police officers who beat Rodney King dominated the news. Racial tensions flared, even though most citizens were still outraged. At the end of April, I went to New York to discuss story ideas with the *Times.* On April 29, the verdicts were handed down: all four officers were found not guilty.

And so the worst riots in L.A. history broke out.

I watched in horror on CNN as flames swept up Hollywood Boulevard, not far from my home. On the third day, I flew back to L.A., thinking maybe a chapter would be added to the book. Everyone was blaming Gates. (Some said he organized the riots to promote his forthcoming book.) Friends called me and asked if Gates had warned me to leave town. When I got to his office, he looked ravished. He had lost maybe 20 pounds. Although he had prepared for riots, he hadn't prepared for the massive outburst that lasted six days, killed 63 people, injured 2,383, and resulted in more than 12,000 arrests. It took the California National

Guard, the Seventh Infantry Division and the First Marine Division to help the LAPD quell the riots.

Gates had already announced he was stepping down. But there was so much ill will toward him that when our book came out two weeks later, some bookstores refused to carry or promote it. But for six weeks, it did top the *New York Times* bestseller list. The 100,000 first run sold out, but Bantam refused to do a second printing.

I stayed friends with Gates. One day he said to me, "Two women officers are suing the department for sexual harassment by their male partners. I don't get it. The first thing we teach is how to control situations, how to look out for yourself. Why didn't they just take their billy clubs and whack their partners? I still love movies from the forties. Lauren Bacall, Katharine Hepburn, Roz Russell. Those women didn't let men push them around. Where are those women today?"

In 2004, I ended my bicoastal life and moved permanently back to New York. But I did stay in touch with Gates. Early in 2010, his lawyer and my friend Jay Grodin called to say Daryl had cancer. Daryl and I spoke on the phone several times, and he was still upbeat, urging me to start writing another book with him. When Jay told me he was going into hospice care, I called Daryl and said I'd see him the next week.

"So we can finally start a book?"

Yes, I said, definitely.

I made arrangements to take an early-morning train from L.A. to Dana Point, where Daryl's brother would pick me up. But just as I was leaving my hotel room, my phone rang. It was Jay. Daryl had passed away in the night.

I often think about him. The pressures he faced, the humor that made me laugh. I am still surprised—flabbergasted—that I had become friends with the redneck Nazi chief of police. Who, I learned, wasn't that man at all.

47

The KGB and Me

THE FIRST TIME I VISITED MOSCOW WAS TO COVER THE 1980 Summer Olympics.

I was terrified.

The Soviet Union was still our Cold War enemy, and tensions only grew worse when President Jimmy Carter announced the United States would boycott the games to protest the Soviet Union's invasion of Afghanistan. Although our athletes would not be competing, hundreds of US reporters submitted visa applications, still hoping to go.

The Soviets took their time getting back to us. Finally, 10 days before opening ceremonies, we got word. Only 17 US reporters were granted visas, including—who knew why—me and my *Newsweek* colleague Pete Axthelm.

My fears were justified. Two months earlier, Russian authorities—KGB?—had roughed up a couple of Western photographers. My grandfather had been conscripted into the Russian army as a teenager during World War I and, knowing that Jews were sent to the front lines first, somehow escaped by walking out of Russia. I had visions of being thrown into the notorious Lubyanka prison. And since Carter still hadn't been able to free the US hostages being held by Iran, I knew my government would not rescue me. I began imagining dramatic ways to break out of prison. Then I typed up a will and left it on the desk in my apartment.

Arriving in Moscow and then at the 6,000-room Rossiya Hotel, the first thing I had to endure was the search of my luggage by KGB agents in the lobby. I watched helplessly as an agent retrieved a Tampax from the suitcase of a woman in front of me, held it up, and demanded to know

"What is this?" The woman had no idea how to explain and stood there miserably shrugging her shoulders while the agent continued to shout at her. Finally, he tossed the Tampax back into her suitcase and sent her, red-faced, on her way.

That evening, Bill Schmidt, *Newsweek*'s Moscow bureau chief, picked me up at the hotel and drove me to his apartment. All summer, he had been sending me amusing files on how Moscow was preparing for its time on the world stage. Any car with a dent was taken away, dogs were hidden from view, as were children; building exteriors were painted; and the Russian people had been deprived of meat for six months—the meat stockpiled so it could be used to impress their Olympic guests with Russia's splendid cuisine.

Bill's place was like a modest New York City two-bedroom apartment. Casually, he lifted a poster from a living room wall, stuck his forefinger in a hole in the wall, and grinned. "That's where we found one of their bugs." He showed me two more holes. "We pick the bugs out, they come back when we're not home and put in more."

"They can listen to everything you and your wife say?"

"Yes."

"But doesn't that make conversation difficult?"

"Not really. We talk as we would normally. The only thing we never talk about are other reporters."

I arrived one week before the games started, and six days later, Pete Axthelm arrived. I went to the airport to meet him and, knowing he would be grumpy, I brought him a bottle of Courvoisier and a box of Cuban cigars. Pete was ashen as he strode down the gray marble halls of the airport. He had written a *Newsweek* column supporting President Carter's boycott, and now he was sure the KGB would get him.

Since Americans weren't competing—and our coverage would be limited—Pete immediately located a muddy, rutted racetrack outside Moscow, and there he retreated almost every day. Nothing did Pete like better than the ponies. Meanwhile, I ran from event to event. The parts I liked best were the so-called "press conferences" with a gold medalist, often a Russian. This is how these sessions typically went. "Mr. Gold Medal Winner, which of the gymnastic routines did you find most difficult?" Or something like that. And the answer, invariably, would be,

"Moscow is a beautiful city. I hope you are enjoying your stay here." And then he would stand and walk out, never to be seen or heard from—by us—again.

Newsweek had procured a car and driver for me, and whenever I could, I offered rides to other American reporters. The driver spoke no English. Indeed, when he returned me to the hotel at night, I would have to move the hands on the dashboard clock to indicate what time I needed to be picked up in the morning.

If I was in the car at noon, he would turn on the radio to hear a newscast. There were two anchors, one male, one female, both of whom would deliver the "news" in perfect American English. "The unemployment rate in the United States is 78 percent," one would report. The numbers of homeless would be given—in the millions, of course. Food prices had reached astronomical highs. Inflation was climbing daily. The average income was dropping, etc.

I would laugh, as would the reporter I was sitting with in the back seat.

Then the driver would turn off the radio. He seemed like a nice guy, and I brought him cigarettes, pens, gum, even pieces of fruit, which the government was allotting only to Olympic visitors. Shyly, he would smile and say, *"Spasiba."*

Dinners were always tedious. We could go to restaurants, which were mostly empty. We would be handed a phone-book-size menu. Page after page of dishes were pictured. But no matter the restaurant, only three dishes were ever available, chicken Kiev being one. The meal would last a good three hours, then a waiter would appear with an abacus and figure out the bill. The food was so awful that I lived on caviar and bakery goods, which were delicious.

There was a rule—or law—that said a man could not go into a woman's hotel room and vice versa. Unaware of this, I went into Pete's room one night after dinner to discuss who would cover what the next day. Pete, still terrified, had broken out in hives. I stayed maybe an hour.

When I opened the door to leave, I was jolted by the sight of a KGB agent stepping back from the door. Apparently, he had been told of my indiscretion and had been listening. He allowed me to walk out of the room, and he followed me down the hall to my room. He stood there until I was inside.

But the most unsettling experience came on Saturday, the day before the Final Ceremonies.

There was a belt I wanted to buy, black leather with a brass hammer-and-sickle buckle. The military guys all wore them, and I thought it would be cool to have one. Someone said I might try an army/navy store. And so, on that Saturday morning, I set off with two fellow journalists to find this store. We approached Red Square. To our left was the Kremlin and Lenin's Tomb; to our right was the blocks-long GUM department store. What lay in front of us was a long walk across the red-brick square.

We had gone maybe one-quarter of the way when suddenly, flames shot up from the far end of the square. A fire! But what was burning? We could see nothing but the flames seemingly issuing from the red bricks. We started running toward it, along with the few other people in the square. I lifted the camera that hung around my neck and slowed so I could snap pictures. Then, seemingly popping out of the bricks and from all sides came the military police, pushing us back. One officer tried to grab my camera. I had borrowed it from my father and, without thinking, I tried to pull away from the man. He was shorter than me, and I kept resisting, desperately hanging on to my camera. Now we were in a tug-of-war. One of my friends shouted, "Just give it to him!" But I wouldn't. I couldn't. My hands, my arms weren't listening to my brain. Then, to my surprise, this officer let go of my camera and raced off to harass someone else.

We obeyed the order to leave the square, circling behind the GUM department store. I doubted 20 minutes had elapsed by the time we reached the far end of the massive store and could look back at Red Square. We stared in silence. The square was deserted—no people, no police, no fire, no ashes. Not a single sign there had been any fire at all. (I did find the store and buy the belt.)

That night, correspondent Ann Compton of ABC News hosted a party for American journalists. The bureau chiefs from some of the news organizations attended. And they all told the same story. Each had phoned sources in the Kremlin. *What caused the fire?* they asked. And each was given the same chilling reply: "But there was no fire in Red Square today."

Later I heard that an Australian coach had self-immolated, but I never saw this confirmed.

Still, the Kremlin's denial of the incident shocked me. Our government could tap dance around things, bend facts to make a point, but deny something had happened when it had been witnessed by dozens of people? (Okay, this was pre-Trump.)

I had one last surprise after I returned home. Bill Schmidt sent a message saying that my sweet little driver was an English-speaking KGB agent who, after dropping me off at night, reported everywhere I went, everything I did, and everything I said to another reporter in the back seat.

48

The Moscow Police and Me

THIRTEEN YEARS LATER, AND I AM BACK IN MOSCOW, RIDING in a patrol car with three cops, each with a Kalashnikov submachine gun laying across his lap.

Much has changed. In 1991, the Soviet Union dissolved, and its many republics claimed independence. Soviet head of state Mikhail Gorbachev's *glasnost* and *perestroika* policies, intended to democratize the economic and political systems that had endured since the Russian Revolution, had thrown the country into turmoil, and his successor, President Boris Yeltsin, was only making matters worse. Though I was neither an economist nor an expert on political systems, even I could see that the Russian people were flummoxed, even scared. The apartments they had occupied, rent free, were now being turned into pricey condos. "They want me to pay $300,000 for my apartment," my translator told me. "Lots of people are leaving Moscow to live in the countryside with family members." Each morning, Russians discovered the price for basics, like bread, had gone up from the day before.

A friend, film director/producer Paul Maslansky, had called me from Moscow, where he was producing *Police Academy 7: Mission to Moscow.* "They're cobbling together a police department," he said. "There's like two rusted police cars and some old Kalashnikov rifles, and it's more like a Marx Brothers movie with a bunch of cops running around trying to arrest criminals."

What fun, I thought, a story about Moscow's Keystone Kops. I called the *Los Angeles Times* Sunday magazine and asked if I could write a story about the Moscow police. Since I figured they would turn me down because of the expense, I offered to use mileage for my plane ticket and I could stay for free because Paul had an extra room at his hotel. I was given the okay.

Please note that under the Soviet regime, "There is no crime in Russia," it was said. Only now, that was gone, and some democratic institutions had to be swiftly created—a functioning police department being one of them. The problem was—actually, there were many—the Duma was not churning out new laws fast enough. Two months before my arrival in Moscow, seven submachine-gun-toting men had robbed a bank. People were horrified. "This was our first bank stickup," said one high-ranking police official. "The state took it very hard." Although six suspects were apprehended, no law had yet been enacted to make bank robbery a crime.

Oh, one more thing. No longer were the police the scary guys—now it was the mushrooming Mafia. They weren't hard to detect. They were the ones driving black Mercedes, which sped by ordinary Russians pulled over to the side of the road, car hoods up as they tried to fix their broken-down Ladas.

—◦◦◦—

Inside a ramshackle brown-brick police station, Lieutenant Colonel Mikhail Sergeivich Pertsev absorbs the latest news crackling over the police radio band. "A man with a submachine gun just threatened a man in a car," he says gloomily. "The man lost the car."

A carjacking? Where?

"Not far from here. An area that used to have a lot of construction. Huts were built for the workers to live in, and there was lots of fighting with knives." Pertsev pauses. "We call this district Chicago."

As chief of one of Moscow's smaller police stations in the northern part of the city, Pertsev seems to possess a bottomless store of good humor, which he needs. He presides over 110 officers and a fleet of seven squad cars, two of which don't work. "They are like the Aurora boat that started the Bolshevik Revolution and is now a museum in St. Petersburg," he says wryly. "They do not move."

Sitting behind the desk in his gray, functional office, Pertsev proudly hoists a new police radio. "It's a Motorola, and we have our American

colleagues to thank for it," he notes. "Seven came last week. Unfortunately, we need 40 or 50." Before the radios arrived, Pertsev's men relied
on Hungarian-made sets. "The Hungarians probably felt hurt with us
after 1956," he offers slyly. "Their radios only caused trouble."

As Russia becomes more capitalistic, it can boast one of capitalism's
ancillary fruits: big-time crime. Vladimir Vershkov, a ruddy-cheeked
lieutenant colonel in charge of press relations, gloomily recites recent
crime statistics, which have been increasing at an alarming rate. When
the year began, five or six cars were stolen a day; during one recent night
in Moscow, 102 cars vanished.

"How many auto thefts do you have in Los Angeles?"

"About 70,000 a year," I reply.

Vershkov blinks. "Oh."

"But we've been at it longer."

More interesting are the Moscow police regulations for shooting
people. "We are allowed to shoot at people if we order them to stop and
they don't," explains Alexander Shestakov, a veteran of Moscow's traffic
police. Which explains why, a few months after the Rodney King beating
incident, a member of a delegation of Russian police visiting Los Angeles
told Chief Daryl Gates, "We don't understand all the fuss. In Russia, we
would have shot him." (America seems to have borrowed this strategy.)

Another distinction that still stands: if some Angelenos call LAPD
officers brutal, almost *all* Muscovites call their cops criminals. "Money,
money, money!" shouts Alex Belabin, my driver in Moscow, every time
we pass a white-gloved traffic cop standing over a doomed motorist. It is
a common sight. "Russian people hate the police," says Belabin with passion. "Every day, they pull me over. 'Hello, Alex! Money, money, money!'"

Fines for traffic infractions must be paid on the spot. If the motorist
doesn't have the cash on him, the officer may follow him home to collect
it or confiscate his license. But everyone knows you can buy your way out
of almost any violation, even drunk driving, by slipping the cop several
thousand rubles (which equals several dollars). Russians refer to traffic
cops as milkmen—people who milk the public.

"We have jokes about the police," says one young woman. "An officer
tells his superior he's getting married and he needs more money. The
superior hands him a portable stop sign."

Space in Moscow is so tight that police stations turn up in the oddest places. One I visited consumes half of an apartment building; another is in a taxi park. Mikhail Pertsev's municipal police station is in a former school built in 1946. Dark, dank, and dungeonlike, it's a prime example of Russia's crumbling infrastructure. Stairs are broken, floor tiles are cracked; paint peels off walls, hallway ceilings are a mass of tangled wires. Many overhead fixtures lack bulbs; the bathroom is beyond description.

Pertsev, a stocky, dark-haired 43-year-old, tackles his job with an old-fashioned sense of pride and responsibility. The chunk of Moscow he watches over, a "sleeping district" of 70,000, is where he grew up and where he still resides with his wife and two sons. But, as is true everywhere in Russia, the neighborhood has grown more violent. "When I was young and lighter in weight, I could bring back five or six criminals at a time," he recalls. "I didn't need to carry a gun. They wouldn't resist me. Now, we all walk around with submachine guns."

On cue, two officers burst into Pertsev's office to show me. Each wears a helmet and, over his clothes, a bulletproof vest that seems a closer relation to knight's armor than to the light Kevlar vests common in America. Strapped to each belt is a nine-millimeter pistol. In their hands, Kalashnikovs. "Wherever we get a call that a crime is in progress, these are the men we send out," Pertsev says.

Do they use motorcycles?

Pertsev grins. "We have some, but they're old and can't be used in a chase." He jumps up. "Come, I'll show you around."

He flings open a door and announces proudly, "This is our gym. Our officers built it themselves." The drab room, maybe 15 feet by 10 feet, is two-thirds consumed by blue floor mats enclosed by ropes. A makeshift slant board, balanced on the seat of a broken-back chair, is crammed between two rusting sets of barbells.

It gets worse. The forensics lab, housed in a tiny, gray, damp room with a single fluorescent bulb, contains only an ancient photo enlarger. More sophisticated work, such as analyzing fingerprints, must be done at headquarters. In December 1992, Pertsev's station was issued three new Russian-made Moskvitch police cars. "By January," he says, "we were making repairs." Although the cars are serviced at a friendly auto shop, where the owner charges for parts but not labor, Pertsev confesses, "After we use up our budget, we have to pay for parts out of own pockets."

But—how? Pertsev makes 150,000 rubles a month, about $150, although the steady decline of the ruble makes it worth less every week. In addition, he is eligible to collect 25 percent of his pension, which amounts to another 7,000 rubles ($7) a month. "A kilo of sausage costs 10,000 rubles," Persev says bleakly, "if it's a good sausage."

He brightens. "But let's talk about crime."

Back in his office, he removes a VCR from a locked cabinet. He plugs it into the TV and pops in a cassette. A bright, clear tape shows officers searching 25 "Mafia people" who had been brought in for questioning. Each of the bad guys wears a black leather jacket over a bulletproof vest. Many carry wads of US dollars. Painstakingly, the officers study each man's passport.

"Look at this one," Pertsev says, tapping the TV as the camera focuses on the passport of a young, dark-haired man. Pertsev laughs. "The photo is of Yeltsin!"

But proving someone is guilty would stretch one 60-minute episode of *Law & Order* into a full season. "The police probably forgot to tell you that it's not really the laws that are holding them back," says Sergei Litvinov, a former Siberian police detective who now works as an investigator in San Francisco. "Five or ten years ago, when Russia had a conviction rate of 99 percent, they didn't need to collect evidence. Now, with the slight democratization that's going on, they must fingerprint and nail their case down. They're still not used to this. Like everything in Russia, the police are inefficient."

—⁓—

Petrovka 38—police headquarters—is a six-story yellow building set behind a wrought-iron gate. It too desperately needs a makeover. Long stretches of hallway are dark; the elevator may or may not work. The building contains administrative offices, forensics labs, and some city-wide units. In room 335, heavyset Lieutenant Colonel Anatoly Ilchenko, wearing a dark suit, dark shirt, and dark tie, looks to be just what he is: deputy head of the organized crime department. "Moscow is like America in the '30s," he says, "I think."

Almost everyone I encounter in Moscow has a Mafia-type story. According to the police, even banks hire racketeers—to find the criminals who steal their money.

———

Again I climb the stairs at Petrovka 38 to witness yet another Russian crime innovation: a weekly press conference. I am amused as I watch an officer crank out pages of crime statistics on a mimeograph machine and hand them out to the dozen local print reporters seated in a small auditorium. They are taking copious notes. Freedom of information, Russian style.

Sitting on a dais and flanked by seven other police officials is Vladimir Objedkov, head of the department of economic crime. "Credit robbery is something new," he says. "A young entrepreneur will set up a company using false documents. He'll get credit from banks, then disappear, changing the money into hard currency and transferring it abroad."

Often, Objedkov adds, the banker is in cahoots with the entrepreneur, accepting false documents for a piece of the profits. "But then," he says with a quick smile, "the Russians have always been inventive."

———

Also in Petrovka 38 are the telephone switchboards, housed in a large room where cops can monitor the city. It is noon, and, according to Colonel Alexander Denisov, the unit chief, 7,000 cops are on duty. He points to an enormous relief map of Moscow that covers the far wall. Small light bulbs indicate the positions of cars on duty. The city's emergency response system is upstairs. Ten phone lines are hooked to 02, the Moscow equivalent of 911, staffed by ten policewomen. "Men can't stand working here," Denisov volunteers. "But women are very good at it." Three of the women look up and smile.

Women are trained in nonphysical work at the police academy then carefully slotted into jobs that keep them behind desks. They operate the new computers that run fingerprints, while men are assigned to the crime scene to collect the fingerprints. Asked about this, Victor Petchnikov, the tall, curly-haired head of criminal police at one *okrug*, or district, says, "The criminal police have no regular hours. Women need to be home to take care of their husbands and children. They prefer it."

So it is women who handle the 20,000 to 24,000 calls that are made to 02 each 24 hours. All calls are handled efficiently and promptly, Denisov boasts.

"Then how come people complain they can never get through?" I ask.

Denisov smiles benignly. "Obviously they have dialed the wrong number."

—◦◦◦—

It is 9:00 p.m. on a chilly Moscow night. I am in a squad car along with three patrol officers. In Moscow, cops go out in threes. All ride in the car with submachine guns across their laps. I am in the back seat next to one; on the other side of him is Svetlana, my translator. A call comes over the radio. A man with a submachine gun and several automatic weapons is terrorizing someone in an apartment building. "Practically every day, criminals use automatic weapons," says Captain Vladimir Kulkov, fingering his own.

These officers are part of a new unit that strictly does patrol duty. They work 12-hour shifts for two days then have two days off. Their new station, now under construction, will contain a locker room, sauna, shower, gym, shooting range, and garage. They even have their own shrink. "She knows when someone needs her," Junior Lieutenant Nikolai Shliaptsev says. "She makes you feel better."

Their territory, just north of the city center, includes woodsy residential streets, from which cars are routinely stolen, as well as the Central Exhibition Center and a major metro stop ringed by numerous robbery-attractive kiosks. Most are open until 11:00 p.m., some all night. "Before, nothing was open at this hour," Shliaptsev says. Tonight is eerily quiet, although a crime was at least being *discussed*, I later learn. Five Brooklyn cops, in Moscow on an exchange program, were in a bar talking of a crime scene they had just witnessed. "There was a dead woman lying on the street," one officer noted. "Right out in front of a crowd, the cops lifted her skirt and shoved a rectal thermometer up her . . . you know, to gauge how long she'd been dead. We were shocked. Man, these Moscow cops can be cold."

Eventually, the three-man patrol stops at the side of a deserted road. Three doors pop open, the men jump out, and each lights a cigarette. They are taking a break, they explain. What, no coffee? No doughnuts?

Shliaptsev laughs. "I don't know what you mean, *doughnut*. But for coffee, there's no place to stop. This isn't like America. A restaurant takes two hours."

—◦◦◦—

It has been easy to see that Russia, dipping its toe into shallow democracy, might have tried to do too much too fast. But then Vladimir Putin came along, and most people's lives improved. I returned to Russia in 2017, as a tourist this time, and I will only report two things. First, the grim GUM department store, which in 1980 had mostly empty shelves except for those holding fur hats, had now become the fanciest mall I had ever seen. Armani? Prada? Tiffany? Step right in! And the Russians retained their sense of humor.

As my group rode on a bus to tour the Kremlin, we were stuck in L.A.-type traffic. Our guide grabbed the microphone. "What do you think is the favorite car of the rich?" she asked.

We threw out guesses: Porsches? Lamborghinis? She shook her head. "It's a Russian-made car."

That had us stumped. Finally, I said, "A police car?"

She grinned. "You're close."

Someone then shouted, "An ambulance?"

"Yes! Rich friends of Putin get their own ambulances. So in traffic they turn on the lights and the sirens and off they go."

I could only hope Mr. Putin has not shared this information with President Trump.

49

Some Things Don't Change, Part I

The Cattle Call

RECENTLY, STORIES HAVE BEEN WRITTEN ABOUT THE POOR working conditions, minimal pay, and sexist practices NFL cheerleaders have to put up with. Several have filed lawsuits. Some teams are pledging improvements. I began to wish I could add my voice today, and then I remembered—wait!—I already had. The following is a column I wrote in 1983.

―――

"Hi! My name is Diane," the young woman said. "I'm 5-foot-3, 120 pounds. My hair is brown, and my eyes are black."

Then, having said all she was allowed to, she twirled round, displayed her backside, paused, twirled again, and stood there, in skimpy leotard and tights, grinning fiercely at 11 male observers.

Behind her was draped a familiar black backdrop. "Raiders," it read. "World Champions."

After Diane came Deirdre, Marilyn, Mary, and about fifty Cheryls and Debbies. For four hours, 152 women (or girls, as they call themselves), each with a large number pinned to her hip, paraded across the wooden stage in a hotel ballroom before the unwavering gaze of Our Los Angeles Raider judges.

By session's end, 75 would be ferreted out for a return call next Saturday. The 35 who survive that tryout, during which they will actually have to dance, will become Our Raiderettes.

Okay, so I never made cheerleader in high school, a morale-shattering defeat I'll carry with me to the grave, even if I win the Nobel Prize. And okay, the thought of young women in 1983, parading in the barest of nothings before 11 pairs of coolly appraising male eyes, to get a job, makes my blood turn cold. Just so you know where I stand.

They arrived in all shapes and sizes . . . and ages. The youngest were 18; the oldest age given on an application blank was 32, though one "girl" privately admitted she had gone to school with retired running back Jim Kiick, who is at least 35-ish.

Beside each judge lay a piece of paper entitled Raiderette Judging Code. It ran from the proverbial 10 (Superstar category), or "Sensational Prospect, Has it all. Few of this caliber in any league. Should be in movies or national TV," down to a (sigh) Two-One, "Not a prospect for a unit of this high caliber."

On they came, and off they went. Some bolted across the stage shouting, "Yea, Raiders!" Others seemed frozen with fright. One woman, who should win an award for bravura, announced, "I weigh 170 pounds."

Standing off to one side was Raiders running back Marcus Allen, brought in, no doubt, to lend glamour to the proceedings. But he seemed remarkably baffled by what he was witnessing.

"This is like a cattle call," he said in disbelief. Then, "Actually, they did the same thing to us, only worse. Before they sign you, they really give you the once-over. I mean, they take pictures. I don't remember, but they may have checked my teeth."

Lending as much dignity as possible to such an event was Al LoCasale, Raider executive assistant. Always his voice was gentle and reassuring. "Everyone take a deep breath," he would say to each new batch of arrivals. "Nothing we are going to do today is fatal." Outside the ballroom swarmed dozens of prospects, some of whom sat in front of mirrors, lathering their cheeks with blusher. Among them were a social worker, a psychologist and, imagine my surprise, the assistant manager of my bank. Nevertheless, the atmosphere was college dorm room.

"I'm really 25, but I said I was 23," admitted Peaches Johnson, a striking black woman who said she was an unemployed actress and dancer. "I want this job mainly because it leads to TV sports and promotional things. That's why most of the girls are here," she stated.

In fact, almost never does a football cheerleader go on to fame and dancing fortune. And for that, they devote a lot of time. Not counting game time, the Raiderettes will practice 16 to 18 hours a week. They will be paid $35 per game, along with two free tickets, a parking pass, and lunch. There are shopping mall appearances and such, but nobody's going to wind up on *Dynasty*.

Mary Watkins, a 32-year-old cashier at Ralph's, eyed some of the competition angrily. "I went to Rams' cheerleader tryouts too," she said. "They told us to wear workout clothes. Then all these women show up wearing sexy things, and they're the ones that made it."

The ones who made it this day were accurately predicted by Mary Weber, a six-year Raiderette vet. "Now, she's cute," Mary said, nodding approvingly at one perky blonde. And, "She'll make it," at a redhead. "She's the only redhead here."

Mary insists there is no Raiderette type. "A full-figured girl of 160 pounds could make it," she said. "Al knows some men like that."

The morning wore on. The parade continued, with the judges pretending this was an honest day's work and the contestants pretending this was necessary for their careers. I was just beginning to convince myself that maybe they were right, when one of the judges, a self-proclaimed womanizer, pulled me aside.

"Who would do this?" he said. "What normal girl would do this? I mean, there's got to be something wrong, don't you think? I ask you, would you do this?"

Later, 75 glowing finalists shrieked with delight. And went home to practice their routines.

50

Some Things Don't Change, Part II

The Donald

I SET MY ALARM CLOCK FOR 6:00 A.M., L.A. TIME. AT 6:30 A.M., I was supposed to call Donald Trump at his office in New York (9:30 a.m.), and I needed a half-hour to pour enough coffee down my throat to prepare. This phone interview had been weeks in the making because—I was repeatedly told—Mr. Trump was a *very* busy man. "There is no way I can schedule an appointment for you to speak with Mr. Trump, since he keeps his appointment book with him and he is not here," is what his secretary/gatekeeper, Norma, told me the first time I tried to reach her boss. This was 1983.

Although I knew all the tabloid stuff—buildings, marriages, wealth— what brought him into my line of vision was his purchase of a USFL team, the New Jersey Generals.

The United States Football League, which premiered in 1983, was designed to play games in the spring, so as not to compete with the NFL. Trump, who had long desired to be an NFL owner—but was rejected— eagerly jumped into the USFL.

"If you call him at 6:30 a.m. your time, tomorrow, you should reach him," said Norma after half a dozen more phone calls that day. At 9:30 the next morning, his time, Trump was not in his office, Norma told me, without a twinge of apology. Over dinner the night before, our unpre-dictable Donald had made an unscheduled breakfast date. Another round of coast-to-coast phone calls eventually produced this dictum. "If you don't mind calling him tomorrow morning, he'll definitely be in," she said.

Her idea of morning was 5:30 a.m., my time.

At 5:30 a.m., the phone in Donald Trump's office rang and rang. I dialed four or five more times. At 5:50, there was still no response. Later, Norma said Trump had been sitting behind his desk waiting and waiting for me to phone. "And you didn't," she said accusingly.

I repeated the number she had given me and she confirmed, yes, that was Trump's number. "Which you obviously didn't call."

That afternoon, I did get a few words with the building mogul. Basically, he told me in no uncertain terms that if I knew *anything* about New York, I would know what prime locations his properties commanded. I bit my lip and did not mention that I was bicoastal and had an apartment, not far from his properties, in the city.

Anyway, the column I wrote in November 1983, began this way.

Donald Trump is a very busy man. Oh, yes, he is.

In the almost, but not quite, eight weeks that he has owned the New Jersey Generals, he has courted and angered Miami Dolphins' coach Don Shula, courted and angered Los Angeles Raiders' quarterback Marc Wilson, courted and angered Cleveland Browns' quarterback Brian Sipe, offered an ungodly price for the Cleveland Indians baseball team—then pulled out yesterday—and recently met with Frank Hawkins, the Raiders' running back, whom, Trump says, he just might like to see in a Generals' uniform. Where shall we begin?

Trump, I wrote, seemed to be wooing everyone except Wayne Newton. And each little woo would produce a very large headline. Indeed, the almost self-made almost multi-multi-multi-millionaire created a bigger stir in the sports world, faster than any newcomer ever has. Known in real estate for his self-promotion, grandiose schemes, and knack for infuriating people, he brings the same qualities to sports. In its first jury-is-still-out season, the USFL lacked one essential ingredient: personalities. It hadn't produced even one slightly outrageous character. Trump, the owners thought, might just be the answer. As he told the *New York Times*, "At 37, no one has done more than I in the last seven years."

But since his flamboyant leap into sports, he has displayed a quality, which, depending on one's point of view, is either perfect or so imperfect as to be idiotic. The quality is inconsistency.

Three examples.

Although the Raiders' Marc Wilson says Trump made him an offer to play for the Generals, Trump claims he did not. "Was I interested in Wilson?" he said in the phone interview. "Interest can mean a lot of things."

"Did you make him an offer?'

"He was injured."

I remind Trump that Wilson injured his shoulder *after* he signed a five-year, $4 million contract with the Raiders.

Trump pretends he doesn't hear and laughs. "People are now calling me a great football sage. I was smart enough not to sign him."

But was there an offer?

"There was no offer. And Wilson signed for what I consider to be an exorbitant sum. I don't know why Al Davis felt he had to pay so much."

Davis may have paid him that much because Trump offered almost the same. While not confirming any figures, Howard Slusher, Wilson's attorney, says only, "Trump made an offer to Marc, which he refused."

Example two. A week ago, Trump flew Cleveland quarterback Brian Sipe to New York and, whisking the quarterback into his limo, gave Brian a tour of his holdings. Later that evening, after Sipe had departed, Trump announced, "We're no longer interested in Brian Sipe."

The next day, Tony Grossi, a reporter for the *Cleveland Plain-Dealer*, was in Trump's office. "He got a phone call from Brian," says Grossi. "It was clear from what Trump was saying that Brian was asking him to reconsider and that he would be willing to take less money. Trump later said to me, 'I get all these messages from NFL quarterbacks. They all want to play for me.' He said he wasn't interested in Brian."

Yesterday, Trump, speaking from his office on the 26th floor of his monument to New York City, Trump Tower, told me, "I'm interested in a number of quarterbacks. Brian Sipe is one of them."

Example three. He offered Dolphins coach Don Shula a five-year contract worth $5 million, plus a 10 percent interest in the Generals. He would call Shula on Monday nights a half-hour before *Monday Night Football*.

"Jeez, I can't believe all the publicity we're getting from this," he would say.

Shula describes the conversations as, "him trying to convince me to take the job. He seemed interesting. I was impressed by his success. As far as his knowledge of football, he sounded like he had just taken a crash course on owning a professional football team."

According to Shula's story, he had asked Trump if housing would be part of the deal. "I didn't specify Trump Tower and certainly not a triplex," Shula says.

Then, on the same Sunday that Trump denied he had any interest in signing Wilson on NBC-TV, he said he and Shula were a condominium away from agreement, and there was no way he would give away one of his apartments. "I called him the next day and said I didn't appreciate his remarks," Shula says. "Besides, all I'd ever told him was I was interested in his deal. I don't think I ever got to the point of seriously considering it."

Trump says, "Those condominiums are worth more than money. They're gold. It's the most valuable real estate in America. I'm not going to give them away to sign a coach."

The man is *busy.*

So far, he has bid on the baseball Giants, Mets, Royals, and Mariners. For the last four weeks, he has been in mad pursuit of the Indians, offering $24 million, or $9 million more than two local groups bid. Rumor surfaced that he intended to move the Indians to New Jersey, which he denied. Then yesterday, he suddenly ended his pursuit. "It wasn't worth the hassle," he says.

So now he can devote his sports energies to the USFL. "I've been a little bit more aggressive than the other owners," he says proudly. "After we reach parity with the NFL, we will have the option of playing our season in the fall."

He sounds excited about the prospects. But, alas, he must go. There are people waiting for him, meetings to go to, phone calls to take.

Donald Trump is a very busy man.

—◊—

Thirteen months later, I tried to speak with him again. In the interim, Trump had removed Chet Simmons as USFL commissioner and installed Harry Usher. He had signed the amazing but rather short Boston College quarterback Doug Flutie to a towering contract. Also, I wanted to know if it was true the USFL was in trouble, since no television network seemed to want to broadcast its games. And maybe I would ask about his picture on the front of *New York Magazine* for a story about his attempts to evict residents from a building he had purchased on Central Park West so he could develop a new project on the spot.

"Don't you understand how busy he is?' said the erstwhile Norma over the phone. "He's doing a whole city."

Apparently, she was referring to Trump's recent purchase of 100 acres on the West Side and his efforts to get development underway. "One hundred acres is the size of many cities," Norma pointed out.

Six weeks later, I tried again. This time in person.

I walked into Trump Tower and stared at the six-story lobby, which looked like it had been imported from the Land of Oz. Everything was just a little too bright to look at very long. The floors and the soaring walls are pink marble. What isn't marble is gold-tinged mirror. At the back of the lobby—stop; make that *atrium*—a cascading waterfall descends from a secret source 100 feet above. Looking at this décor, which can best be described as High Glitz, it is clear what Donald Trump's problem is. He is an L.A. kind of guy trapped in a New York zip code.

What I have before me is six full floors of Guccis and Puccis and Lina Lee's, a Rodeo Drive all fancied up and rearranged vertically.

"Whether the sophisticated gourmet, the extravagantly wealthy, or Walter Mitty of the adventurous jet set—Trump Tower has *something* for you," is what it says in "Talk of the Tower," the building newspaper. "The Trump Tower is 'the spirit' of New York City—the 'heart' of the Big Apple as the World's foremost City approaches its fourth century," the article goes on. "Encapsulating the sense of rapid change, energy and elegance, lust for the 'new' and nostalgia for the old, Trump Tower's atrium embodies the upward yearning of twentieth century man's reach for the very best life has to offer."

I had called ahead. A second secretary had been contacted by a friendly intermediary. Second secretary said no problem; an interview would be scheduled. But when this secretary was recontacted, she quickly switched me to Norma.

"I'm sorry," said Norma sweetly. "Mr. Trump is out of town and won't be back until Thursday afternoon." From Thursday on, he didn't have a single half-hour *ever* that could be given over to an interview, Norma said.

"Maybe I'll just stop up and see his office," I said.

"Oh, that won't be necessary," Norma said. "I can send you a brochure."

—〜〜—

The following week, I decided to try to find Trump.

In the elevator up to the 26th floor, the elevator operator, dressed in black slacks with tuxedo-ribboned legs, a black bow tie, and a gray wool coat, asked if it was cold outside.

I did not answer. I was too busy studying myself from all angles. Every square inch of elevator, including the ceiling, was covered in gold-tinged mirror.

The elevator deposited me in a corridor of more gold-tinged mirrors. At one end were glass doors. I walked in. A receptionist was poking out of a high, maroon-colored round desk. Behind her, set on a mirrored wall, were the words, "The Trump Organization," made—naturally—of mirrored letters.

I sat down to wait. Down a hall, men in work clothes were carrying paintings, either new ones going up or old ones coming down. Outside the windows, you could glimpse the barren trees in Central Park. Eventually, the second secretary came out.

"Oh, Mr. Trump is just on his way out to lunch," she said. "Why don't you call Norma this afternoon and see if she can squeeze you in?"

"Great," I said.

"While you're waiting, why don't you go down to the atrium and do some shopping?" she said, smiling.

"Terrific," I said.

"But don't spend too much money," she said. And giggled.

I promised I wouldn't.

I rode the elevator down to the lobby and took a cab home.

The story did not end there. Trump pressed the other owners to sue the NFL for monopolizing TV broadcast rights. Trump was convinced the USFL would win and force a merger with the NFL. The heated trial lasted 42 days, and when it was over, the jury shockingly decided the NFL had indeed broken the law. More shockingly, the jury awarded damages of $1. Actually, $3 because damages in antitrust suits are tripled.

Wiped out financially, the league folded.

During a press conference, Trump blamed the other owners.

51

Some Things Don't Change, Part III

Me

IT IS TRUE THAT I NO LONGER WRITE ARTICLES, THOUGH occasionally I'll do a book. Still, every morning I sit at my desk and log on to my computer. It is where I am most comfortable, where I am truly happiest. Writing. I am not a patient person. I get no pleasure standing over the stove, cooking up some yummy concoction—it takes too long! But writing—I can't remember ever being impatient when I write. Hours disappear, the room darkens. I look at my watch, surprised. It's that late.

Why writing? I have asked myself this so many times. And I can offer only one explanation: escape. School didn't interest me, so I daydreamed during class. I daydreamed through the ballets and symphonies my parents dragged me to. In fact, I daydreamed a lot. I still do. Perhaps it's because I prefer the worlds that I mentally concoct better than the real one I am stuck in. Early on, it hit me that writing was an escape. Fiction is obvious. I can make up whatever I want to. But when I discovered journalism, I found that it, too, was an escape. I could immerse myself in whatever story I was working on, slip momentarily into other people's lives. I was there, not here.

Writing about sports—this was an accidental gift. But I discovered that in a complicated world with so many factions and countless interpretations, games were such a welcome relief. Someone wins, someone loses. End of story. This, too, I realized, was an escape from the everyday world. This I should have known, for I had escaped into baseball as a child.

Abetting me in my various escapes were Indiana University professors, a handful of remarkable editors, and several inexplicable lucky breaks. One example. When Roscoe Born chose to put me on staff at the *National Observer*, rather than fire me, the only editor who would take me on was Lionel Linder. And it was Lionel's praise and encouragement that made me feel special. I realized this years later when, one day, the travel editor asked to borrow me to write a short piece. He handed me several clips and press releases. After I turned the story in, he dropped the edited version on my desk. "Take a look," he said. Heavy black lines filled the pages. Sentences cut, rewritten, his words added, the story completely rewritten. I was stunned. The story wasn't important, yet I couldn't help thinking: *What if he had been assigned my editor? Would I still come to work every day with a smile? Would my job thrill me? Would I have been fired?* Lionel was my first lucky break, only months into my career, and the confidence he gave me sent me places I never could have imagined.

I am so grateful that I was able to chase my dream—the real one—sitting at this desk or a seat in the press box, tapping a keyboard, telling a story.

And as I sit here now, at my desk, I can only wonder: *whose world will I plunge into next?*

Acknowledgments

WHOM TO THANK FOR HELPING ME, BESIDES SO MANY instances of inexplicable good luck? Oddly, in this era of bad men getting caught doing bad things, I realize most of the people who opened doors for me—were men. (Of course, women were still in short supply back then.) In the beginning, there was Bruce Shah, always assuring me that I could do anything I set my mind to, and whose patient reading—and rereading and rereading *again*—of drafts of my first mystery novel was so instrumental in getting the damn thing published.

There was managing editor Roscoe Born at the *National Observer*, who took a big chance hiring me, and my editor, Lionel Linder, who always made me feel I had produced an amazing story. And when sports teams tried to bar the door, these men, plus Editor-in-Chief Henry Gemmil, quickly formed my posse. I had so much to learn during those early years, and I could not have imagined a finer mentor than our sensational writer, the late Wesley Pruden Jr. At *Newsweek*, they handed me a sportswriting job without a second thought. I must also mention Jim Bellows, editor of the *Los Angeles Herald Examiner*, who hired me as the first female sports columnist in the country, when even I didn't think it was a job I could do. Later, a new editor, John Lindsey, was always there to back me up. And even though some didn't like me, I am grateful to my colleagues in the sports department who did their best to give me any help I needed.

I must also thank former *New York Times* sports editor Joe Vecchione, who reached out to me in Los Angeles to do a myriad of stories for him. And Art Cooper who called on me to write cover stories for *GQ* magazine. From John Walsh, first at *Inside Sports* and later at *ESPN the*

Magazine, I learned so much, even though I was a perennial no-show at his infamous A-to-Z bar tours in Manhattan. I was also so lucky to have the friendship of sports columnist John Schulian, *Playboy* editor Steve Randall, TV broadcaster Charley Steiner, and especially to Don Fehr and Gene Orza of the Major League Baseball Players Association.

Those who helped me ages ago, and should have received my thanks back then, were the journalism professors at Indiana University who never once—like so many folks—told me what I *couldn't* do. More recently, I owe a great debt to Dan Smith, president of the IU Foundation, who helped make this book possible. And I so appreciate the considerable help from Indiana University Press acquisitions editor Ashley Runyon, head of the copyright program Naz Pantaloni III, editorial project manager Allison Gudenau, and all who made the publishing endgame so easy on me. Also many thanks to Neil Leifer, who encouraged me to write this memoir. And most of all to Bob Roe and his hippos for so many helpful suggestions to improve my manuscript.

Text Credits

The following chapters, or portions thereof, previously appeared in other publications:

Chapter 4, portions reprinted with permission, September 7, 1970, © Dow Jones & Company, Inc. All Rights Reserved Worldwide.

Chapter 5, portions reprinted with permission, September 2, 1972, © Dow Jones & Company, Inc. All Rights Reserved Worldwide.

Chapter 6, portions reprinted with permission, 1972, © Dow Jones & Company, Inc. All Rights Reserved Worldwide.

Chapter 9, portions reprinted with permission, June 15, 1974, © Dow Jones & Company, Inc. All Rights Reserved Worldwide.

Chapter 10, reprinted with permission, 1974, © Dow Jones & Company, Inc. All Rights Reserved Worldwide.

Chapter 12, portions reprinted with permission, September 13, 1975, © Dow Jones & Company, Inc. All Rights Reserved Worldwide.

Chapter 14, from *Newsweek,* December 18, 1978, © Newsweek Media Group. All rights reserved. Used under license.

Chapter 15, portions originally published in *Inside Sports,* October 1979.

Chapter 16, portions originally published in *Inside Sports,* July 31, 1980.

Chapter 17, portions originally published in *New York Magazine,* April 21, 1980.

Chapter 20, portions reprinted with permission of Hearst Communications, Inc., August 9, 1981.

Chapter 24, portions reprinted with permission of Hearst Communications, Inc., March 9, 1982.

Chapter 25, portions originally published in *GQ,* January 1986.

Chapter 30, portions originally published in *GQ,* August 1987.

Chapter 31, portions reprinted with permission of Hearst Communications, Inc.

Chapter 32, reprinted with permission of Hearst Communications, Inc., May 16, 1984.

DIANE K. SHAH is a former journalist and the first female sports columnist for a major daily newspaper. She is the author of four mystery novels and the coauthor of *Chief: My Life in the LAPD*, a *New York Times* bestseller with police chief Daryl Gates, and *Relentless*, photographer Neil Leifer's memoir. She lives in New York City.